JOHN HICK

John Hick

A Critical Introduction and Reflection

DAVID CHEETHAM
The University of Birmingham, UK

ASHGATE

Published by
Ashgate Publishing Limited
Gower House
Croft Road
Aldershot
Hampshire GU11 3HR
England

Ashgate Publishing Company
Suite 420
101 Cherry Street
Burlington, VT 05401-4405
USA

Ashgate website: http://www.ashgate.com

British Library Cataloguing in Publication Data
Cheetham, David
    John Hick : a critical introduction and reflection
    1. Hick, John, 1922-
    I. Title
    230'.092

Library of Congress Cataloging-in-Publication Data
Cheetham, David.
    John Hick : a critical introduction and reflection / David Cheetham.
        p. cm.
    Includes bibliographical references and index.
    ISBN 0-7546-1599-5 (alk. paper)
        1. Hick, John. I. Title

    BL43.H35 C48 2003
    210'.92--dc21

                                                                2002032695

    ISBN 0 7546 1599 5

Printed and bound in Great Britain by MPG Books Ltd, Bodmin, Cornwall

Contents

Acknowledgements

I am grateful to the following journals for permission to reproduce material. To *New Blackfriars* for permission to use 'Evil and Religious Pluralism: The Eschatological Resolution' (May, 1997) and 'Religious Passion and the Pluralist Theology of Religions' (May, 1998). To *The Expository Times* for permission to use 'Hell as Potentially Temporal' (Vol. 108, No. 9, June 1997). To the Modern Churchpeoples Union for permission to use material in their journal *Modern Believing*: 'Pulp Fiction, a God of Love and an Authentic World' (Vol. 27, No. 3, 1996). To *Sophia* for permission to use 'John Hick, Authentic Relationships and Hell' (Vol. 33, No. 1, 1994).

A number of people have commented on drafts of the chapters or the entire book (at various stages). In particular, I wish to thank Prof. Paul Badham, Rev. J. Andrew Kirk, Dr. Peter Fulljames, Youngsoek Cho and Prof. John Hick. They are, of course, not responsible for the book's defects (for which I alone am to blame).

Introduction

History will probably judge John Hick to be one of the great philosophers of religion of the twentieth century. During his distinguished career, his thought has had a tremendous influence on debates in the philosophy of religion. This influence does not just reside within academic circles but extends into the classrooms where young people are studying commonly disputed questions in religion. A survey of Hick's work will show that he has not just focussed on one particular area within his chosen field, rather he has made substantial contributions to just about every aspect within this field. Thus, terms like 'experiencing-as', 'epistemic distance', 'eschatological verification', 'Irenaean theodicy', 'the replica theory', 'many lives in many worlds', 'the Real' have been woven into the very fabric of contemporary religious philosophical thought. In fact, most textbooks or 'readers' in the philosophy of religion will contain some reference to Hick's distinctive contributions.

Hick's work could be described as a journey. Readers of his books will not find a static thinker, rather his work might be characterised as an ever-expanding exercise. His thought has undergone many changes and shifts of emphasis - the evangelical student at Hull University slowly over time became the controversial pluralist 'guru'. Nevertheless, the changes did not involve the wholesale discarding of what might be called the foundational aspects of his thought - his view of religious belief in the context of 'experiencing-as', the Irenaean intuition of a soul-making universe, the affirmation of a life beyond death have remained. Instead, Hick sought to adjust his thinking within certain limits in order to accommodate an increasingly pluralistic outlook. However, to what extent he has managed to coherently retain such 'foundations' has been the subject of intense scrutiny over the years and some critics have questioned his consistency. Hick himself is critical of those commentators who have ferociously seized upon an aspect of his thinking and viewed it in isolation from the rest of his thought, or have neglected to take into consideration changes or qualifications that he may have added at a later date. Thus, when undertaking a study on a particular aspect of his thinking one has to take care that such later qualifications are properly considered.

The methodology I have followed is one which takes a quasi-historical approach in that I have sought to rehearse some of the arguments that occurred at the time when Hick published his works. This study begins where Hick began - with the problems of religious language, and ends where he has arrived - with the questions of religious plurality. The effect of this is that I have often chosen to use terms that Hick has qualified (or altered) in his later work. The most important instance of this is the way Hick refers to the divine. In earlier days he was content to use the term 'God' in the Christian theistic sense; but in his later work he adopts 'the Real' as his preferred term which he thinks is more 'transcategorial'. For this reason, some of the discussions (for example in chapter two) might be considered anachronistic in light of Hick's later pluralistic thinking; but, again, my justification is that I have sought to take a quasi-historical approach and stay within the parameters of the time his thinking on such topics emerged. Moreover, many of his books have been reissued and as they contain very little in terms of revision (except for new prefaces) one can only assume that they are acceptable to Hick in virtually their original form. However, this is of course subject to the qualification that they may be regarded by the *later* Hick to speak of 'true myths' rather than literalities. In most chapters I have weaved in my own critical observations and have included a brief summary at the end of each. Sometimes, particularly in discussions of Hick's eschatology, I have made suggestions and added speculations of my own that I feel could be developed further. However, in a book that is primarily a discussion of a particular thinker's work, I decided that it would be inappropriate to embark on extensive speculations of my own on this occasion. Additionally, although the topics of the chapters are intended to follow Hick's intellectual contribution and development in a chronological fashion, it is also possible to read each chapter as a separate unit. This might be of use to readers who are only interested in particular areas of Hick's thought (e.g. epistemology, theodicy, eschatology or religious pluralism).

A great deal of writing about Hick's work has been polemical, some of it deliberately corrosive and recalcitrant. Hick does not provoke this because of his tone - which is mostly measured and balanced. However, his work is often challenging and controversial. Throughout this book I have sought to adopt a positive tone. This does not necessarily imply that I agree with Hick, rather it is an appropriate stance for a book which purports to introduce its readers to a thinker's work.

Life

John Hick was born in Scarborough on the 20th January, 1922. His first academic studies were in law at Hull University (then University College, Hull), and it was during this time that he was converted to Christianity. His early Christian experience 'was Calvinistic orthodoxy of an extremely conservative kind'.[1] From Hull he went to Edinburgh University in 1940 to study philosophy. However, it was not long until his studies were interrupted by the war during which he served in the Friends Ambulance Unit. He returned to Edinburgh to resume his philosophical studies and graduated in 1948 with a First. During this time his initial fundamentalist fervour had begun to wane. He was unimpressed with what he has described as 'a lack of intellectual integrity in fundamentalist circles, in that any potentially unsettling questions were regularly suppressed rather than faced'.[2]

Hick decided to proceed to Oriel College, Oxford University to research for a doctorate in the philosophy of religion. He undertook this research under the supervision of the philosopher H.H. Price (who's work he was later to refer to in his studies on the possibility of disembodied minds). The thesis that emerged from this time was later to become his first book, *Faith and Knowledge* (1957).

In 1956, Hick moved to America to take up his first academic position at Cornell University. Three years later he took up another position at Princeton Theological Seminary, and it was here that Hick's 'other' career as a controversial theological figure began. Already a minister in the English Presbyterian Church, he wished to transfer to the American Church. However, his orthodox views had 'slipped' somewhat and he felt unable to confess such things as the literal six-day creation, predestination, the verbal inerrancy of the Bible and the Virgin Birth. This led to controversy, and the issue was only finally settled in Hick's favour when it reached the national Assembly.

After seven years of teaching in America, Hick returned to Britain in 1963 and took up a lectureship in the philosophy of religion at Cambridge University. It was here that he developed his now famous Irenaean theodicy (influenced by the early church father, Irenaeus), and published what is widely reckoned to be one of the definitive works on the problem of evil, *Evil and the God of Love* (1966).

In recognition of some of these outstanding early achievements, Hick was appointed to the H.G. Wood Professorship at the University of Birmingham in 1967. Birmingham is one of the most multicultural cities in Europe and the experience of living and working in this city was to shape the future orientation of Hick's philosophical theology (or, more accurately, philosophy of *religions*). During the early 1970s he was to become involved in (often 'chairing') community relations projects. This was a turbulent time in British immigration politics, and some of Hick's colleagues in these projects were physically attacked. In such eventful times, he found himself working in partnership with Muslims, Jews,

Hindus and Sikhs, and this began to affect his religious and philosophical outlook. He writes that 'it was not so much new thoughts as new experiences that drew me, as a philosopher, into issues of religious pluralism, and as a Christian into inter-faith dialogue'.[3] In 1973, Hick published *God and the Universe of Faiths*, in which he argued that there needed to be a revolution in religious and theological thinking which saw all religions as equally valid. Further to this, and largely as a result of his Birmingham experiences, Hick felt drawn to investigate the different religious traditions more deeply, and he made a number of study visits to India and Sri Lanka. The result was another major work in which Hick explored the different religious accounts concerning the future/afterlife, *Death and Eternal Life* (1976).

The ideas that Hick had been developing on the question of religious pluralism meant that whole areas within Christian theology had to be re-examined. With his next book (which he edited) he brought together a series of contributors who, in their various different ways, challenged one of those areas - the traditional views of Christ. *The Myth of God Incarnate* (1977), was destined to be one of Hick's most controversial projects.

Hick returned to America in 1982 to take up the Danforth Chair in the Philosophy of Religion at Claremont Graduate School in California. It was here that he developed and extended his thinking which resulted in the Gifford Lectures of 1986, and the publication of what many estimate to be his *tour de force*: *An Interpretation of Religion* (1989). He retired in 1993 and returned to Birmingham as a Fellow of the Institute for Advanced Research in Arts and Social Sciences at the University of Birmingham.

Work

What is John Hick's theological position? This is not that easy to answer. The reason for this is that his work extends over almost half a century and is contained in well over twenty authored and edited books. During this time, as we have said, his work has shifted and changed. Thus, in the earlier part of his career it would have seemed accurate to describe him as a fairly orthodox Christian philosopher preoccupied with making sense of the Christian faith. His first two books, *Faith and Knowledge* (1957) and *Evil and the God of Love* (1966), appear to inhabit largely a Christian worldview. However, as we proceed chronologically through Hick's output, for example *Death and Eternal Life* (1976), *The Myth of God Incarnate* (1977) and *An Interpretation of Religion* (1989) (and perhaps latterly *The Fifth Dimension*, 1999) we see an increasing broadening out of his worldview and an embracing of a pluralistic outlook.

Following on from this, a related question about Hick's work is whether it can be seen as a unified whole or should be regarded as inconsistent. Two critics of Hick's work, Gerard Loughlin and Chris Sinkinson, adopt different points of view on this matter.[4] Loughlin points out the discontinuities in Hick's thinking. He maintains that with every new publication Hick may have advanced too far beyond his earlier work, even cancelling it out. Particular examples that Loughlin draws attention to are Hick's notion of eschatological verification, his Christology and his Irenaean theodicy. When these were first formulated they appeared to be founded on a fairly 'orthodox' Christian understanding, however with the development of Hick's pluralistic hypothesis they have been rendered 'mythological'. It is possible that such mythologising may actually disturb the cognitive sense behind Hick's earlier work, leaving it virtually unrecognisable. Thus, one might ask if Hick's previous work should be radically revised or even discarded altogether?

Chris Sinkinson believes that there is an essential unity to Hick's work. This unity is to be found in Hick's epistemology. For example, Hick's early emphasis on the voluntary nature of religious experiencing (first expressed in *Faith and Knowledge*) was actually the seed-bed for Hick's final arrival at his pluralistic perspective. Sinkinson suggests that Hick's work has never in fact been 'Christian' because its prior loyalties have always been to an Enlightenment or Kantian philosophical tradition. In fact, he suggests that Hick's *first-order* language is his philosophy with Christian (or other religious) discourse coming second. This being the case, what we see in Hick's work is the slow working out of his first-order commitments to their inevitable pluralistic conclusion.

Both these evaluations have strong arguments in their favour, and it is probable that they are both valid within the terms of their different points of departure. So, we can indeed observe that Hick's work is unified by his basic epistemological structure; however I would disagree with Sinkinson with regard to describing Hick's philosophy as his own first-order discourse. In fact, Hick has explicitly described his pluralistic interpretation of religion (which contains much of his philosophical framework) as a second-order explanatory discourse in contrast to the first-order commitments of the different religions.[5] Admittedly, it is questionable whether this is a tenable position to hold and we shall be discussing this more closely in chapter five. Loughlin is also right to point to the difficulties that have come to the surface with Hick's development. Hick has repositioned his work into a mythological framework and it is possible that the result is too sophisticated or abstract to have real meaning. Nevertheless, it would be wrong for us to conclude that Hick's earlier work is irrelevant. He is able to argue that this work has value - for example, he would see his Irenaean theodicy (even in the form it takes in *Evil and the God of Love*) as a helpful myth for Christians when it comes to making sense of evil and suffering. His pluralistic hypothesis does not seek to cancel out first-order religious discourse, rather it is a second-order meta-theory *about* that first-order discourse. Again, we shall have more to say about this in chapter five.

In following a quasi-historical methodology, then, we begin in chapter one by looking at Hick's earliest work on epistemology. The basic structure of his epistemological notions remain constant throughout his work, thus one can feel justified in treating his work across the years on this issue as a unified whole. This chapter considers Hick's view of religious belief (in fact, *all* beliefs) as experiencing-as and proceeds to consider some of the defences he made on behalf of religious language against the prevalent positivist mood of the middle of the twentieth century. Hick's orientation is realist in that he is committed to the fact-asserting character of religious statements; however, he adds the important rider that he does not adhere to the sort of naïve realism that might seek to advocate a crude literalism. Rather, he prefers a *critical* realism which maintains that the real world enters the consciousness through our interpretative experience. Furthermore, Hick argues (from a philosophical-explanatory perspective) that the world is religiously ambiguous in that neither the arguments for a religious or naturalistic interpretation of it are conclusive. However, *experientially*, people are able to perceive a significance in the world which, for them, can be overwhelming and 'given'. Thus, Hick draws a distinction between philosophical and theological-experiential modes of discourse. In his epistemological work it is an experience-encounter model that he favours over more propositional models of revelation. Such an empirical emphasis in his thinking can also help to explain a characteristic methodological feature of his major writings - the endeavour to consider *all* the available evidence (especially empirical) when investigating a given topic. Thus, those familiar with Hick's work will know that major works such as *Evil and the God of Love* and *Death and Eternal Life* are exhaustive in their scope.

Chapter two looks at the next major concern which followed Hick's early epistemological work: the problem of reconciling the fact of evil and suffering with the existence of a loving God. Hick presented a definitive treatment of this topic in *Evil and the God of Love*. His response is forward-looking in the sense that it envisages the resolution of evil to reside in the notion of a limitlessly good outcome to human existence. Developing the ideas of the early church father, Irenaeus (130-202 CE), Hick interprets the suffering of life as part of a soul-making journey in which persons are perfected over time. He rejects an Augustinian model which looks back to a time when human beings fell from grace and thus brought evil into the world; instead he sees evil as part of the divine intention to mould souls into the likeness of God (*similitudo dei*). This is a limitlessly good outcome that will be experienced by all (universalism).

According to Hick, the idea of soul-making requires an extension of the normal human lifespan, for human beings are rarely perfected in a single life. Thus he next turned his critical attention to the idea of life after death. This became the extended investigation that culminated in the publication of *Death and Eternal Life*. Hick's eschatology (or more accurately, his *par*eschatology) is an impressive philosophical and speculative venture. It is no mere proposal for the possibility of life-after-death, but a systematic and imaginative attempt to postulate far beyond present existence. As we have just hinted, his eschatology is no idle exercise, it does not emerge from his thinking for just the reason that he prefers that there be an afterlife rather than there not be. No, the 'forward look' has been a vital ingredient in much of his thinking. In his case, the reasons for his speculative eschatology are threefold. Firstly, when seeking to uphold the basic cognitivity of religious language he suggests an eschatological verification of religious expectations. Secondly, as we have just said, his Irenaean theodicy seeks to justify the existence of evil on the basis that it is a utility to soul-making. But, as a single life is too short, Hick maintains that there needs to be further development after death. Finally, his response to the fact of religious diversity, which we examine in chapter five, has resulted in a hypothesis which postulates that there will be some sort of movement towards a unity in the eschaton. Thus, in chapter three we will look in some detail at the philosophical arguments that surrounded Hick's suggestions concerning disembodied existence and resurrection bodies. Then, in chapter four we will begin to look ahead to Hick's pluralism by considering his now famous notion of 'many lives in many worlds' in which he prefers to speak of a series of limited or 'bounded' existences following our earthly existence rather than the idea of one continuous everlasting life. This eclectic eschatological picture connects the soul-making ideas considered in chapter two, the discussions about the coherency of life after death in chapter three and the pluralistic hypothesis in chapter five.

As we have said, Hick's work has provoked a great deal of reaction and debate, perhaps the controversy that surrounded the appearance of *The Myth of God Incarnate* is the supreme example of this. But this work foreshadowed a much more significant contribution. This was his philosophy of religious pluralism that began to emerge in 1973 with his call for a 'Copernican' revolution in theology and later became highly developed in *An Interpretation of Religion* (1989). Hick's philosophical journey has culminated in the grand proposal that we should see all the major world religions as equally valid responses to the same ultimate reality (the 'Real'). In saying this, he has suggested that all religions are different human and cultural expressions of this reality. Being true to his earlier epistemological work, and incorporating a kantian-influenced distinction between *things in themselves* and *things as perceived*, Hick suggests a difference in the way the Real is *in itself* and as it is perceived by the various religions. Thus, religions in their various discourses can only speak *mythologically* of the Real *in itself*. However, some of Hick's critics suggest that it is as if he has been going up the speculative ladder without looking down to check whether those things he positioned to steady it are still taking the strain. Thus, a great deal of criticism has focused on Hick's ability to reconcile his pluralistic hypothesis with his earlier work. These issues, amongst other things, are considered in the final chapter.

Finally, when seeking answers to the question of what unifies Hick's work, it is perhaps not to the actual consistencies in his arguments across the decades, or to the 'foundational' aspects in his thought that we should look. In fact, if we look at things differently, it seems that Hick's work has always addressed questions that *interest* people: What does my religious talk mean? Why do we suffer? Shall I live after death? What about other religions? Perhaps the common thread in Hick's work is that his questions (and his pursuit of answers) seem to make *religious sense*; that is, they are issues eminently worth bothering about.

Notes

1. J. Hick, *Disputed Questions*, p.139.
2. Ibid.
3. Ibid, p.141.
4. See, G. Loughlin, 'Prefacing Pluralism: John Hick and the Mastery of Religion' (Hick responds in 'A Response to Gerard Loughlin'), also G. Loughlin, 'Squares and Circles: John Hick and the Doctrine of the Incarnation' in H. Hewitt, (ed.), *Problems in the Philosophy of Religion*. See C. Sinkinson, *The Universe of Faiths: a critical study of John Hick's religious pluralism*; also, within this book Sinkinson draws attention to P.L. Barnes, 'Continuity and Development in John Hick's Theology'. Sinkinson's book is an excellent critique of Hick's religious pluralism from an evangelical perspective.
5. Also, when speaking personally, Hick maintains that on an *experiential* or theological level he is a Christian (even if *as a philosopher* he is also a pluralist): 'But I have myself been formed by the Christian vision of God as revealed in the life and teaching of Jesus as reflected in the Gospels, and continue to be most at home in this...' *Disputed Questions*, p.145.

Chapter One

Faith and Knowledge

It is perhaps not surprising that a philosopher as profound as John Hick should begin his philosophical career by concerning himself with one of the fundamental questions of philosophy. This is the question of what we can know, the preoccupation of *epistemology*. His first major work, *Faith and Knowledge* (1957), is a developed investigation of this issue, but his epistemology has undergone various refinements throughout his career. Nevertheless, as there is a sense of continuity in his thinking on this matter, we shall be taking his work together.

Although Hick's primary focus is the meaning of religious faith, his thinking extends to all aspects of belief and knowledge. This is because he does not believe that one can, or should, separate religious *knowing* from other forms of knowing. Religious knowledge is embedded in the totality of our knowing. Moreover, he does not think that beliefs necessarily arise from pure 'intellection', rather they arise out of personal experience. Another way of putting this is that, for Hick, religious cognition should take place in 'presence' rather than 'absence'.[1] By this he means that he seeks to portray knowledge as something we are *acquainted with* rather than 'knowing-about'. The irony, as Hick sees it, is that much academic (western) systematic theological work has been about examining religious beliefs as distant *propositions* whereas the inspiration behind them were lived encounters with, and experience of, the divine.

In this first chapter, then, we shall be considering Hick's contribution to the questions of religious belief and knowing. To begin, we shall look at his view that all experience is 'experiencing-as'; secondly, we shall proceed to consider his commitment to the basically factual character of religious belief. Thirdly, following on from this second concern, Hick's distinctive response to the 'verificationist' debate of the 1950s will be considered; but in order to contextualise (conceptually) Hick's response we shall also briefly allude to the responses of R.M. Hare and R.B. Braithwaite. Finally, a number of criticisms of Hick's thinking will be looked at.

Experiencing-as

As we have said, Hick does not uphold the view that religious faith is a
matter of assenting to a set of propositions; or that 'salvation' is reliant on
our ability to be correctly cognizant of a certain creed. This does not mean
that Hick is advocating an irrationalism as far as religious belief and faith
are concerned. Rather, we should broaden our understanding of rationality.
For Hick, rationality is not solely instantiated by a set of logical arguments
or written propositions on the page. To be 'rational' is something human
beings do (or not); or, as Hick says: 'It is *people* who are rational or
irrational, and derivately their states and their actions, including their acts
and states of believing.'[2] Thus, being rational is connected to the whole
web and totality of experience. *Experience* is an important starting point
for Hick. This being the case, we might characterise his orientation as
empiricist in that there is an emphasis throughout his work on the evidence
of the senses and experience. Moreover, as an interesting corollary, we
cannot, thinks Hick, divide into neat compartments our various beliefs; all
beliefs are in some way connected or affected by our *total experience*. So,
the experience of God does not arrive as something separate from the rest
of our environment. It is not a 'pure' or direct knowledge, but is mediated
through other objects. He writes:

> The ordinary believer does not, however, report an awareness of God as
> existing in isolation from all other objects of experience. His consciousness of
> the divine does not involve a cessation of his consciousness of a material and
> social environment. It is not a vision of God in solitary glory, filling the
> believer's entire mind and blotting out his normal field of perception[...] He
> claims instead an apprehension of God meeting him in and through his
> material and social environments.[3]

Another way of speaking about this comprehensive experience is what
Hick calls *significance*. He explains significance in the following: 'By
significance I mean that fundamental and all-pervasive characteristic of our
conscious experience which *de facto* constitutes for us the experience of a
"world" and not of a mere empty void or churning chaos.'[4] This experience
of a 'world', or seeing a significance in things, also says something about
our interpretative freedom. This is not to imply that the 'real' world
changes at our interpretative whim. Hick is not advocating *solipsism* (the
belief that the world is wholly a creation of our minds). Rather, the world
enters our consciousness through an interpretative filter. Thus, an atheist
and a believer inhabit the same world, but this world appears different to
them; that is, it has a different *significance* for each. Hick writes:

For there is a sense in which the religious man and the atheist both live in the same world and another sense in which they live consciously in different worlds. They inhabit the same physical environment and are confronted by the same changes occurring within it. But in its actual concrete character in their respective 'streams of consciousness' it has for each a different nature and quality, a different meaning and significance; for one does and the other does not experience life as a continual interaction with the transcendent God.[5]

Hick characterises *all* experience as 'experiencing-as'. Here he has borrowed and developed the concept of 'seeing-as' put forward by the modern philosopher, Ludwig Wittgenstein (1889-1951). In this context, Wittgenstein was interested in drawing attention to the complex nature of changing perceptions, for example he writes: 'I contemplate a face, and then suddenly notice its likeness to another. I *see* that it has not changed; and yet I see it differently. I call this experience "noticing an aspect".'[6] Moreover, Wittgenstein pointed out that it is possible to see the same thing differently. He made reference to 'picture-puzzles' such as a picture which, depending on how you looked at it, was either a duck or a rabbit. That is, it is perfectly possible to see the picture in two different but equally legitimate ways - as a duck or a rabbit. Hick extends the somewhat mono-dimensional idea of seeing-as to 'experiencing-as'. Furthermore, he wants to say that 'experiencing-as' is not just something that occurs in special puzzle cases (like being confronted by a 'duck-rabbit' picture), but it refers to *all* our seeing and experiencing; that is, it is something far more all-embracing or, as we have said, *significant*.

According to Hick, the amount of freedom we have in respect to interpreting our world varies in proportion to the sphere in which we are operating. There are different degrees of freedom in interpretation. For example, our interpretative freedom is most restricted (or involuntary) at the level of everyday sense experiences. We may choose to interpret a bus speeding towards us as an illusory creation of our imagination, but the bus will tend to ignore such mental sophistry and assert its reality! Thus, Hick notes that for us the *significance* of the physical world is that it is something objective who's 'laws we must learn, and toward which we have continually to relate ourselves aright if we are to survive'.[7] At the level of inter-personal relationships and morality our freedom is less restricted. However, it is still closely connected to the most basic kinds of sense perception and interpretation just mentioned because such things take place within the natural environment. That is, our moral experience does not take place in an abstracted world, but within our physical world. Hick writes that the 'world of moral significance is, so to speak, superimposed upon the world, so that relating ourselves to the moral world is not distinct from the business of relating ourselves to the natural world but is rather a particular manner of so doing'.[8] And finally, as we have said, there is religious experience which is yet another layer of interpretation. At this level there is great freedom to interpret the world in many different ways; that is, we might say that seeing or perceiving religious significance (or none) is 'a voluntary act of interpretation'.[9]

To explain further, we start at the level of perceiving our natural environment and build up layers of interpretation (that we have 'learned' through our experiences) which together constitutes for us a significant 'world'. The important thing to reiterate is that Hick characterises *all* belief as a matter of 'experiencing-as', not just religious belief. To say this may seem exaggerated or brashly all-encompassing, for example it is surely the case that at least basic perceptual beliefs are 'directly' encountered? But Hick's point is that no object or experience, however basic, merely enters our consciousness without some interpretative process. So, the simple fork might be interpreted as just an interesting metal object to those unfamiliar with its use. A tuft of grass on a field may be mistakenly experienced-as a rabbit instead. The existence of a person struggling in heavy seas at the base of a cliff can be experienced-as merely a description of a state of affairs or it can be experienced-as a moral imperative to seek help. An immense waterfall with a rainbow glimmering in its spray may be theistically significant for those experiencing it as evidence of design, but it will perhaps only have aesthetic significance for the atheist. In saying all this, Hick is giving religious beliefs the same pedigree as all beliefs. That is, by describing *all* experience as 'experiencing-as', Hick has given religious beliefs a validity that can only be denied at the cost of questioning all beliefs. Put bluntly, if a criticism of religious belief is that 'it's just a matter of interpretation, so it cannot be trusted', then Hick's riposte is that all our beliefs are the result of interpretation! Thus, despite its complexity, religious belief is not a special case requiring separate justification. In an appreciation of Hick's work, the Christian philosopher William Alston commented on the force of Hick's point:

> One cannot demand an independent warrant for the interpretative scheme of religious experience without, in parity, making such a demand for the other areas of experience as well. And since the demand cannot be met anywhere, the logic of the criticism would lead us to reject the epistemic credentials of all experience.[10]

Nevertheless, if all our knowledge is characterised as 'experiencing-as' does this not also mean that everything (even natural belief) is cast into subjective uncertainty? Hick responds by saying that although the existence of a *real* world external to our senses presents a notorious philosophical conundrum its existence is, for all practical purposes, taken for granted. Or rather, the real world is not a propositional certainty, it is an experienced reality. Furthermore, our sense-experiences have an involuntary character; that is, there is a 'given-ness' about such things, and by acting in accordance with such perceptual beliefs we find that we live successfully in the world. So, when we choose to step out of the path of buses (because we trust that our sense-experiences are accurate about the existence of buses), we find that such choices have proved correct! Given the involuntary character of our sense-experiences, and our 'successful' living, Hick concludes:

> These characteristics [...] constitute a sufficient reason to trust and live on the basis of our perceptual experience in the absence of any positive reason to distrust it, and our inability to exclude the theoretical possibility of our experiences as a whole being purely subjective does not constitute such a reason.[11]

Our interpretations, then, are not simply made-up. It is our experiences (and successful engagement with the world) that give rise to our interpretations. Moreover, according to the principle of credulity,[12] in the absence of strong countervailing reasons there is no good reason to doubt our senses.

As we have seen, religious beliefs are part of the same epistemological framework that Hick applies to perceptual beliefs. Thus, the rationality of religious belief is connected to the rationality of basic perceptual beliefs. There is a parity between them, or a similar justification for each. So, Hick argues that just as it is impossible to regard our perceptual beliefs as illusory, so it is similarly impossible for those with overwhelming religious experience to deny the reality of those experiences. Thus, the great saints of the past were so completely aware of their relation to the divine that they took their experience of the divine for granted; for them, the divine presence was almost a mundane fact. Furthermore, their religious experience could be characterised as *involuntary*; and to deny such experiences would seem from their perspective to be as insane as someone who denies their basic perceptual experience of the world. Given this, these great saints were just as rational in accepting the veridical nature of their experiences as we all are in accepting that our natural beliefs are accurate. However, we should not misunderstand Hick to be proposing an argument for the existence of God on the basis of religious experience. Rather, he is only seeking to demonstrate the *rationality* of religious belief on the basis that it is connected to the total epistemological framework of experience in general.

Nevertheless, there are clearly some complications with this. For example, is the analogy with perceptual beliefs somewhat overstretched? We have just seen that although Hick connects all levels of experience it is nevertheless the case that our freedom to interpret becomes greater as we progress from natural to moral to religious levels. In fact, this freedom at the religious level of interpretation is clearly evidenced by the sheer variety of often contradictory beliefs held throughout the world's religions. Does not this phenomenon suggest that religious experience is largely illusory? This is of course a possibility, and Hick recognises this. Nevertheless, he responds by suggesting that such variety in human religion, rather than causing difficulties, is actually indicative of the immensely complex and unfathomable nature of the ultimate reality that lies behind the various different religions. However, this is taking us into Hick's pluralistic hypothesis and we shall have more to say about this in chapter five.

A related difficulty is the question of insanity. For it is clear that insane people also experience the world in ways compelling to themselves, but they also see things erroneously. There may be only a tiny minority of such people, but then the number of 'great saints' is pretty small as well. Why cannot we simply say that the overwhelming religious awareness of great religious people is of the same stuff as the deluded or insane? In response, it would appear that Hick's epistemological structure militates against such a verdict. To repeat, all our experiences are connected in a *total experience* which encompasses our natural, moral and religious (or none) interpretations. The *significance* that the world has for us is not an isolated epistemological activity, rather it is something that includes all our experiencing. Hick therefore asks us to consider the total impression we get of such great religious figures. Do they appear mad? Hick answers: 'On the contrary the general intelligence and exceptionally high moral quality of the great religious figures clashes with any analysis of their experience in terms of abnormal psychology'.[13] That is, Hick's recommended methodology is to consider the whole picture of a person - not just what that person believes or says about religious matters.

However, if overwhelming religious awareness is the experience of a few special people, how are ordinary religious believers justified in their beliefs? By 'ordinary' religious believers we are not intending to sound condescending, rather we are merely referring to those who would not claim to be as advanced as the great exemplars of their faiths. Here Hick again speaks of building up layers of experience that collected together make the religious perspective a rational choice. So, the ordinary believer's own modest religious experience (perhaps with occasional 'peak experiences'), 'makes it both possible and reasonable to be so impressed by the reports of the *mahatmas* that one's own experience is supported by their much more massive awareness of the transcendent'.[14]

Whilst we may speak of the overwhelming religious awareness of great religious persons and the commitment of their 'ordinary' followers, we should not lose sight of the fact that our interpretative faculties play an important role in constructing *significance* or a 'world' and, as a result, we have a great degree of freedom and autonomy at the religious level. Looking at human experience in general, Hick thinks that at the religious level human beings have the ability to interpret the world and its choices in any way that they prefer. That is to say, the world does not have built into it some inherent proclamation of God's reality or a contrary naturalistic character; rather, it is ambiguous and human beings can experience it as different things. Moreover, as Hick prefers to talk of knowledge as 'acquaintance-with' rather than 'knowing-about', he is doubtful about the philosophical validity or religious value of 'proofs' for the existence of God. In fact, he argues that all the classical proofs (cosmological, teleological and so on) fail to conclusively demonstrate God's existence and they tend to result in a stalemate between believer and sceptic. This is, says Hick, what one might expect in a religiously ambiguous world. Moreover, he believes that even if one of the proofs for God's existence actually succeeded it would probably have only a *notional* rather than religious effect. Intellectually we can assent to something whilst remaining emotionally and religiously untouched. Actually, for Hick, the religious ambiguity of the universe is something desirable because it permits a great deal of freedom. This ambiguity is another important starting point for Hick in terms of giving creatures freedom in relation to the transcendent:

> In creating finite persons for fellowship with himself, God has given them the only kind of freedom that can endow them with a genuine (though relative) autonomy in relation to himself, namely cognitive freedom, the freedom to be aware or unaware of their creator.[15]

This 'cognitive freedom' to be aware or unaware of the reality of God is something that Hick calls *epistemic distance* and we will speak more about this in the next chapter. However, the picture that Hick presents of a religiously ambiguous world which is capable of being experienced in many different ways means that there is little room in Hick's system for divine revelation. This is further underlined by his emphasis on experiential rather than propositional knowledge where the picture is one of human beings freely experiencing (voluntarily) the *significance* of the world as opposed to conforming to a set of divinely revealed truths. Moreover, in his later writings Hick borrows from the epistemology of Immanuel Kant

(1724-1804) in drawing a distinction between the world as it is experienced (*phenomena*) and the world as it is in itself (*noumena*). Kant's main point was that we cannot perceive the world as it actually is, we can only experience the world through our own interpretative lenses. We simply cannot get beyond this. Thus, Chris Sinkinson, a critic of Hick, points out that for Hick 'revelation is not primarily a declaration from an objective divine being, but is the felt response or the awareness of the individual to that divine being'.[16] Clearly, Hick's epistemology does not seem compatible with the notion of a divine being revealing propositional truths to humankind and this has consequences with regard to ways of doing theology. Given this, his empiricist style of thinking will probably not satisfy those committed to propositional models of revelation.

At this point it is important to draw attention to a distinction in Hick's thinking. This is the distinction between philosophical *explanation* on the one hand, and the world as it is actually experienced or lived on the other.[17] These are two levels of discourse that help us to understand what Hick is saying about the religious ambiguity of the universe. On the first level, the philosophical-explanatory, we can say that the world is ambiguous with no one explanation being more demonstrable or intellectually provable than another. On the second level, that of our conscious experiences, the world is capable of being experienced *intensely* (religiously or naturalistically) so much so that for the great religious figures (apostles and prophets) within the theistic traditions:

> God was known [...] as a dynamic will interacting with their own wills; a sheerly given personal reality, as inescapably to be reckoned with as a destructive storm and life-giving sunshine, the fixed contours of the land, or the hatred of their enemies and the friendship of their neighbours.[18]

These two levels (the philosophical-explanatory and the experiential) are crucial in Hick's thinking, and it is possible that some of Hick's critics have overlooked the distinction.

Realism and Non-Realism

An interesting feature of Hick's work is that he sometimes seems to embrace views that could be perceived as significantly different or even opposed.   Thus, his emphasis on personal experience rather than propositional knowledge in religious faith ('acquaintance-with' rather than 'knowing-about') could lend itself more readily to a merely poetic, mythological or subjective account of religious faith. However, despite the presentation of religious faith as experiencing-as and talk of a religiously ambiguous universe, Hick also wishes to defend the basic factual nature of religious language. That is, he is committed to the *reality* of the human encounter with the transcendent. The development of his thought in his later writings has not altered this basic feature (although it has undergone a degree of qualification). This means that Hick is committed to the idea that objects or persons (e.g. God) exist independently of human beings thinking about them. Moreover, to say 'God exists' is not to utter mere poetry, it is meant to be *factually* significant. This does not mean that he thinks that we can directly experience such objects, if this were the case then Hick would be a *naïve* realist. Rather, as we have already seen, the objects that exist in the real world reach us through the interpretative apparatus of our minds and cultures: thus Hick calls himself a *critical* realist. He writes:

> Realism then [is] divided into naïve realism, holding that the world is just as we perceive it to be, and critical realism, holding that there is an important subjective contribution to our perceiving, so that the world as we experience it is a distinctively human construction arising from the impacts of a real environment upon our sense organs, but conceptualised in consciousness and language in culturally developed forms.[19]

Applying this to religions themselves, Hick maintains that they are complex mixes of cultural responses to the transcendent - the culture filters the 'real' experience. In advocating a critical realism, Hick is opposing non-realist alternatives where religious language expresses the deepest human spiritual emotions and morals but does not actually refer to independently existing realities. Thus, the founder of modern non-realism in religious language - Ludwig Feuerbach (1804-1872), characterised 'God' as merely the projection of the highest human ideals. God was a concept that human beings used to concentrate all the things that they viewed as excellent. Feuerbach thought that religious language revealed more about humanity than 'God': thus theology should be turned into anthropology.

It is non-realist interpretations of religious language of the Feuerbachian type that Hick thinks are especially inadequate. Underlying Hick's rejection of this sort of approach is his view that the great religions embody a 'cosmic optimism'[20] that must go beyond a purely naturalistic account of human existence. This cosmic optimism is expressed in different ways within each of the religions, but there is a sense in them all that human beings are advancing towards a limitlessly good outcome. Hick writes:

> By divine grace or divine mercy, or by a gradual transcending of the ego point of view and a realisation of our own deepest nature, we can attain or receive

our highest good. And in so far as this limitlessly better state is said to be available to everyone, the message of each of the great religions constitutes good news for humankind.[21]

Furthermore, as this is a future hope in which *everyone* can share - including those presently living in desperation or poverty - it suggests future opportunities that extend beyond the single lifetime that the naturalist (and therefore the non-realist) is able to grant. Looking at Christian eschatology in particular, Hick insists that with the teaching of Jesus comes also the affirmation of life after death. He writes that 'the teaching of Jesus is so pervaded by the belief in a life after death that it is hardly possible to base one's religious faith upon him, as the revelation of God's love to man, and yet to reject so integral a part of his conception of the divine purpose ...'.[22] He argues that it would seem to be an inexplicable contradiction to claim that God loves and values each human being and desires them to reach their highest potential and good, and at the same time to maintain that God has ordained their extinction before they have had the chance to fully enter into the divine will. Hick believes that the historical Christian faith is unintelligible without some notion of life after death. A non-realist or a reductionist view (though the two should not be considered identical) 'claims that the meaning of the various Christian doctrines can be wholly stated in terms of present experience and involves no claim that goes beyond this'.[23] In Christian existential statements there is an understanding that the eternal is present now and is within us.[24] That is, the 'eternal' existence does not necessarily mean something yet to come in the context of a future existence, rather, it represents a quality of existence in this present life. But Hick claims that in most cases of such reductionism there is a reducing of 'the metaphysical to the psychological, or the ontological to the existential, or the transcendent to the immanent. In contrast to this, theological realism affirms both dimensions and refuses to reduce the one to the other'.[25]

It is these convictions about the future life to come, in addition to a supra-naturalistic account of the universe, that persuades Hick towards critical realism and away from non-realism. For Hick, the non-realist descriptions of faith merely affirm naturalistic accounts of human existence by denying the supra-naturalistic character of the universe and, in particular, a real future (after death) for the human journey towards salvation or liberation or enlightenment. Thus, for Hick, non-realist accounts are merely dressing up in religious terminology the naturalistic conviction that human beings are just 'complex animals who live and die'.[26] In addition, we shall see in a moment that Hick seeks to defend the notion that religious statements make factual statements about the world and reality. We must choose between non-realist accounts that seek to endorse the language or narrative of religion without the corresponding supra-naturalism, and critical realism which embraces the whole package (supra-naturalism, life after death and so on).

A possible initial criticism of this is Hick's tendency to polarise the choice between realism and non-realism when it may be argued that there are intermediate alternatives. Is the choice between realism and non-realism really that clear? Hick thinks that it is, rather than seek to dissipate the issues through over qualification, he thinks that it is important to clarify the root assumptions of realist the non-realist accounts so that we can appreciate the fundamental significance of each position. He writes:

> May there not be intermediate possibilities? I think not. There can be endlessly different and endlessly complex and subtle variations on either theme, no doubt with all manner of new options yet to be developed. But in the end they will all fall on one or the other side of the distinction between naturalistic and supra-naturalistic understandings of the universe.[27]

However, it may be that Hick is allowing his perspectives on religious language to be somewhat governed by value judgements concerning facts and fictions. For example, if religious language is described as merely poetic fiction, then it seems possible to interpret Hick as saying that this is a sort of cosmic *pessimism* in comparison to an optimistic view which is associated with *fact-asserting* religious expectations. And yet, some recent non-realist thinkers seek to portray their views as breathing new life into old and dead conventions. That is, there is a positive and life-affirming character in the way they express their non-realist vision. For example, Don Cupitt, a recent non-realist, writes:

> The world is only an endlessly shifting purely contingent order of signs of motion, a Sea of Meanings [...]And just the ability to see this and say it is precisely what gives us our new and joyful freedom [...] Your God is only your faith in him, your values are only your commitment to them. That is liberation. You're free.[28]

Cupitt is speaking of liberation from the idea that there are fixed norms and foundations that are imposed on the world from without. For him, holding a non-realist perspective on religious language means 'reclaiming' such language for the individual thus allowing individuals to create themselves and design their own meanings. Another thinker, D.Z. Phillips, makes a similar point when he writes: 'If we say that language, as such, refers to reality, the concept of reference employed and the reality supposed to be referred to are *entirely* unmediated. They have no context in which to have any sense.'[29] That is, Phillips is arguing that to say that there are metaphysical realities *apart* from human language is to divorce human language from those realities. Phillips, like Cupitt, seeks to repossess 'reality' and place it into the realm of human language. That this should not be understood as a loss or a reduction is conveyed when he says: 'According to the conception of philosophy shown in Wittgenstein's work, our task is to rescue the wonderfulness of the ordinary from the grip of metaphysical tendencies to which we are all prone.'[30] Phillips asks the question: if we believe in God and yet do not act as if we do then how *real* is our belief? That is, for Phillips, *real* belief is acting and behaving in a certain way not just assenting to the existence of metaphysical realities.

Nevertheless, Hick argues that just because thinkers like Cupitt and Phillips are seeking to emphasise the meaning and importance of religious practices and dispositions rather than metaphysical realities does not mean that both cannot go together. Realists do not have to separate beliefs from actions. In fact, we have seen that as Hick is a critical realist he is committed to the idea of the 'real' world entering our minds through our own imaginative, cultural and interpretative filters. Religious beliefs are a result of 'experiencing-as'. Thus Hick is able to affirm the presence of the metaphysical in the ordinary (Phillips), and the freedom that we have in our personal religious 'appropriations' (Cupitt). However, there is an important factor in a realist interpretation that Hick argues makes it more preferable. He writes: 'To the extent to which someone genuinely believes in God, that person lives in trust, obedience and answering love. It is thus impossible [...] to know what is meant by God without knowing something of the difference that God's existence makes for our lives.'[31] Furthermore, 'the theistic belief which properly affects one's whole life is belief in a God who exists independently of human belief and whose goodness and ultimate sovereignty give final meaning to our lives'.[32] So, it is the importance of a reciprocal relationship ('answering love') and the fact that this relationship makes a difference to our lives (e.g. it involves 'trust and obedience') that is crucial.

Logical Positivism - Verification and Falsification

Although Hick is not persuaded of the religious validity of 'proofs' for the existence of God, we have seen that he sees the importance of affirming the factual nature of religious language and expectations. When we say that 'religion is fact-asserting'[33] we are saying that religious language has a *cognitive* character. This is in contrast to a fictional (even if poetic/mythical/ethical) language which is *non-cognitive*.

Placing things into a historical context, Hick's defence of the cognitive character of religious language was largely in response to a philosophical movement in Europe (influenced by the early Wittgenstein) called *logical positivism*. This was a philosophical system devised in the 1920s that was to extend its influence into the latter half of the 20th century. Its tenets included the claim that 'metaphysics' was a meaningless philosophical activity because metaphysical propositions were neither verifiable by empirical observation nor demonstrable as analytic statements. Thus, philosophy was conceived as being an activity of logical analysis - properly confined to logical, mathematical and scientific discourse rather than the ambivalent fantasies of moral and religious whim. That is, most logical positivists regarded religious and moral utterances as 'metaphysical' and therefore incapable of proper empirical and analytical investigation.[34]

The logical positivists were seeking to make statements and philosophical propositions meaningful or meaningless by a principle of *verification*. In 1929 in a journal called *Erkenntnis*, the logical positivists, as represented by the Vienna Circle, published their 'manifesto'. They claimed that:

> the scientific conception of the world does not acknowledge any insoluble riddles. The clarification of traditional philosophical problems leads to the result that they are partly shown up as pseudo-problems and partly transformed into empirical problems and thus subject to the verdict of empirical science.[35]

Similarly, the British philosopher A.J. Ayer - who championed logical positivism in his early book *Language, Truth and Logic* (1936) - wrote concerning verification:

> We say that a sentence is factually significant to any person if, and only if, he knows how to verify the proposition which it purports to express - that is, if he knows what observations would lead him, under certain conditions, to accept the propositions as being true, or reject it as being false.[36]

For example, suppose there is a man who claims that there is a pencil in the next room. Such claims are in principle capable of verification because we can verify that there is indeed a pencil in the next room by going into it and finding out. Thus, his statement 'there is a pencil in the next room' is a meaningful statement because it can be empirically verified or falsified. But, say the man claims that 'God exists'. What tests are there for a statement like this? He might say 'look how the world is ordered!'. Now, we can verify that the world seems to be regular and ordered - that could be a meaningful statement therefore - but should we leap from this and say

'God exists'? Ayer would claim that to say 'God exists' here would be unwarranted by the evidence at hand and was therefore meaningless. However, it is important to get something clear here. Ayer is not claiming that God does not exist, but rather that we cannot talk sensibly (or factually) about things which cannot be verified or falsified. If we are to make sure of what we can know, Ayer claims that there must be clear guidelines as to what kinds of language are acceptable, otherwise we end in confusion.

Following on from this, in the early 1950s, Antony Flew threw down a challenge to theologians, and asked whether such statements as 'God loves mankind' are ever falsifiable. It seemed to him (and he expressed some degree of frustration) that theologians were not prepared to admit that any set of circumstances could arise that would demonstrate that the above statement was false. To illustrate the fluid character of religious statements, Flew employs a now famous parable (first suggested by John Wisdom)[37] concerning two explorers who enter a jungle and find a clearing in it which contains many flowers and many weeds. One of the explorers asserts that there must be a gardener, but the other does not believe this. After setting up watch, no gardener appears, so the believer postulates that the gardener is in fact invisible. They therefore decide to erect an electrified fence around the perimeter of the clearing, so that even if the gardener is invisible he will be noticed by the reaction of the fence when he touches it. Once again, there are no results. Nevertheless, the believer is still not convinced. Instead of admitting defeat, the believer decides to further qualify his/her belief in the gardener by postulating an invisible and intangible figure who has no scent or sound. At this point the sceptic despairs - just what remains of the believer's original assertion? Crucially, what is the difference between the believer's intangible and invisible gardener and one that has no actual existence?[38]

By this parable, Flew hopes to demonstrate that theologians have a tendency to widen the goal posts almost infinitely so that their beliefs are not nullified. He relates his parable to the problem of evil and suffering, and observes that it is as if there were no event or circumstance (however horrible) that would be conceded by the theologian as having the effect of nullifying belief in a loving God.[39] In fact, rather than conceding such dogmas, Flew maintains that theologians often make an endless stream of qualifications in order to hold on to their cherished beliefs, he writes:

> Someone tells us that God loves us as a father loves his children. We are reassured. But then we see a child dying of inoperable cancer of the throat. His earthly father is driven frantic in his efforts to help, but his Heavenly Father reveals no obvious sign of concern. Some qualification is made - God's love is 'not merely human love' or it is 'an inscrutable love' perhaps, -

and we realise that such sufferings are quite compatible with the truth of the assertion that 'God loves us as a father (but, of course...)'. We are reassured again.[40]

Flew claims that this constant manoeuvring and readjustment dissipates the original assertion, and 'a fine brash hypothesis may thus be killed by inches, the death by a thousand qualifications'.[41] So, the question that is being posed to the theist is, 'what difference would we expect to see in the universe if there is no God?' If there is no difference made to the world by asserting that there is a God or by insisting that there is no God, then 'does theism constitute a genuine assertion?'.[42] Hick elucidates:

> the underlying principle may be stated as follows: if a proposition p is to constitute a (true or false) assertion, the state of the universe which satisfies p must differ, other than in the fact of including this assertion, from any state of the universe that satisfies not-p.[43]

The challenges of Ayer and Flew have been responded to in broadly two different ways. One is the non-cognitivist ('religious language is not meant to be factual'), and the other is cognitive ('religious language is factual'). Again, we are somewhat polarising things here, but (following Hick's style) making straightforward distinctions can sometimes help us to identify the significance of each more readily. In the context of the logical positivist debate, the non-cognitivist view is represented by thinkers like Hare and Braithwaite, whereas we have seen that Hick supports a cognitivist view.

Before looking at these responses, one option might be to merely brush aside the demands for verification or falsification by pointing out that logical positivism as a philosophical movement has been largely discredited. Ironically, it seemed to collapse under the weight of its own demands. For example, how can we verify the 'verificationist principle' itself? Are we expected to accept its logic and method as self-evident or, even, analytically true? If not, then is it empirically verifiable? It seems difficult to specify how we can verify or falsify it, and therefore it appears to be meaningless according to its own criteria! Moreover, due largely to the innovations of Wittgenstein, the logical positivist criteria for meaning came to be seen as inadequate, and was replaced by the method of linguistic analysis. That is, instead of meaning being verified by empirical verification and falsification, meaning was to be found in the use of an expression in its varied contexts. Moreover, there seemed to be no agreement on what kind of verifiability principle to uphold. The verification principle's seeming inability to cope with criticism even led Ayer himself to confess that 'most of the defects were that nearly all of it [the verificationist principle] was false'.[44] Thus, some responses to the positivist challenge have been undisguisedly dismissive.[45] Nevertheless, Hick feels that the positivist challenge by Flew cannot be brushed aside so swiftly.[46] Moreover, he recommends that the whole notion of the cognitivity of religious propositions needs to be taken seriously and a response to the basic *sense* behind the verificationist principle is therefore required. In an important point, Hick maintains that:

> one does not have to have achieved a definitive formulation of a verifiability or falsifiability criterion to see that a supposedly declarative statement is pointless if it fails to claim that the facts of the universe are in some respect thus and not otherwise; and also that it is important for the theologian to be able to show that the central propositions with which he is concerned are not empty or pointless.[47]

However, not all scholars would agree with this, and they believe that there are many examples of things being meaningful apart from being described as factual or non-factual. Taking up Flew's challenge from a non-cognitivist perspective, Hare admits that Flew 'seems to me to be completely victorious'.[48] Hare's own response is a non-cognitivist option. He accepts that Flew has shown that religious statements seem to resist factual demonstration, but argues that this does not make them meaningless. He coins the term, *blik*, which means a way of looking at the world which 'although unverifiable and unfalsifiable, is also unshakeable'.[49] He argues that 'it was Hume who taught us that our whole commerce with the world depends upon our *blik* about the world; and that differences between *bliks* about the world cannot be settled by observation of what happens in the world'.[50] Hare gives a witty example of an Oxford academic who thinks that all his fellow academics are plotting against him. He will not allow any evidence (e.g. the outstanding friendliness of academics toward him) to count against his suspicions. In this sense we might say that he has a *blik* about academics, and we can see the meaning this has for him in his behaviour and attitude towards them. Or, as another example, one may be convinced that the steering mechanisms of cars are inherently faulty. Again, no amount of persuasive cajoling will convince one that this is not the case; one simply has a *blik* on this issue and thus prefers not to drive cars. Hare's point is that although *bliks* cannot be verified or falsified, they are nevertheless meaningful; or, as Dan Stiver puts it, they are 'existentially significant'.[51] Flew wants there to be an 'explanation' (in the empirical sense) of meaningfulness which settles matters with total certainty, but Hare's point is that we accept things as having meaning with a lot less stringent criteria.

Hare thinks that we *all* have *bliks*, so to speak: 'But it is nevertheless true to say, as Hume saw, that without a *blik* there can be no explanation; for it is by our *bliks* that we decide what is and what is not an explanation.'[52] So, returning to our examples, as well as the quaint academic who thinks that all his colleagues are against him, the rest of his colleagues have there own *blik* about the matter - that their friend is mistaken about academics. Or concerning the man with a paranoid *blik* about steering mechanisms, the 'rest of us' have a *blik* - that he is too overly cautious. Again, referring to the former example, Hare writes: 'Let us call that in which we differ from this lunatic, our respective *bliks*. He has an insane *blik* about dons; we have a sane one. It is important to realize that we have a sane one, not no *blik* at all...'[53] However, it is here that the problem with Hare's non-cognitivist response to Flew becomes apparent. It seems difficult for Hare to resist the charge that his *bliks* are purely arbitrary. There seems to be no safeguard which allows us to properly identify irrational or insane *bliks*. In which case, how does Hare distinguish in the quote above between sane and insane dons? Does he have a criterion which will judge the matter? And, if so, might this not take us right back to a form of empirical criteria, thus falling into Flew's hands?

Tackling the positivist challenge somewhat differently, Braithwaite claims that religious beliefs do not fit into 'truth-testing' empirical methods, but this does not mean that they are insignificant or meaningless. Rather, they are unfairly judged by narrow cognitive criteria. In fact, Braithwaite maintains that religious statements do not seem to be well characterised as being 'cognitive'. This does not mean that religious language is meaningless. Braithwaite points out that there are many things in human existence that we would see as being meaningful besides them being capable of strict rational analysis or empirical verification and falsification. One such thing is ethics or morality. It does not seem that moral exhortations are intended to be seen under the light of strict logical analysis or empirical verification. Instead the meaning and value of moral statements are gauged in relation to their 'fitting-ness' within the living community, and their purpose in guiding human conduct and life. If moral statements have a use in human life then surely they cannot be regarded as meaningless? But this does not mean that Braithwaite is seeking to lift religious statements out of the arena of empirical testing, so to speak. They still have meaning in our day to day lives and experience. That is, they are still empirical statements but we have transferred the criteria for meaningfulness away from the need to verify or falsify them and adopted the idea of use. This is what Braithwaite means when he writes: 'the only way of discovering how a statement is used is by an empirical enquiry; a statement need not itself be empirically verifiable, but that it is used in a particular way is always a straightforwardly empirical proposition'.[54]

Braithwaite does not think that religious statements (like moral statements) are merely emotive, rather they are *conative*. That means that religious statements show forth intentions to perform a course of action, or to follow a set direction in life. In a way, this means that religious statements are, in a sense, capable of being verified according to the principle: 'By their fruits ye shall know them.' Again, this is the sense that Braithwaite intends when he writes: 'This account is fully in accord with the spirit of empiricism, for whether or not a man has the intention of pursuing a particular behavior policy can be empirically tested, by both observing what he does and by hearing what he replies when he is questioned about his intentions.'[55]

Leading on from this second factor, Braithwaite argues that a person's decision to act in a certain way is not just illustrative of his/her sincerity, but is also a criterion for the meaningfulness of his/her assertions. Braithwaite writes that 'the meaning of a religious assertion is given by its use in expressing the asserter's intention to follow a specified policy of behaviour'.[56] Now, in saying this, Braithwaite, is suggesting that verifying or falsifying the factual content of religious statements isn't the real issue. The real issue is the intention to act in a certain way - and this is the real criteria for meaningfulness. Therefore religious statements should be regarded 'as being primarily declarations of adherence to a policy of action, declarations of commitment to a way of life'.[57]

Such a view has had its critics, and not necessarily from the likes of Flew and Ayer but from theologians themselves. Those committed to cognitivist or realist accounts of religious language, like Hick, will argue that religious statements are not intended to be just non-cognitivist guides towards a certain way of life, they are also meant to reflect the truth about the way things are. That is, it is not good enough to describe religious statements as fictional but meaningful because it is argued that what gives religious statements their real distinction is that they make real factual claims about the way the world is. For example, 'God exists' doesn't sound very like a mere commitment to a way of life - it is perhaps interpreted better by saying that it intends to be a statement about facts.

Indeed, Hick himself would agree with this criticism. He believes that Hare's *blik* is cognitively vacuous, it expresses 'a way of feeling and thinking about the world which expresses itself in pseudo-assertions, pseudo because they are neither verifiable nor falsifiable and are therefore factually empty'.[58]   Furthermore, responding to Braithwaite, Hick writes: 'In order to render a distinctive style of life both attractive and rational, it seems that religious beliefs must be regarded as assertions of fact, not merely as imaginative fictions.'[59] As we have seen, the underlying insistence by Hick is that religions make claims about the world and reality that are in principle capable of being true or false. If Christianity, in particular, is not to 'deny itself' it must 'insist on the properly factual character of its basic affirmations'.[60] However, it is interesting to note that in his later work Hick has increasingly qualified the factual nature of religious statements, such that much that he says about religious statements resembles Braithwaite's position that we have just outlined. For example, in *An Interpretation of Religion* (1989) he develops the view that religious statements are 'mythologically', rather than literally, true of the transcendent reality. Their primary purpose is to engender an appropriate response or disposition towards the transcendent and their 'truthfulness' should be judged by the 'fruits' evidenced in the religious followers of the various religions.[61]

Hick is concerned to meet Flew's criticism on Flew's own terms. His own response to the verificationist challenge is to point to the possibility of *eschatological verification*. If the naturalistic position is correct then we should expect that death constitutes an end to our individual existence: we live and die - that's all. If, however, we continue our conscious existences after death then both the believer and non-believer will be able to verify the fact and this could be taken as confirmation of religious expectations. For example, take the expectation of 'life after death', Moritz Schlick put it bluntly when he wrote:

> We must conclude that immortality, in the sense defined (i.e. 'survival after death', rather than 'never-ending life'), should not be regarded as a 'metaphysical problem', but as an empirical hypothesis, because it possesses logical verifiability. It could be verified by the following prescription: 'Wait until you die!'.[62]

If religious expectations can be experientially verified after death, then the demands for empirical verification can be met. That is, there can be an experience that will serve to verify religious statements and therefore confer upon them a factual status. Nevertheless, this raises the question of the nature of such verification. How is it to be done? Hick turns to the question of what might be called the 'mechanics' of verification.

What does it mean to verify something? Hick believes that verification is 'primarily the name for an event which takes place in human consciousness'.[63] That is, something is verified when somebody is there to do the verifying.[64] However, verification is not just a psychological notion, it is also a logical activity, therefore verifying is like knowing. Perhaps more importantly to Hick's scheme, some verification is conditional. That is, one has to go through a process, or take a specified route of action, in order to accomplish the verification of something.[65] For example, if you go into a conjoining room you may find certain objects - but *only if you go* into that conjoining room will you verify or falsify whether those certain objects are in fact in there. Such considerations are then utilised by Hick to propose a way by which religious statements can be shown to be cognitive. He places such things into an eschatological context. So, take the hypothesis of life-after-death, it has built into it a prediction that one will, after the date of one's bodily death, have conscious experiences - including the experience of remembering that death.[66] What follows from this is the notion that theism is to be verified in the eschaton, its verification relies on what might be called the eschatological experience which serves to show that theism contains the correct view of reality.

In verifying whether or not 'God loves humankind' is a correct proposition, there is the question of whether some definitive experiment can be undertaken which would settle matters.[67] An answer to this question is difficult to provide due to the fact that we are not in a position to see the whole picture. Getting into the correct position to judge such things is to have travelled more completely along life's journey, including (crucially) the post-mortem journey. Again, I. Crombie, another important contributor to the verificationist debate, believes that we are not yet in the position to decide whether or not God is a loving God. Similarly to Schlick, he writes: 'For the Christian the operation of getting into position to decide it is called dying.'[68] And again, 'the Christian...looks for the resurrection of the dead, and the life of the world to come; he believes, that is, that we do not see all of the picture, and that the parts which we do not see are precisely the parts which determine the design of the whole'.[69]

Hick follows very much the same line. In verifying the claims of Christian theism, he argues that one must be permitted to take into account the entirety of the Christian 'explanation' rather than following a reduced version of it or even employing a critique which might be considered 'external' to the Christian worldview. By this Hick is meaning to direct our attention particularly to the eschatological dimension of the human/divine story *as is contained in the Christian hope.*[70] Therefore, the resources available to demonstrate the cognitivity of Christian theistic claims are not to be located solely in this earthly life and existence, but in the life to come also.

However, with the possibility of life after death also comes a disruption of the 'symmetrical' concept of straightforward verification and falsification. That is, the notion of life after death in theism, is a verification of an *asymmetrical* kind says Hick. By way of explanation, it could be said that *symmetrical* verification and falsification is a simple case of something being manifestly true or manifestly false, like both sides of a coin. For example, the statement 'there is a table in the next room' is capable of verification (if indeed there is a table in the next room), or falsification (if there isn't). However, Hick points out that the prediction of life after death cannot be falsified, only verified. A religious statement which predicts that there shall be a life after death:

> will be verified in one's own experience if it is true, but which cannot be falsified if it is false. That is to say, it can be false, but that it is false can never be a fact which anyone has experimentally verified. The circumstance does not undermine the meaningfulness of the hypothesis, however, since it is also such that if it be true, it will be known to be true.[71]

If we return for a moment to Flew's parable of the gardener, Hick counters it with a parable of his own. He describes a journey by two people along a road, one believes that at the end of the road there is a Celestial City, the other does not. The believer in the Celestial City interprets the trials that they both face along the journey as 'purposeful' in order to develop their characters into worthy citizens. The other interprets such events as part of an aimless ramble and just enjoys the good and endures the bad. During the course of the journey the two companions do not necessarily have different theories about the details of the journey or the experiences along the way, however they do differ with regard to the ultimate destination and meaning. When at last they turn the final corner and suddenly view the Celestial City it will turn out that the believer was correct - that is, there has been an 'eschatological verification'.[72]

Nevertheless, there are further problems to be addressed. For example, to whom will it be 'known' to be true? Or, will the supposed expected verification be unambiguous? In fact, the existence of an afterlife, if there is one, may not serve as a verification of theism in any way at all and Hick recognises this in an important statement:

> It [an afterlife] would not be a state of affairs which is manifestly incompatible with the non-existence of God. It might be taken as a surprising natural fact. The atheist, in his resurrection body, and able to remember his life on earth, might say that the universe has turned out to be more complex, and perhaps more to be approved of, than he had realised.[73]

What afterlife experiences would serve as a verification of theism? Hick opts for the concept of the Kingdom of God which he envisages as a 'situation which points unambiguously to the existence of a loving God'.[74] However, what does this unambiguous situation constitute? He believes that it would involve firstly an awareness of the completion of God's purposes in us, and secondly, an experience of communion with God as revealed by the person of Christ. That is, to avoid resurrected persons seeing their post-mortem experiences as purely natural phenomena, there will be an 'experience of communion with God as He has made Himself known to men in Christ'.[75] Clearly, such expectations and experiences are tailored specifically for a verification of Christian theism. In light of Hick's pluralistic hypothesis (which was to come later in Hick's career and philosophical/religious outlook and is considered in chapter five) these Christian-specific expectations would have to be modified.

Eschatological Verification, Certainty and Ambiguity

Could one say that Hick's notion of eschatological verification turns religious faith into a provisional certainty? Put crudely, does the notion of 'wait until you die' actually seem to run counter to the sentiments of faith and certitude that we might commonly associate with committed faith? Here there are a host of related problems and objections. For example, the idea of a provisional attitude towards an eschatological hope might seem to run counter to concepts of worship and thanksgiving. Can sincere worship take place within a context of *provisionality*? Indeed, Alasdair MacIntyre has said that 'religious faith...is never provisional...the gladness of the Easter morning is never a conditional joy'.[76]

Clearly, this criticism has some force in the context of committed faith. It can be maintained that the believer may consciously aspire to have an allegiance to his/her religion which is unconditional. Thus, if that believer is awaiting some sort of confirmation or verification by an anticipated situation in the eschaton then it is almost as if his/her beliefs cannot be unconditional.   Or rather, for those believers who have wholeheartedly 'grasped' their faith/tradition it can sound almost patronising to ask a believer if he/she is awaiting a *verification* of their beliefs. This is not necessarily to say that believers perceive their faith to be beyond reason, but that they hold that their faith is perfectly reasonable in this present life. For them, their faith is already verified by their religious experience (and, perhaps also, reasoned argument); indeed faith in the 'unseen' would seem to be commended in the Gospel of John when the resurrected Jesus confronts Thomas: 'Then Jesus told him, "Because you have seen me, you have believed; blessed are those who have not seen and have yet believed".' (Jn.20:29). Thus, we might argue that eschatological verification conveys the idea that the cognitive validity of religious language and experience has been effectively *postponed*.

Nevertheless, to pursue this line of criticism is also partly misleading. Hick's commitment to the religious ambiguity of the universe means that any religious 'knowing' is a matter for the individual's own experiencing-as, in this sense it is not *public* knowledge. Or else, we should remind ourselves of Hick's two levels of discourse: the 'philosophical-explanatory' which describes the universe as religiously ambiguous with no worldview being more probable; and the 'theological-experiential' which speaks of our own religious experiencing of the world. Hick is not doubting that the religious person is convinced of the truth of their beliefs, neither is he claiming that their faith is tentative and provisional. In fact, when characterising religious faith as 'experiencing-as', Hick acknowledges that 'prophets' and 'apostles' (examples he employs) can experience the world in overwhelmingly religious terms.[77] That is, he acknowledges that there are people for whom God is a given or 'lived' reality. So, to respond to Hick's eschatological verification theory by saying that it underlines agnosticism is a mistake. What Hick is doing is trying to lend to religious statements a *cognitive dignity*. His theory is not directed towards the believer but to those who would claim that religious language is cognitively meaningless; put another way - his theory is a defence on behalf of religion to its cultured despisers. On a strictly theoretical basis, Hick has satisfied Flew's verificationist demands with his proposal of eschatological verification.

However, in light of the admission by Hick that religious people (e.g. 'prophets' and 'apostles' etc.) can be overwhelmingly convinced in this life by their religious 'experiencing-as', T.R. Mathis in his book *Against John Hick*, critically examines Hick's putative eschatological verification and concludes that it is not necessary in Hick's system of thought. In an excellent summary of his argument, Mathis writes:

> Faith is a human response to God's self-revelation in the history of the world which becomes actual through a person's religious experiencing-as. Hick believes this experience makes possible an uncompelled cognition of the presence and purpose of God while preserving the freedom and responsibility of the individual in relation to God's infinite, omnipotent nature. Knowledge of the presence and purpose of God is in this way supposedly revealed to people in this life. Conceivably therefore, any rational person could acquire (as did the prophets and apostles) an awareness of God's loving purpose with regard to any set of this-worldly circumstances. Presuming this is possible, eschatological verification is then not necessary to establish theistic statements as factual, for one could experience the circumstances of the world, including its evils, in conjunction with the presence and purpose of God.[78]

Mathis' point is cogent. If people can indeed come to a place of religious certitude in this life, which Hick admits, then it can only be that this present environment is capable of enabling such certitude. Thus, if theism can be verified here and now then an eschatological verification is surplus to requirements. Here, Mathis is speaking of an experiential confirmation of theistic belief. (This might be contrasted with a purely rational or notional belief in God acquired through reasoning and argument.) It is at the experiential level that religious people can feel intensely aware of the reality of their faith, and it is this level that Mathis appears to be speaking of with regard to a 'this-worldly' verification of religious faith.

Nevertheless, although Mathis argument seems strong, in my view Hick is still right to assert that the variety of evidence available is capable of both a naturalistic and theistic interpretation and so we must await an eschatological resolution. Moreover, it also seems possible to reverse Mathis' point. For can we not suppose that there are atheists (or non-religious persons) whose experiences have *convinced* them that there is no God? Perhaps such experiences might be characterised as harrowing personal circumstances, or an overwhelming sense of human suffering, or being witness to some horrific wartime incident, or else sheer indifference or being a 'convinced' naturalist. If it is possible to be fully persuaded that there is no God due to this-worldly circumstances then, following the form of Mathis' reasoning, there is no need for eschatological *falsification* because theism has been falsified by experiencing the circumstances of the world. The point is not that this present world is incapable of allowing people to have an 'awareness' of the truth of their stance, it is that it is *capable* of somewhat experientially verifying contradictory stances. This, as Hick might say, is typical of the ambiguous nature of this world that awaits an eschatological resolution. In short, there may be strong evidence for theistic *and* atheistic claims in this world. And, perhaps the kind of verification that Hick is suggesting is the type that cannot be interpreted as suggesting *anything other* than the truth of the religious worldview.

However, is such verification still possible in the present? Mathis also thinks that some prominent scholars clearly believe that there are 'evidences' within the present existence that should serve to demonstrate/verify theistic belief. Indeed, the famous Christian promise 'seek and you will find' (Matt.7:7) might seem to run contrary to the notion that theism can only be verified after death. Mathis' point is that for some thinkers like F.R. Tennant, Richard Swinburne or Hugh Montefiore the evidence for theism 'is in principle knowable by others, that is, that others confronted with the same evidence should similarly be led to the same conclusion'.[79] Thus, one can get into a position (presumably by examining the available evidence) of seeing that theism contains the more probable (or economic) explanation for the universe - the scales may be tipped in favour of theism after all. Nevertheless, to merely indicate that the balance of probability (in the minds of sophisticated scholars rather than the *hoi polloi*) leans towards theism seems to fall short of the sort of full, unambiguous eschatological verification in the sense that Hick is intending. That is, even if a theologian were to stumble across a particularly effective 'proof' for God's existence this might still not be experientially or existentially compelling.

Perhaps the fact that this world seems to present an ambiguous message with regard to a theistic worldview (e.g. the problem of evil), shows that clear verification has not taken place? Somewhat endorsing a similar standpoint, Peter Donovan writes that so-called 'evidences' for theism in this present earthly life 'are not evidence in the sense of observations tending to verify, or put beyond reasonable doubt, the truths of the statements in question. For it is quite open to the non-believer, and in no way irrational for him, to see things as fully accounted for in natural terms'.[80] And this, surely, seems to be Hick's warrant for eschatological verification (or 'resolution'): a situation (existential and rational) in the eschaton that can put beyond reasonable doubt the truth of theistic belief, to settle matters once and for all.

As already indicated, a related question concerns ambiguity and freedom. We saw earlier that Hick makes a connection between the religious ambiguity of the universe and the freedom of human beings. But it is possible to question the validity, or necessity, of this connection. For example, would the removal of ambiguity affect freedom? Perhaps much depends on the manner rather than the fact of disclosure. It is surely not uncommon that a person can learn the truth about something but nevertheless ignore the truth that is staring them in the face? Similarly, Terence Penelhum argues that it is possible to disambiguate the universe without destroying freedom:

> [A]ll that is necessary is the removal of grounds for reasonable doubt, and this does not require being overwhelmed. It could happen when a conclusive argument was produced, or a miracle occurred, or a past life was systematically remembered. Such events would not take away the freedom of those who were aware of them. For they could *refuse to accept* them.[81]

Thus, Penelhum maintains that Hick is mistaken if he thinks that some sort of total religious ambiguity is required for freedom to be upheld. He is suggesting that a slight adjustment to the fine balance of ambiguity or the 'removal of grounds for reasonable doubt' would not seriously upset human freedom.

However, it is possible that Penelhum's criticism reflects a misunderstanding with regard to Hick's conception of the world as religiously ambiguous. This misunderstanding is located in a failure to distinguish between the philosophical-explanatory and the experiential-theological modes of Hick's thinking. The kind of ambiguity that Hick is speaking of is not an anodyne, featureless ambiguity; or rather, a 'neutral' world which is pivoted exactly in the middle between religious and naturalistic interpretations. Or rather, even though this might be maintained as a theoretical or philosophical interpretation, it is not an *experiential* one because human beings don't live their lives in such non-partisan ways. We have seen that Hick *does* acknowledge the idea that some people can live their lives so totally convinced of their theistic beliefs that their whole experiencing-as is *saturated* with the divine presence. But, equally, a non-believer can feel certain of their naturalistic perspective. Thus, for Hick, the world is ambiguous in the sense that it is capable of experientially supporting contradictory stances and religious passions. In an important clarification, Hick writes:

> For whilst the objective ambiguity of our environment consists in the fact that it is capable of being interpreted in a variety of ways, its consciously experienced and actively lived-in character consists in its actually being interpreted as meaningful in a particular way which, whilst it operates, excludes other possible ways.[82]

Nevertheless, Chris Sinkinson makes a point which is related to Penelhum's when he draws attention to the fact that Hick characterises the experiences of great religious figures like Jesus as *involuntary*. That is, the experience of God for Jesus was as compelling as natural experience. Thus, Sinkinson asks how Hick reconciles this idea of an involuntary religious experience with his other idea that religious interpretation is a voluntary act; that is, a voluntary experiencing which is compatible with a God who maintains an epistemic distance from his creatures in order to facilitate an uncompelled free response? Was Jesus not free in his religious response to God? Is he the exception in Hick's religious epistemology? Sinkinson thinks that there is a tension in Hick's thinking here between freedom and certainty in faith. He argues that Hick is wrong to maintain that religious ambiguity is required for freedom. Even though religious figures like Jesus were overwhelming aware of God's presence they were nonetheless free. He suggests that 'there is nothing incoherent in a free moral agent adopting a religious belief, even though compelled to do so by reason, revelation or miracles'.[83] Thus, once again, Hick does not require ambiguity for freedom.

Sinkinson seems to have uncovered a difficulty in Hick's thinking. However, it is possible that it is double-edged because, in criticising Hick's view, it seems that Sinkinson (who argues from a Christian theistic perspective) must face up to a question that he begs: If religious freedom is compatible with an awareness of God's presence, then why is God's presence not unambiguous to all? For, if we accept Sinkinson's point, we should all be able to be like the great religious figures and still be considered free agents. Consequently, switching to matters of theodicy, God's choice to remain hidden from the human race as a whole is unjustified. Obviously, this problem can also be directed at Hick himself, but it might be suggested that he faces a lesser difficulty because in his later pluralistic work he seeks to draw attention to the overwhelming religious experience of *all* the great figures of the world's religions. This presumably means that although he recognises the compelling nature of some religious experiences this does not compel belief in just one of the religions because of the sheer *diversity* of experiences that there are. Thus, despite the overwhelming nature of some religious experience the world still remains religiously ambiguous due to the varieties of religious experience. This might not be the case if overwhelming religious experience in general was seen to be endorsing one particular religion's views.

In another criticism, Penelhum points out that Hick seems to present things as a choice between naturalism and religious belief. Contrary to this, Penelhum draws attention to immense variations and subtleties that exist even in the western cultural scene where such a two-fold distinction seems most at home. Thus he maintains that:

> we are not faced with a simple theist-naturalist ambiguity, in which each side can justify itself, at least negatively, in relation to the other; we are faced, rather by a world that exhibits *multiple* religious and ideological ambiguity.[84]

It is true that Hick presents the religious ambiguity of the universe as a choice between religious and naturalistic interpretations, and this may be a weakness in Hick's deliberations on this matter. However, if Hick has a tendency to use polarities when discussing epistemic distance, he certainly would agree with the sort of multiple ambiguity that Penelhum suggests is the case. This becomes readily apparent when one glances at Hick's pluralistic hypothesis that we shall deal with more closely in chapter five. In this hypothesis, Hick is clearly presenting a picture which speaks of the multi-faceted nature of the human response to the transcendent. Thus, the fact that Hick draws attention to such multiple religious interpretations of the universe and human existence seems to make Penelhum's criticism somewhat redundant. However, speaking of such multiple religious interpretations could pose problems for the coherency of eschatological verification. For example, in Hick's later writings (having advanced towards a pluralistic perspective) he tends to speak of the 'religious' rather than the theistic interpretation. And, this religious interpretation is contrasted with a naturalistic interpretation. However, within Hick's pluralistic hypothesis the religious perspective includes Buddhism in its broad remit and as Buddhism is a non-theistic religion it is difficult to distinguish it from naturalism in any clear way. Thus, it seems that the clearly drawn lines (e.g. theism versus atheism) that characterised his earliest epistemological work become more fuzzy as we progress towards his later work.

Summary

Hick's earliest work was concerned with religious epistemology. He suggested that religious beliefs resemble sense perceptions rather than propositional beliefs. Moreover, he argued that religious beliefs should not be seen as wholly different from the rest of our perceiving, it is closely connected to our experience of the world. In fact, all experience is *experiencing-as*, and if this is the case then even our basic perceptual beliefs share the characteristic of 'experiencing-as' with religious beliefs. Hick believes that all objects or events arrive in our minds not in a pure and unmediated form but shaped and filtered through our interpretative mental structures.

It is this fundamental building block in Hick's thought that has profoundly affected his subsequent philosophical and theological work. It probably finds its most significant final expression in his *An Interpretation of Religion* (1989), where he presents his view of religions as representing multiple human experiences of (rather than literal propositions about) the transcendent.

Nevertheless, although he wishes to stress the nature of religious beliefs as involving personal experience, he also argues for their cognitive (or realist) status as 'fact-asserting'. That is, *contra* non-cognitivists like Hare and Braithwaite, religious beliefs are not just vacuous poetry or edifying moral stories, they also make factual statements about the world and reality. We might also connect this with a basic affirmation in Hick's writings of the supra-natural character of religious expression in contrast with naturalistic perspectives which limit the human journey to this life only. Hick regards such naturalistic pictures as profoundly pessimistic, and argues that the cosmic optimism present in the majority of religious expectations should point to a life after death. Hick utilises the idea of a future fulfilment of religious expectations and proposes (in response to the 'verificationist challenge') an eschatological verification of religious statements and expectations. In such a way Hick provides the empirical criterion for rendering religious statements factually meaningful. However, criticisms of this idea have questioned the seeming *provisionality* of eschatological verification. For example, is such a notion actually foreign to the religious mind with its sense of commitment in the here and now? Is it overly sceptical with regard to the availability of convincing evidence in favour of the theistic worldview in the present? Moreover, are related ideas such as the basic religious ambiguity of the universe (or 'epistemic distance') strictly necessary in order to preserve the freedom of human beings? And, in what way is the universe ambiguous - is it a straightforward choice between naturalism and religious belief? As we have seen, some of these questions may reflect a misunderstanding of Hick's thinking.

The basic idea of an eschatological verification of religious statements leads us to ask about the plausibility of human survival beyond death, but an extended treatment of this subject did not follow until after Hick had turned his attention to another question – the problem of evil and suffering. So, it is to this question that we now turn.

Notes

1. See Hick, 'Religious Faith as Experiencing-As' in P. Badham, (ed.), *A John Hick Reader*, p.34.
2. Hick, 'Rational Theistic Beliefs Without Proofs' in Ibid., p.56.
3. Hick, *Faith and Knowledge*, pp.95-96.
4. Ibid., p.98.
5. Hick, 'Religious Faith as Experiencing-As' in P. Badham, op.cit., p.37.
6. L. Wittgenstein, *Philosophical Investigations*, p.193.
7. Hick, *Faith and Knowledge*, p.107.
8. Ibid.
9. Ibid., p.123.
10. W. Alston, 'John Hick, Faith and Knowledge' in A. Sharma, (ed.), *God, Truth and Reality*, p.28.
11. Hick, 'Rational Theistic Beliefs Without Proofs' in P. Badham, op.cit., p.58.
12. See an account of this principle in R. Swinburne, *The Existence of God*. See also, Hick, *An Interpretation of Religion*, pp.214-220.
13. Hick, 'Rational Theistic Beliefs Without Proofs' in Badham, op.cit., p.62.
14. Hick, *An Interpretation of Religion*, p.223.
15. J. Hick, *God and the Universe of Faiths*, p.67.
16. C. Sinkinson, *The Universe of Faiths*, p.144.
17. For a detailed examination of this distinction, see S. Twiss, 'The Philosophy of Religious Pluralism: A Critical Appraisal of Hick and His Critics'.
18. Hick, 'Rational Theistic Beliefs Without Proofs' in Badham, op.cit., p.59.

19. Hick, *Disputed Questions*, p.4.
20. Ibid., p.12.
21. Hick, *The Fifth Dimension*, p.52.
22. Hick, *God and the Universe of Faiths*, p.185.
23. Ibid.
24. Thus, for example, H.J. Richards writes, 'The good news is not that resurrection of the body is a guaranteed future bonus, but that it is a present reality.' *Death and After*, p.38.
25. Hick, *God and the Universe of Faiths*, p.184.
26. Hick, *Disputed Questions*, p.13.
27. Ibid., p.15.
28. D. Cupitt, *The Time Being*, p.66.
29. D.Z. Phillips, 'Great Expectations: Philosophy, Ontology and Religion' in J. Runzo, (ed.), *Is God Real?*, p.206.
30. Ibid., p.207.
31. Hick, 'Belief in God: Metaphysics and Values' in J. Runzo, op.cit., p.132.
32. Ibid.
33. See Hick, 'Religion as Fact Asserting' in P. Badham, op.cit.
34. Defining logical positivism, A. Quinton writes: 'A body of philosophical doctrine developed from the late 1920's by the Vienna Circle under the leadership of Schlick and Carnap. It asserted the meaninglessness of metaphysics, which it held to consist of all propositions that are neither verifiable by empirical observation nor demonstrable as analytic, and conceived philosophy as consisting purely of analysis, conducted with the assistance of formal logic with a view to the logical reconstruction of mathematical and scientific discourse. Most logical positivists regarded religious and moral utterances as metaphysical and thus meaningless.' 'Logical Positivism' in A. Bullock and O. Stallybrass (eds.), *The Fontana Dictionary of Modern Thought*, p.35.
35. O. Hanfling, *Logical Positivism*, p.34.
36. A. J. Ayer, *Language, Truth and Logic*, p.35.
37. See J. Wisdom, 'Gods' in *Proceedings of the Aristotelian Society* London, 1944-45. See the same piece reprinted in Hick, (ed.), *Classical and Contemporary Readings in the Philosophy of Religion*.
38. A. Flew, 'Theology and Falsification' in A. Flew and A. MacIntyre (eds.), *New Essays in Philosophical Theology*, p.96.
39. Ibid., p.98.
40. Ibid., pp.98-99.
41. Ibid., p.97. (Emphasis mine.)
42. Hick, *Faith and Knowledge*, p.167.
43. Ibid., p.166.
44. A.J. Ayer remarking in *The Listener*, March 2, 1978, p.270. Cited in W.J. Abraham, *An Introduction to the Philosophy of Religion*, p.20.
45. For example, Plantinga writes: 'If the notion of verifiability cannot be so much as be explained, if we cannot so much as say what it is for a statement to be empirically verifiable, then we scarcely need worry about whether religious statements are or are not verifiable.' A. Plantinga, *God and Other Minds*, p.168.
46. Hick feels Plantinga's response (in the note above) is 'unhelpful philosophical pedantry', Hick, *Problems of Religious Pluralism*, p.114.
47. Ibid.
48. See R.M. Hare's discussion in 'Theology and Falsification' in A. Flew and A. MacIntyre (eds.), op.cit., p.99.
49. Hick, *Faith and Knowledge*, p.162.
50. Hare, op.cit. p.101.

51. D. Stiver, *The Philosophy of Religious Language: Sign, Symbol and Story*, p.51.
52. Hare, op.cit., p.101.
53. Ibid.
54. R.B. Braithwaite, 'An Empiricist's View of the Nature of Religions Belief' in Hick (ed.), *The Existence of God*, p.236.
55. Ibid., p.237.
56. Ibid., p.239.
57. Ibid.
58. Hick, *Problems of Religious Pluralism*, p.110.
59. Hick, *Philosophy of Religion*, p.96.
60. Hick, *God and the Universe of Faiths*, p.24.
61. See Part V of Hick, *An Interpretation of Religion*, for an extended discussion about the ethical criterion.
62. See M. Schlick, 'Meaning and Verification' *Philosophical Review*, 1936. Cited in Hick, *Faith and Knowledge*, p.179.
63. Hick, *Faith and Knowledge*, p.171.
64. Ibid., pp.170-171.
65. Ibid., p.173.
66. See Ibid., pp.173, 175.
67. See I. Crombie's discussion in 'Theology and Falsification' in A. Flew and A. MacIntyre (eds), op.cit., pp.124-125.
68. Ibid., p.126.
69. Ibid., p.129.
70. For example, he writes: 'the possibility of experiential confirmation is thus built into the Christian concept of God; and the notion of eschatological verification seeks to relate this fact to the problem of theological meaning.' *Faith and Knowledge*, pp.176-177.
71. Ibid., p.175.
72. See Ibid., p.177.
73. Ibid., p.186.
74. Ibid., p.187.
75. Ibid.
76. A. MacIntyre, 'Faith and the Verification Principle' in A. MacIntyre and R.G. Smith (eds.), *Metaphysical Beliefs*, p.181. Further, if things are *provisional* then: 'religious beliefs could never be anything more than as yet unconfirmed hypotheses, warranting nothing more than a provisional and tentative adherence. But such an adherence is completely uncharacteristic of religious belief...For part of the content of Christian belief is that a decisive adherence is given to God. So to hold Christian belief as a hypothesis would be to render it no longer Christian belief.' Ibid.
77. See, 'Rational Theistic Beliefs Without Proofs' in P. Badham, op.cit., p.59.
78. T.R. Mathis, *Against John Hick*, p.84.
79. Ibid., pp.76-77.
80. P. Donovan, *Religious Language*, p.49.
81. T. Penelhum, 'Reflections on the Ambiguity of the World' in A. Sharma, op.cit., p.172.
82. Hick, *An Interpretation of Religion*, p.129.
83. C. Sinkinson, op.cit., p.61.
84. T. Penelhum, op.cit., p.170.

Chapter Two

Evil and Soul-Making

Having a forward look is crucial, Hick thinks, for an adequate response to the problem of evil and suffering. The problem, at least for Christian theology, is a matter of reconciling the existence of evil with the existence of an all-loving and all-powerful God. A truly optimistic view of human life in the context of a purposeful, all-loving Creator, surely possesses an eschatological resolution or completion as a vital feature? Hick turned his attention to such issues in *Evil and the God of Love* (1966). This book is widely considered to contain the definitive historical survey of Christian responses to the problem of evil. It also contains a developed argument which represents Hick's own contribution and suggestions concerning the age-old conundrum. Hick does not seek to present a solution to the problem of evil, and he is clear about the limitations of theodicy as an intellectual activity. Thus, his own theodicy 'offers an understanding of our human situation; but this is not the same as offering practical help and comfort to those in the midst of acute pain or deep suffering'.[1]

In *Evil and the God of Love* Hick identifies two different streams of argument in the concern of theodicy: the Augustinian and the Irenaean. It is with the latter type that Hick has greater affinity. The Augustinian theodicy forms the backbone of the traditional Christian account of evil in that it traces the origin of evil to the primordial misuse of freedom by created beings. According to this view, angels and humankind were originally made free and perfectly good and lived harmoniously with God. That is, evil was not created by God, and, moreover, evil has no real substance of its own at all. Instead, evil can be described as the malfunction of something good, or the privation of goodness (*privatio boni*). The creatures went wrong, they used their freedom to disobey God and hence corrupted the goodness that had been divinely installed. Evil is the result of created beings misusing their freedom and therefore bringing about the evil and suffering that we experience in the world - it is the creatures' responsibility, not the Maker's.

However, Hick has a number of objections to the coherence of this view. Firstly, he thinks that this kind of theodicy achieves only a 'Pyrrhic victory' because it appears to rest on a literal understanding of the story of the Garden of Eden. As such, then, the Augustinian theodicy can only make *theoretical* sense. It is logically possible, but stumbles when it comes to an assessment of likelihood. Hick points out that any plausible theodicy should properly consider evolutionary accounts of human origins, and thus acknowledge our creation as immature rather than perfect beings.

Secondly, Hick wants to question the possibility of the origin of evil from Augustinian premises about the pre-Fall condition of created rational beings who are supposedly morally good and perfect. Augustine wrote concerning the original immortality and perfection of human beings: 'God created certain beings immortal in the sense of being unable to die: man was created immortal in a different sense, being able not to die, an ability given to him from the Tree of Life, and not from a natural endowment.'[2] Furthermore, 'The first man had the ability not to sin, not to die, not to desert the good...This was the first freedom of the will, the ability not to sin.'[3] Hick replies: 'The notion that man was at first spiritually and morally good, oriented in love towards his Maker, and free to express his flawless nature without even the hindrance of contrary temptations, and yet that he preferred to be evil and miserable, cannot be saved from the charge of self-contradiction and absurdity.'[4] Also, 'The basic and inevitable criticism is that the idea of an unqualifiedly good creature committing sin is self-contradictory and unintelligible.'[5] To be clear, Hick does not deny that perfect beings are free to sin, but he is denying that it is possible for perfect beings to *choose* to sin. If they were perfectly good then it should be impossible to make such a choice unless some sort of imperfection was already present in the creature which allowed the errant choice to be made! Thus, Hick reinterprets the notion of original perfection to mean that the 'original' creation was perfectly geared towards producing the perfect result, or outcome, that God desired. He accords with Schleiermacher's conception: 'For him [Schleiermacher], the "original perfection" of the creation is its suitability for accomplishing the purpose for which God created it.'[6]

Thirdly, Hick wants to question the success of the Augustinian type of theodicy in attempting to 'shift the blame for the occurrence of evil from the creator to the creatures'.[7] Hick believes that the Augustinian theodicy fails because it does not succeed in shifting the blame away from God for the existence of evil. Augustine essentially pulls the carpet from under his own feet with his ideas on predestination. According to the classical picture, everything that occurs does so because God wills it. Things and events are therefore predestined in advance. Take for example this quote from Augustine (one which Hick selects): 'Therefore they (the saved) were elected before the foundation of the world with that predestination in which God foreknew what He Himself would do; but they were elected out of the world with that calling whereby God fulfilled that which He predestined.'[8] Now, if God foreknew the choices his free creatures would make, then God cannot be successfully displaced by his creatures for the responsibility for evil's existence. Hick feels, therefore, that theodicy is more successful if it does not try to shift responsibility away from God but instead fully acknowledges that responsibility from the outset.

Above all, the fundamental difficulty that Hick has with the Augustinian theodicy is that it is oriented towards the past, and seeks to justify the existence of evil by the misuse of freewill in prehistoric times. Hick believes that this is the wrong orientation - theodicy should be forward looking. He writes:

> The Augustinian type of theodicy looks to the past (i.e. explaining evil in terms of a misuse of freewill eons ago)...in contrast, the Irenaean type of theodicy is eschatological, and finds justification for the existence of evil in the infinite (because eternal) good which God is bringing out of the temporal process.[9]

Thus, Hick prefers an 'Irenaean' strategy. Irenaeus distinguished two stages in the human story. First of all, humanity has been created in the 'image of God' (*imago dei*). This is indicative of the potential and 'specialness' of humanity. However, the destiny of human beings is to become like God (*similitudo dei*). The outworking of the process from the first of these stages to the second is a long arduous struggle with sin towards the likeness of God. For Irenaeus, there was an initial innocence in the Garden of Eden. Sin was not a fully conscious rebellion of 'perfect' beings, but an act of weakness. Here, evil and suffering are understood as remedial rather than punitive. Sufferings are divine utilities towards helping us reach *similitudo dei*.

Hick's theodicy is a contemporary reading of these basic ideas. In agreement with Irenaeus, he does not wish to look back to a cosmic mistake made by human beings, but rather speaks of a divine purpose to bring a limitlessly good outcome in the future from the evil that has been weaved into the ways things are. He places a great deal of importance on human freedom. As we saw in chapter one, he maintains that human beings are placed into a religiously ambiguous world. If God were 'present' to human beings then this would stifle human freedom; human beings would not really be free to walk towards or away from God. Such epistemic distance is a necessary condition for free personal development. Furthermore, the freedom of human beings is inextricably tied up with the physical universe. This world is the environment in which human beings find themselves and which is subject, not to the wills of human beings, but to physical processes. That is, it is a world which is not plastic to our wishes, it can work for or against us: the fire that warms a shivering family against the cold can also destroy another family's house - the fire is not 'swayed' by opinion, it operates according to physical laws. This situation makes the world a challenge to live in. But it is through such challenges that we develop into fuller persons. If the world were pliable to our every whim, then it would be a morally static existence with no demands being made or difficult choices to face. Put simply, a sugary paradise would not be conducive to effective soul-making.

We are animals in our origin, but 'children of God' in our destinies. That is, we are created as an organic part of the world and, common to other creatures, there is a basic survival instinct that has fuelled a self-regardingness at the heart of each human being. For Hick, the 'sinful nature' is to be seen as synonymous with this basic self-regardingness, and furthermore, it is this self-regardingness that is to be overcome as we move towards the divine will.[10]

However, the process of transforming human animals into children of God is something that cannot be realistically achieved in this lifetime. To expect the Irenaean perspective to work within such parameters would result in its failure. Hick thinks that extending the human journey beyond death is essential for the Irenaean theodicy to make sense. Perfecting human beings takes longer than a single lifetime; and evil and suffering can, in the short term, actually work against the soul-making project and destroy souls just as effectively as making them. Of course, Hick cannot really resolve this possibility by just extending the time allotted; but given *unlimited* time, he thinks that the soul-making journey will have produced a limitlessly good outcome for all. Viewing the Irenaean perspective from within a lifetime, we cannot see the full outworking of the process, and it can seem that evil serves only a destructive purpose. Viewed from a much longer period of time, we may see many peaks and troughs, so to speak, but they will have eventually brought about a good end. This means that Hick is suggesting that the environment following death provides similar challenges to our present environment so that the process of soul-making can continue. However, we will have more to say about this in chapter four.

Following on from this, it is perhaps hardly surprising that Hick is committed to the idea of universal salvation. There will be no loose ends, rather (in the words of Mother Julian of Norwich) 'all shall be well, and all shall be well, and all manner thing shall be well'.[11] The alternative picture, that some will find themselves eternally damned, can only serve to obstruct the possibility of a viable theodicy. Hell's existence would only perpetuate an unresolved dualism. That is, however bright the enjoyment of the blessed, the deepest darkness would still be eternally present in the misery of the lost. Moreover, if God is all-loving and all-powerful then it seems unthinkable that the divine will would be unwilling to save all of humanity, or that his loving purposes would ultimately fail for certain individuals. Thus Hick writes that 'the doctrine of hell has as its implied premise either that God does not desire to save all His human creatures, in which case He is only limitedly good, or that His purpose has finally failed in the case of some...'.[12]

However, what of human freedom? One possible question is: Can Hick be committed to the notion of free beings developing in a religiously ambiguous world and at the same time confidently assert the universal salvation of all humanity? In seeking to answer this, it is important to understand that Hick assents to universalism as a *practical*, rather than a scientific or logical, certainty. Universalism is inevitable not because the outcome has been 'predetermined' (thus undermining our freedom), but because God's character and capacities make such an outcome extremely likely. To clarify this, picture a game of chess between a novice and a Grand Master. Although the game has not been rigged in advance, (and at times the Grand Master allows the novice to take the odd bishop), the outcome will almost certainly be a victory for the Grand Master. Similarly, Hick asks us to consider the outcome of a relationship between an all-loving, all-knowing God and a human being. Surely, even if we are not assenting to divine predestination, we can be confident that the outcome will be in accordance with the divine will? In addition, Hick alludes to Augustine's view that human hearts are restless until, ultimately, they rest in God ('...*quia fecisti nos ad te, domine, et inquietum est cor nostrum donec requiescat in te*').[13] This means that our 'natures' are orientated *towards* the divine, and this basic divine 'instinct' will draw us freely into the goodness of the divine will. In the end, all human souls will have arrived, through a long process of difficult and, at times, bewildering soul-making and refinement, into the perfect divine will.

This brief outline of Hick's theodicy will, doubtlessly, have prompted a number of questions in the reader's mind. In what follows, we will be looking at some of the criticisms that have stemmed from Hick's thinking on this issue; this will serve to help us to expand on what has been outlined. In due course we will extend the discussion and consider the notion of person-making and its outcome at greater length. However, it should be pointed out that the following discussions will often speak of God as *personal*. This would have made sense to Hick when he wrote *Evil and the God of Love* in 1966 and thus it seems a reasonable stance in terms of a discussion of Hick's theodicy. However, in later work he would speak of a 'transcategorial' ultimate reality.

Dysteleological Evil and Mystery

Many critics of the Irenaean perspective have sought to draw attention to the fact that at times the amount of evil in our world would seem to exceed the levels one would require to facilitate constructive soul-making. This is the problem of *dysteleological* evil.[14] Take an example of something which is familiar to us in modern times, an example which is used by R.Z. Friedman.[15] There is a terrible drought in east Africa, and it is graphically flashed across television screens in the West; we are informed that 100,000 people will certainly starve. As a result of such distressing pictures, the West is jolted into action and aid begins to flow into Africa. Now, the theodicist committed to some kind of greater-good theodicy could claim that such 'evil' has produced good; that is, some previously hardened Western souls have developed a sense of solidarity with those who suffer, and sympathy for the less fortunate. However, Friedman poses an interesting question: 'let us say the situation worsens, not dramatically but noticeably. The death toll will not be 100,000 as predicted but 101,000. Will this increase actually serve to proportionately boost the amount of aid. Would 100,000 dead not "do the job" of 101,000?'[16] The challenge is for a theodicist like Hick to show that there is no more evil in the world than is necessary to provide the environment for effective soul-making. Could God make do with less evil?

A similar criticism comes from D.Z. Phillips, however Phillips does not focus on the *amount* of evil as such, but on the fact that God allows certain evils to take place for the sake of some future good. He asks us to consider a child dying of inoperable throat cancer. The fact that such an evil can exist at all is bad enough, but to say that God has planned such an evil, or that it has some pre-ordained purpose, is even worse. A premeditated crime is considered to be particularly heinous. God's 'evil nature is revealed',[17] says Phillips.

Hick does not shy away from these issues, in fact he himself draws attention to a haunting question that is posed in Dostoevsky's classic work, *The Brothers Karamazov*:

Imagine that you are creating a fabric of human destiny with the object of making men happy in the end, giving them peace and rest at last, but that it was essential and inevitable to torture to death only one tiny creature - that baby beating its breast with its fist, for instance - and to found that edifice on its unavenged tears, would you consent to be the architect on those conditions?[18]

The response to such problems is not easy, and, for some, to even seek to provide answers is itself inappropriate. Firstly, the issue raised by Phillips and Dostoevsky really pivots on making value judgements as to whether it is possible for some evils to be compensated by a good outcome or consequence. It is possible that such value judgements can only be personal decisions and moral opinions on the matter. However, to prevent misunderstanding, Hick does not think that every individual evil that has occurred will receive some kind of appropriate eschatological answer as a riposte. One is not seeking to accurately balance the pluses and minuses. To suggest a suitable good consequence from, say, the Jewish holocaust is probably a crude and tasteless exercise. Hick, quite properly, does not seek to propose suitable outcomes to various historical evils, instead he keeps to general statements. So, he writes that the final outcome 'must be good beyond our present imagining - and must be far more positive than the mere "peace and rest at last" of which Dostoevsky speaks'.[19] Here, then, we are speaking of a good outcome which is so limitless that it is beyond present comprehension. Or else, we are being asked to appreciate the *sense* of such an appeal to a good outcome without speaking of concrete instances. Admittedly, the nature of value-judgements means that this will satisfy some, but not all. However, it is hard to decide who is right on this issue.

Secondly, Hick actually seeks to provide a more substantial answer to this kind of problem, (and, perhaps, the question about arbitrary 'quantities' of evil exemplified by Friedman's analogy), and he does so ingeniously. He quotes H.H. Farmer's comment when he said 'paradoxically, the failure of theism to solve mysteries becomes part of its case!'.[20] Hick thinks that pointless, irrational and undeserved suffering is in fact the very kind of suffering that motivates sympathy and unselfish kindness in people. Gratuitous evil can bring out the noblest characteristics in the human spirit. So, he freely admits that it is difficult to try to answer such problems as dysteleological evil, and in the end he appeals to mystery, and its positive value. That is, the actual impenetrable and baffling mystery of undeserved suffering has the positive outcome of motivating highly valued actions. Paradoxically, it is the sheer inexplicable nature of some evils that prevents human complacency and indifference.

However, one critic, R. Puccetti, thinks that Hick's appeal to mystery exposes an important admission. He writes:

> Does one not detect a small white flag waving in the smoke there? For if, on the one hand, innocent suffering presents a mystery the rational mind cannot penetrate; or on the other, its compensation in a future life requires conjectures beyond all present experience, then surely the "problem of evil" remains unsolved?[21]

Expanding this point further, Puccetti asks why the problem of evil is a problem at all if Hick concedes that, when all things are finally considered, it is an insoluble mystery? That is, Hick still believes in the plausibility of his view of God (as benevolent and loving), despite admitting the sheer mystery of evil.[22] However, this is hardly a generous criticism. Hick's use of mystery in his theodicy is in the context of the *wider comprehensibility* of the overall picture he presents; that is, he seems to use mystery as a utility rather than as an explanation. The overall picture includes, for example, the Christian notions of faith and trust in the face of the incomprehensibility of evil. Thus, Hick's theodicy 'does not expect to be able to see in detail how "all things work together for good" for God's creatures, or how it can be that by wrestling with evil we are ultimately being created through it'.[23]

When considering dysteleological evil in the context of his overall theodicy, it turns out, following Farmer's reasoning above, that this very stumbling block may actually help Hick's theodicy to work. To repeat, the idea is that excessive, seemingly unfathomable and *un*-soul-making evil is actually essential for a soul-making environment to work at all. For Hick, as we have just alluded to, the sheer excess of evil is necessary for us to be mystified and work towards overcoming evil. That is, if we understood all instances of evil and its utility for some good, we would not be motivated towards its destruction - evil would become acceptable.[24] Or else, if evil is *always* comprehensible it becomes somewhat anodyne.[25] Another critic of Hick, William Rowe, uses a marathon runner as an analogy to illustrate Hick's point. In order to win a marathon, the runner has to feel that the odds are stacked against him/her in order to train hard and actually win. Thus, paradoxically, 'rationally believing that he won't win is, after all, required if he is to win'.[26] Similarly, thinking that the amount of evil is excessive for the soul-making project is paradoxically necessary for effective soul-making.

The appeal to 'mystery', however, remains a possible weakness, and we should acknowledge some validity to Puccetti's complaint. For, despite such sophisticated manouevering, Hick has to be confident that the process is going to work in order to say that the Irenaean strategy is justified. Nevertheless, to make such assurances would appear to sit uncomfortably when combined with assertions of mystery. Put simply, to be *certain* (practically or otherwise) that the Irenaean process will succeed is not to take such 'mysteries' seriously. There still seems to be some point in asking why Hick should propose a comprehensible outworking of the process if he can make a frank appeal to mystery? Why not just draw a line under *mystery* and leave it at that? Such a conclusion might also remove the necessity for life after death as a solution to the problem of evil, because the solution is located not in a comprehensible outworking of the process, but in the appeal to mystery or human limitations in comprehending the divine purposes. The need to assert that the Irenaean strategy will reach a successful conclusion (that is, all human beings finding salvation), also poses a possible problem when we consider the implications of the criticisms of the 'free-will defence' made by A. Flew and J. Mackie.

The Criticism of A. Flew and J. Mackie

Flew and Mackie do not believe that the free-will defence is successful. Furthermore, they do not believe that it is possible to reconcile the idea of a good God with the existence of evil. Their arguments for saying that the propositions 'God exists' and 'evil exists' are mutually contradictory rests on the proposal that God could have created creatures who would freely choose the right in all circumstances. Their arguments (formulated independently of each other) are based on a compatibilist conception of freedom. It is the case, as Flew acknowledges, that the notion of creatures possessing freewill is central to the free-will defence. Now, a person is free, according to the compatibilist, when he or she is 'unconstrained'. Additionally, 'there is no contradiction involved in saying that a particular action or choice was: both free, and could have been helped, and so on; and predictable, or even foreknown, and explicable in terms of caused causes'.[27] Our actions are not wholly undetermined, if they were then we would have no control over them and they could hardly be called *our* actions. Flew and Mackie are maintaining that our actions are determined by our nature. It follows, therefore, that 'Omnipotence might have, could without contradiction be said to have, created people who would always as a matter of fact *freely have chosen to do the right thing*'.[28] Flew concludes, 'the keystone argument of the free-will defence, that there is a contradiction in speaking of God so arranging the laws of nature that all men always as a matter of fact freely choose to do the right, cannot hold'.[29]

Hick thinks that such criticisms are, in fact, successful in showing a major problem with the free-will defence. He thinks that it is entirely possible that God could have created people that they always freely choose to do the right things. If such right actions flow freely from the nature of human beings, then there is no problem, at least under a compatibilist model of freedom. Having said this, Hick thinks that the Flew-Mackie critique reveals the need for theology to adopt a 'stronger conception of human liberty'.[30] His own suggestion is what he calls 'limited creativity'. Here he means to argue that even if we say that our actions proceed from our natures, there is still room for spontaneous (perhaps, even, 'unexpected') decisions that take place at the very moment of decision. Thus, he writes that:

> [W]hilst a free action arises out of the agent's character it does not arise in a fully determined and predictable way. It is largely but not fully prefigured in the previous state of the agent. For the character is itself partially formed and sometimes partially re-formed in the very moment of decision.[31]

In addition, he thinks that the criticisms of Flew and Mackie ultimately fail because they misunderstand, or underestimate, the importance of an 'authentic' relationship between God and human beings.[32] Put simply, although it may be possible for God to create beings who freely do the right things, it is not possible for God to *guarantee* such actions and at the same time have an authentic response from human beings. To clarify this, Hick gives the following analogy: If we were, according to Flew and Mackie, pre-programmed always to choose the right, then God:

> would be in a relationship to His human creatures comparable to that of the hypnotist to his patient. That is to say, He would have pre-selected our responses to our environment, to one another, and to Himself in such a way that although these responses would from our point of view be free and spontaneous, they would from God's point of view be unfree.[33]

Hick thinks that such relationships would be *second-best* to ones where peoples' responses had not been pre-selected. Looking at the analogy, the patient's post-hypnotic friendship with the hypnotist he might regard as merely a 'technical achievement' and therefore lacking in authentic value. However, the hypnotist would treat as 'real' friendship the friendship of someone whose mind had not been conditioned by hypnotic suggestion, but had become his friend through genuine responses to the hypnotist's character.[34] Hick applies this analogy to the relationship between God and a human being, and he concludes that God 'cannot without contradiction be conceived to have so constituted men that they could be guaranteed freely to respond to himself in authentic faith and love and worship'.[35]

Getting human beings to freely do the right things is one thing; having them do so 'authentically' is quite another. Whereas the former is possible, the latter is not. One can perhaps agree with Hick's intuitions here. Nevertheless, is it possible to detect a tension between Hick's thinking that: a) 'the idea of God's so creating men that they will inevitably [freely] respond positively to Him'[36] is self-contradictory, and b) that it is a 'practical certainty' that all human beings will freely respond, *uncoerced*, to the divine will in the eschaton (universalism)?[37]

Seeking to harmonise such notions, we saw a moment ago that Hick employed Augustine's thought that our hearts were made by God to be restless until we find our rest in God. Furthermore, in an article in reply to Keith Ward,[38] Hick states the following: 'It is an unrealistic understanding of freedom that leads to the conclusion that men cannot be genuinely free and yet be so made and provided for by God that they will all eventually respond to Him in faith and love.'[39]   However, could the criticism be levelled against Hick that he almost stumbles into contradicting this statement with his arguments against Flew and Mackie? Firstly, Hick believes (*contra* Flew and Mackie) that unless people are created significantly free (to choose good or evil), they cannot respond authentically in faith and love to God; it is in fact contradictory, states Hick, to say that beings who are created to freely choose the right, can also be said to authentically respond to God.   Secondly, we have seen that although Hick argues that all people will ultimately find salvation, he makes it clear that God is not intervening in the soul-making process; instead we have been created with a nature *towards* the divine that will lead us, ultimately, to respond positively to God. He concludes: 'God does not have to coerce us to respond to him, for he has already so created us that our nature, seeking its own fulfilment and good, leads us to him. The notion of divine coercion is set aside by divine creation.'[40] So, Hick here seems to argue that God has so created us that it is practically inevitable that we will positively respond in the end. This is because God has, as it were, placed within each of us a homing device. And yet, we have just seen Hick state: 'we must declare to be self-contradictory the idea of God's so creating men that they will inevitably respond positively to him'.

It is possible that if Hick wants to argue in the way that he does against Flew and Mackie then he places his universalist arguments in jeopardy. That is, Hick believes that, in the context of authentic relationships, a state of affairs where all people freely choose the right is *second-best* to one where people can freely choose right or wrong. By logical contagion, is it possible to suggest that a universe where everyone will inevitably freely respond positively to God is *second-best* to a universe where it is not inevitable that everyone will so respond?

To be fair, it could be argued that there is an important difference between saying that there are beings who will always freely choose the right from the moment they are born, and postulating an *inherent bias* in humanity that will eventually over infinite time lead to all human beings performing rightly. But to respond to such criticisms in this manner would be to miss the point of the above argument. This argument is centred on

Hick's own assertion about the importance of an authentic relationship with God. Hick is making the value-judgment that relationships which are *unfixed* in advance are more valuable than relationships that are *fixed* in advance. What is important, according to Hick's own theory, is that from God's point of view a loving relationship between himself and a human being has come about without God seeing to it that such a relationship inevitably occurred. Otherwise, this would be a 'poor second-best' relationship. The argument hinges on seeing that there is no real difference - from God's point of view - between Flew and Mackie's *immediately* 'right' person and Hick's *eventually* 'right' person, in this respect. Flew and Mackie's 'right' person is created to freely choose the right, now; Hick's universalism means that people will, inevitably, choose the right in a million years. And yet, from the divine perspective, what is the difference between a day and a million years?[41] So, is it possible to say that a universe where it is inevitable that everybody will respond positively to God is *second-best* to a universe where it is not inevitable that everyone will so respond? Granted, it is still possible to say that humanity has been created with a bias for God, but not that this means that the free, uncoerced, salvation of every person is guaranteed; because if it is guaranteed then it is of no *authentic* value to God.

Alternatively, perhaps we are exaggerating such difficulties? We have seen that Hick does not want to underwrite such a guaranteed outcome as a logical certainty, but rather as a practical intuition. Therefore, given that there are no *logical* guarantees, Hick could argue that his practical confidence in universalism does not actually upset the demands for authenticity. Nevertheless, it seems clear that in order for the Irenaean theodicy to work then the universal salvation of all creatures *must* be the actual outcome, if one human being were lost then this intended theodicy would have failed. Thus, perhaps Hick has to guarantee universalism more than he admits?

Is it possible to modify Hick's soul-making idea so as to take some account of these observations? A possible approach might seek to speak of the value of person-making as an end in itself rather than appending a universalist conclusion.

Linda Zagzebski and Personal Development

In responding positively to Hick's soul-making idea, the American philosopher Linda Zagzebski suggests a modification that involves the affirmation of personal development without any strings attached. She comments that: 'To love a person logically requires permitting that person to be a person. To allow a person to be a person requires that he be allowed to contribute to his own soul-making through his free will.'[42] Furthermore, a parent: 'loves her child as an end in himself and would continue to do whatever contributes to the development of his personhood whether or not it leads to good. What parent would ever agree to turn her child into a non-person or even less of a person because her child is bad?'[43]

These are provocative observations that Zagzebski makes, and, following them up, we could ask why there should be a resolution of evil in accordance with a universalist model at all? Is that all people will eventually come to freely choose to do the right really a necessary outcome? In order to investigate these questions it might be helpful to set things out in a more propositional framework:

1. God can create beings who are free to do both right and wrong.
2. God can create beings who freely do only the right (Flew and Mackie).
3. It is of greater authentic value to create free beings who being 'significantly' free will not necessarily always perform rightly (or respond positively to God).
4. It is of lesser authentic value to create free beings who even though they are free will be oriented to always freely perform rightly (or respond positively to God).
5. Therefore (2) is of lesser value than (1).

However:

6. It is a 'practical certainty' that all free beings will at the end of the day freely perform rightly (or respond positively to God) however long the process leading to this state of affairs takes.

Is there a possible similarity between (2) and (6)? As we have seen, Hick believes that the relationship that God would have to beings who would be oriented in such a way that they would always freely act rightly (2) is analogous to the relationship between a hypnotist and his patient. That is, it is a second-best state of affairs to (1) where beings can freely perform right or wrong actions or even actions which seem completely out of character. It is more valuable that beings who are free according to (1) respond positively to God, than the alternative situation described in (2) where their positive response is guaranteed anyway. Now, we have seen Hick claim that it is a practical certainty that all free beings will eventually perform rightly. The potential paradox is that if Hick wants to claim that it is a practical certainty then he is subtly endorsing the position of Flew and Mackie.

So, let us suggest that it is a more valuable state of affairs to create beings whose freedom is such that they might perform wrong actions as well as right ones. Moreover, let us accord with Hick that a universe where beings are oriented to always perform rightly is a second-best state of affairs. Now, must we assume that the reason why God created a universe of free beings as in (1), is that they will all eventually freely perform rightly? I think that we must admit that this is certainly possible. Perhaps it is instinctively the hope of the religious believer that God has an unlimitedly good outcome in view for the future of every individual. But if we say that it is certain (because of the demands of the Irenaean 'theodicy') that all beings will come to perform rightly (universalism), then are we lessening the value of God's initial choice to undertake the risky enterprise of creating beings who are significantly free? That is, there is more value in risk concerning personal relationships, than in certainty.

So, following Zagzebski, what if God created significantly free human beings not because he wanted them to develop into good persons, but because he wanted them to develop into *full* persons? We are therefore proposing that:

7. Evil exists so that there can be persons.
8. Creating significantly free persons is more valuable than eradicating evil if eradicating evil means eradicating significant personhood.
9. Maintaining personhood is therefore more valuable than eradicating evil.

If (9) is true then the universalist position is potentially unfounded. What seems to be more important to the universalist is that the resolution of evil requires that all free persons eventually come to respond positively to God. But, if we have said (8), then this is not true.

Might it be suggested that we really do not require an *outcome* to person-making, as such, at all? In the world of loving personal relationships we might suggest that it is the 'world of authentic personal interaction' that matters, *whatever* the outcome. It is important not to describe things in a purely functional way. That is, in the sense that we might say 'the *function* of free persons is to enter into authentic loving relationships with each other and with God'. Perhaps we do not require, as a justifying condition, that this putative 'loving relationship' will ever be realized - the value is located not in the guarantee of such a relationship occurring, but in the circumstances or life-conditions that might *potentially* produce such a relationship.

Elucidating this point further: let us assume total failure. That is, let us suppose that God does *not* manage, at the end of the day, to enter into a single loving relationship with any of his creatures. We might respond and say that God had made a mistake in making the world this way - it had failed its purpose; or that the circumstances that God had created were *unjustifiable* because they had failed to produce the desired outcome (like the salvation of all people). But to say this would, perhaps, miss the point of God creating a free world at all. The reason for having freedom in a personal world is surely not so that such freedom can eventually be tamed or controlled towards some pleasant outcome. That seems to defeat the exercise. Rather, the purpose of freedom is to authenticate personal encounters.

In expressing possible reservations about the notion of universal salvation (or, at least, the guarantee of that outcome), we are not ruling out that there is an extension of life beyond death - nor are we, perhaps, eschewing the idea of there being a good outcome to the process of soul-making. But we are defining that outcome differently. We are suggesting that there is a *limitless value* in the free development of persons without the appended necessity of a universally salvific outcome. Moreover, such 'limitless value' becomes diminished when we attempt to inject *certainty* or *guarantees* into it. Why not just stop at the value of *freedom* and leave it at that?

Nevertheless, the actual consequences of this require further exploration. The universalist standpoint, which Hick supports, presents itself as a more satisfactory choice for those committed to God being love. However, rather than portraying the universalist's loving God as one who is unendingly concerned for the creatures' eternal welfare, is there a reverse or alternative picture? Is the universalist's love self-interested? Perhaps the universalist's love is a love which is too jealous to lose, too sentimentalist to allow free persons to make serious choices. Perversely, perhaps, we might charge the universalist's God as one who cannot tolerate final refusal from any creature. If such action is love then surely it is *possessive* love which in seeking to protect the beloved, protects only itself. This is divine love? Analogously, when we love particular people we value total freedom of action for such individuals - this is what we really mean (and value) when we refer to something being 'real life' or 'true to life'. As we have said, a relationship which is coerced or guaranteed to come up roses, is empty of authentic content.

So, in seeking to uphold freedom and the value of free choices it seems possible that some people might finally resist the beckoning of divine love. If this is asserted then what are the possible outcomes? In rejecting the notion of 'hell', Hick also rejects a third possibility that unredeemed souls will not suffer eternally but just go out of existence. One might call this 'conditional immortality' or annihilationism. Such a position seems to have been taken seriously by the *Doctrine Commission of the Church of England* when they stated that:

> Hell is not eternal torment but it is the final and irrevocable choosing of that which is opposed to God so completely and so absolutely that the only end is *total non-being*...Annihilation might be a truer picture of damnation than any of the traditional images of the hell of eternal torment.[44]

With the talk of 'total non-being' there is a slight ambiguity with regard to the precise meaning. The notion may be analogous to Augustine's view of evil that we saw earlier - the absence of goodness, or a malfunction of something perfect - that is, the notion of non-being can be understood in relation to a detachment from the source of all being, God. Literally, non-being refers to an 'absence' of being. God is perceived as the Sustainer: '..in him all things hold together' (Col.1:17). Thus the result of steering a path away from God is that one's existence becomes increasingly unsustainable, leading eventually into non-being. Or else, non-being may refer to a quality of life which amounts to a total loss of meaning or purpose in existence. In the first case one is possibly speaking of the actual dissolution of some kind of substance, in the second one is referring to a featureless existence without love or value.

The problem of an eternal dualism seems to be alleviated by positing a conditional immortality or annihilationism. Evil is resolved and finished with, there is no place for suffering, the old has passed away. Secondly, whilst rejecting the idea that people may suffer eternally in hell, such a position also does not welcome the universalist's guarantee (like Hick's) that all persons will find salvation. However, it is possible that there is, in fact, a basic instinct that underlies both the annihilationist view and the universalist position, and this is that they both abhor a loose end. Both seek to eliminate any residual dualism. Therefore, in both pictures the end is monistic, or non-dualistic, but with annihilationism there is a proportion of people who will not be present. That is, in both views there is in fact no one who eventually exists *outside* the fold. Admittedly, the annihilationist account does seem to do better when taking stock of the seriousness and significance of personal decisions against God. Under such a scheme a person might still choose, finally, to resist the divine beckoning; they can freely supply their own answer to the question, 'who am I?'. Thus, free choices count for something.

Nevertheless, do they count for enough? It could be argued that true freedom in this context must involve the ability to choose a path not divinely recommended and a lot more besides. Freedom, or more specifically, free personhood, is eventually betrayed in an annihilationist picture. That is, God is not perceived to preserve human freedom so that each human soul is allowed to realise its full potential even if that potential is not ideal. If we envisage the existence of persons outside of God's will as somehow *vestigial* then it is easy to permit annihilationism. But in a world of free personhood, where it is important to maintain the value of being a person, such value is undermined by asserting that these persons are terminated because they have resisted the divine will. Surely it is a mistake to think that persons who will never respond to divine overtures are vestiges of God's plan and require disposal?

If immortality is conditional then God is not really interested in our freedom after all, such interest has been feigned. Instead, could it be suggested that each person has their own positive value? This is not to suppose that the 'self' is only valuable when it has aligned itself to God, but that personhood, or selfhood, in combination with free development is endorsed with a divine 'Yes'; it has intrinsic value. Thus, the notion that by stepping outside of Being-itself persons become *non*-being seems to restrict our appreciation of the eternal value of true freedom. Analogously, such talk is rather like saying that God has erected a sophisticated perimeter fence which will automatically destroy the individual who steps beyond it. Thus, it does not seem right to suppose that God will destroy people because they have freely developed into persons at variance with the divine purpose. There is, perhaps, a divine commitment to the infinite number of eventualities (positive and negative) that can arise out of a free universe.

An important question for the present discussion is 'can choices be *decisive*?' The idea that people can finally and irreversibly choose to reject God and consciously opt for misery would seem to be inconceivable. Thus, T. Talbott asks incredulously: 'But what could it possibly mean to say that some sinners are trying as hard as they can to damn themselves?...What could possibly qualify as a motive for such a choice?'[45] This is a powerful question, nevertheless perhaps one motivating factor may be an overwhelming desire for autonomy or independence. However, somewhat avoiding Talbott's question, there is something else that can be said: do we have to suppose that persons have to make an *irrevocable decision* at all? What if we were to picture hell as a kind of eternal 'procrastination' instead? This procrastination becomes so ingrained that making valuable decisions and taking action becomes increasingly difficult. R. Swinburne, when talking about the possibility of hell, suggests that '..it is possible that a man will let himself be so mastered by his desires that he will lose all ability to resist them'.[46] Might it be argued that persons can mould themselves into something which eschews change? So, when we examine our motivations we might imagine 'putting off a decision until tomorrow' *eternally*. That is, we really have no desire to face up to certain choices or courses of action. However, such a 'realistic' assessment of ourselves does not preclude us actually making that decision or taking appropriate action: this remains as something *potential.* Moreover, at what point might we say that we become *decisively* unable to choose or act? As things proceed the capacity for change recedes into implausibility, but it always remains possible. Similarly, what might be suggested is that perhaps even with hell's inhabitants there is no sense that a decisive choice for evil (or self-destruction) has been made. That is, there is never a point when such persons make a decisive choice to be separate from God, it is just that they never make a choice *for* God. Thus, there is a sense of irreversibility here, but such a sense exists in tension with the additional notion of the *potential* for change. Augustine, when talking about the nature of heavenly existence, thinks that although the potential to sin is logically possible, it will never be actually realised because persons, being in the presence of God, will not be able, consciously, to sin.[47] Thus, in heaven there is the potential to sin, that is - freedom still exists. Similarly, in hell there is the potential for change - freedom still exists. Freedom is not abolished.

The notion of hell as decisive and irrevocable sits uncomfortably with the idea that people choose hell themselves. Such an uncompromising picture seems more at home in the context of God actually shutting people out. However, if we suggest that people shut themselves out then the idea of hell's decisiveness is coloured differently. If people go there by their own choosing then any notion of decisiveness operates from their own perspectives and decisions. Wittgenstein seems to come close to this idea when he writes: 'A man will be imprisoned in a room with a door that's unlocked and opens inward as long as it does not occur to him to pull rather than push it.'[48] A door that is unlocked hardly represents a decisive finality. Thus, let us suggest that hell is *potentially temporal.* Also, following the self-made/person-making sense, hell might be renamed 'autonomy'. That is, hell is properly understood not so much as a place but as an autonomous state; it is also a place that can be escaped from. This is its potentiality, the door is unlocked. Nevertheless, such potentiality exists in a state of tension with the actuality of the situation. Perhaps we might understand such potentiality in a sort of Aristotelian sense. Aristotle defines things in terms of their capacities for certain functions or purposes. With 'autonomy' described as *potentially temporal* we have a place which has a capacity for positive change. However, such a capacity may not alter the fact that 'autonomy' is everlasting. That is, the activation of such potentiality into actuality may lie eternally dormant. This is not to say that potential temporality is therefore incorrectly applied to 'autonomy'. We might clarify this with a mundane illustration: The concept of 'knife' obviously includes the potential for cutting something. However, it is still correct to label something a 'knife' even though it might lie forever unused on the kitchen table. It retains the potential for such a use.

With 'autonomy' as potentially temporal we have a concept which allows for change. Free persons in a potentially temporal 'autonomy' may never change, but we have not decisively underwritten such a tragic possibility by eliminating them. The conclusion here is that the authentic process of free personal development is not short-changed, on the one hand, by a guaranteed universal outcome, or, on the other hand, by some kind of annihilationism. Rather, true to Hick's religiously ambiguous soul-making universe, it follows its free course without intervention.

Nevertheless, it is possible that all this falls foul of the fact that it places far too great a premium on human freedom and neglects the context which, for the present discussion, includes an all-loving, all-powerful God who desires the well-being of all created beings. In which case, if we were to shift the focus away from the precious autonomy of human beings and emphasise instead the God of love who seeks universal well-being, we might see the spirit behind Hick's confidence that the divine love will succeed. Moreover, the idea that people can get themselves into a state where they feel they cannot change hardly seems to represent a good reason to postulate hell/autonomy on their behalf! For, would not a loving God seek to orchestrate ways in which to enable their change for good? Ascribing a limitless value to human freedom and person-making (which has been *decontextualised* from the loving divine purpose) could serve to perpetuate things indefinitely; that is, it seems that there can be no consummation as such, or *closure*. And so, one of the persuasive features of Hick's universalism is that it seeks a conclusion that is ultimately positive. He himself responds to Zagzebski's observations, which motivated the brief discussion above, when he says:

> For is it possible to separate love from a seeking of the love of the beloved? Does not love mean valuing another and seeking that other's good? Surely, if we remove its seeking-of-good aspect, love would have no content or substance, no reason to express itself in one kind of behaviour rather than another. To say that God loves us is, then, to say that God values us and seeks our highest good.[49]

However, our ultimate conclusions about this issue will probably reflect our chosen focus - divine love or human freedom. It appears to be very difficult to do justice to both these concepts when they are brought together in a universalist ending, but Hick has concluded that Love will find a way.

Epistemic Distance and the Irenaean Intuition

Moving on, some critics have concentrated on Hick's notion of a religiously ambiguous universe. As we have seen, Hick maintains that it is important that, in their initial creation, human beings were not made unambiguously aware of God's overpowering presence because they would then have been in the oppressive situation of a cognitive straitjacket; freewill would have been stifled. 'In order to be a person, exercising some measure of genuine freedom, the creature must be brought into existence, not in the immediate presence, but at a distance from God.'[50] If one has been created at an *epistemic distance* from God, then one is in a better position to think and do as one pleases. Given this basic cognitive freedom, a human being can freely walk towards or away from God. So, Hick envisages the emergence of humanity in a natural and ambiguous environment. The epistemic certainty of Eden never existed. The human species develops only gradually a God-consciousness (Schleiermacher), and this consciousness may take much longer than a single lifetime to achieve. Moreover, there is no coercion on God's part, these free beings do not experience an overriding presence of the divine, and they are likewise free to walk in any direction that they choose.

So, the notion of epistemic distance appears to have a significant place in Hick's philosophical theology, it is bound up with an epistemological perspective which stresses the free experiential and voluntary nature of religious experiencing-as. Nevertheless, it is possible that, once again, there are consequences for Hick's theodicy. Firstly, we might ask why the universe is as ambiguous as it seems? We saw in chapter one that one critic, Terence Penelhum, suggested that to say that the truth is clear to someone is not the same as being 'shattered into submission' by that truth. That is, assenting to the truth of something (for example, the existence of God, or the reality of *samsara*), 'does not require being overwhelmed'.[51] So we might ask why the existence of God is not more obvious? Indeed, that God is not more obvious can become a question for theodicists as well as epistemologists. Thus, the humanist thinker, C. Robert Mesle, asks why God seems to hide? He writes: 'I cannot accept Hick's solution that a loving God has intentionally made the world look as if there is no God so that we are free to choose faith. I do not believe that ignorance is the ground for freedom and faith.'[52] This is a powerful point: if the presence of evil and suffering is difficult enough, then God's apparent absence seems to exacerbate the problem. However, Hick could possibly respond by pointing out that Mesle seems to have made a one-sided point. For, Hick's epistemology actually maintains that the world is capable of *both* theistic and non-theistic interpretations, it is not that the world does *not* proclaim

God's reality, it is rather that it conveys an ambiguous message. God thus seems acutely present to (and 'unhidden' from) the great saints who experience the world in overwhelmingly religious terms. However, God's absence seems equally plain to those who experience it naturalistically.

Secondly, Hick's theodicy recognises that this present life is not sufficient for the soul-making process to be completed. Thus, Hick posits an afterlife in which this soul-making journey will continue until all are saved (universalism). Here a problem arises. The final end or 'eschaton' is a scenario that is expected to some extent to verify theism (and thus satisfy the empiricist demand for meaningfulness). The effect of this could lead to the possibility that epistemic distance is to become a lot less distant, as it were, as the journey through many lives proceeds. It would, however, appear crucial to Hick's theodicy that this epistemic distance is maintained in order for the ambiguity of the objective environment to remain in place. Moreover, the notion of human beings freely discovering their Creator without coercion is central to Hick's thesis, otherwise his intended theodicy falters. The question arises, 'if the next lives are to be increasingly less ambiguous, then why the level of ambiguity in this life?'. Thus, there is a tightrope act between coercion and free-realisation and this precarious situation is the focus for Hick's critics. For example, S. Kane writes:

> For the admission that, even if man lived at a lesser epistemic distance from God than he presently does, he would still be free in the manner required for him to be able to fulfil the purpose for which God made him, carries with it the implication that there are instances of evil in the world which cannot be justified in terms of the basic explanatory principles of soul-making theodicy, namely, those instances that make man's epistemic distance from God exceed that required for him to be able to fulfil God's purpose for him.[53]

The very existence an afterlife does a great deal to seriously weaken the materialist worldview, and therefore the idea of an ambiguous universe is compromised. Ironically, it is possible that Hick inadvertently exposes this problem by actually denying that an afterlife would have a profound effect on altering an atheist's world view:

> It [an afterlife] would not necessarily be a state of affairs which is manifestly incompatible with the non-existence of God. It might be taken as a surprising natural fact. The atheist in his resurrection body, and able to remember his life on earth, might say that the universe has turned out to be more complex, and perhaps more to be approved of, than he had realized.[54]

Is this a convincing argument? Perhaps, given the atheist's assumptions about the human person, an afterlife would stretch that worldview to breaking point? To be fair, the mysticism associated with the new physics has opened up a world more flexible than the deterministic Newtonian model. That is, there are enough startling discoveries in contemporary science to allow, within a materialist worldview, for surprising occurrences or states of affairs. However, when we come to discuss parapsychological experience in the next chapter, we shall see C.D. Broad admitting that if the existence of an immaterial self (in connection with parapsychological research) were shown to be a fact then it would 'literally alter everything'[55] with regard to materialistic presuppositions. Moreover, we shall also see in the next chapter that according to Hick's speculations we are talking not just about the possibilities of an immaterial self, but about a fully conscious (and fully re-embodied) afterlife. It is difficult to resist the conclusion that any significant epistemic distance that exists in this present life would become severely diminished in the next life.

However, perhaps the problem of justifying a collapse of epistemic distance in the afterlife is a problem because of the reasons Hick gives for its institution. For Hick, epistemic distance is a divinely instituted situation - right from the very start, God was distant and hidden from human beings. Hick has dispensed with 'the Fall' as a concept in his thinking, and so he can no longer, it seems, say very much about the *role of humanity* in bringing about an epistemic distance. That is, the concept of 'the Fall' provides the narrative that speaks of human beings desiring independence or freedom from their Maker. If we choose to see things this way then epistemic distance is not something which is divinely-driven (even if it serves the divine purpose), it becomes the human choice for autonomy. However, in clearly opting against the Augustinian model, Hick seems to have eschewed the Augustinian idea of human 'sin' which is where such ideas might naturally find their home. Moreover, under Augustine's scheme, Mesle's question about God's hidden-ness might have been tackled by inverting it: why do *we* hide from God? Thus, the shattering of epistemic distance in Augustine's picture might be an appropriate judgement for human pride and independence. However, this would imply a return to a more retributivist, rather than utilitarian, view of God's dealings with humankind which Hick rejects. If we recall, Hick sees humanity as created in a 'fallen' (or neutral) state in a world of challenge and ambiguity for *the purpose of* effective soul-making. In Hick's thinking, then, epistemic distance is part of the framework that God has made and not a result of human sin.

Thirdly, some critics have developed further problems with Hick affirming a universalist stance about the destiny of humankind whilst maintaining no divine coercion. That is, will the divinely-instituted epistemic distance have to be compromised to facilitate a universalist outcome? Again, Kane homes in on this potential Achilles' heel for Hick:

> For, let us suppose that the epistemic distance remains the same for every one of these new methods of divine self-disclosure. But if that is so, then there is no reason for thinking that even the employment by God or infinitely many new methods of self-disclosure in the afterlife would have any other consequences than those achieved by the method he uses of self-disclosure in this life...[56]

Thus, although the practical certainty of universal salvation is essential to Hick's theodicy, when it is brought into connection with the notion of epistemic distance, such a proposal potentially uproots the notion of free personal development inherent in Hick's soul-making idea. Of course, a thinker of Hick's calibre is not unaware of such criticism. He deals with such problems in Chapter 13 of *Death and Eternal Life*.[57] To begin, Hick proposes that all human beings have an innate leaning towards God, so the practical certainty that all shall find salvation derives from the idea that eventually the inherent tendency towards God in each human being will be realised without coercion. As we have seen, Hick draws on Augustine's famous statement that our hearts will be restless until we find our true home, which is God. Thus, Hick argues that an assertion that the universal salvation of human beings is a certainty can be harmonised with a non-coercive God. Nevertheless, we must remember that Hick's religious epistemology speaks of our religious experience as 'voluntary', and therefore there would seem to be a sense that our movement towards spiritual maturity is somewhat self-motivated. Thus, one thing that Hick seems to depend on here is the idea that everybody seeks their own fulfilment and good, and it is arguable that this is an assumption that does not take into account the possibility that some people may deliberately self-destruct, or stubbornly refuse to take a better course.[58]

We shall revisit the question of epistemic distance again in chapter four when we come to look at Hick's pareschatology. Indeed, it is arguable that the development of Hick's later thought towards a more pluralist framework in his eschatology makes it easier for him to deal with questions of the alleged shattering of epistemic distance by the afterlife.

Summary

Evil and the God of Love (1966) contains Hick's definitive historical survey of Christian approaches to the problem of evil together with his own distinctive Irenaean response. Hick has reservations about the Augustinian type of theodicy and prefers an Irenaean approach. He believes that a viable theodicy should take full account of human evolutionary origins (rather than speaking of perfect creatures who went wrong in the distant past). The responsibility for the existence of evil cannot be successfully placed on the shoulders of created beings, instead one must admit that, ultimately, God is responsible for the way the world is. Thus, theodicy should be forward looking and seek to justify the God of Love by a limitlessly good outcome in the future. From the beginning, human beings have been placed into a religiously ambiguous world full of suffering and challenge, and they will eventually emerge from life's journey as perfected souls. However, a single earthly lifetime is not sufficient for the soul-making process to be completed. This means that our earthly lives must be extended into the afterlife where there will be further opportunities for development in another challenging world. The justification of evil (and therefore, God) lies in the eschaton when the soul-making process will have finally yielded up an outcome that will more than compensate for the evil and suffering that has led up to it.

What appeals in Hick's theodicy is the fact that it seems to steer away from tyrannical and juridical pictures of an omni-perfect God who exacts punishments for evil. Instead, it portrays God as very much a personal (even 'parental') Being who wishes to authentically interact with human beings. The effect of this is that it seems to bring God more *into* the world of the sufferer; that is, God accepts ultimate responsibility for evil and is perceived to work *within* the process to bring all people into a limitlessly good outcome for their lives.

Critics have sought to focus upon the sheer amount of evil in the world and the fact that it seems to exceed the requirements of a soul-making world. Or else, there is a refusal to accept that evil and suffering can be justified by good consequences in the future. Moreover, it is possible that authentic human freedom and the promise of universal salvation are two notions that are not easy bedfellows. Perhaps, if human freedom is upheld there must be the possibility of some people deciding to remain at variance to the divine will? However, in assessing the validity of such complaints much depends on the value-judgements of the assessors themselves. Other critics have asked why the universe is religiously ambiguous: why does God hide from us? Moreover, some have questioned whether epistemic distance, or religious ambiguity, can be successfully maintained beyond death. Would an afterlife not make the universe less religiously ambiguous and thus upset Hick's notion of *free and uncoerced* human development continuing beyond the threshold of death?

Nevertheless, all theodicies that are put forward for consideration are subject to attack; and the sheer variety of experienced evils means that there are many additional cases or exceptions that undermine attempts at formulating all-encompassing general theories. The Irenaean theodicy is the work of a philosopher of religion, however it is also an insightful attempt to understand the human condition and its purpose. It is not presented as an abstracted philosophical treatise which is content with a 'Pyrrhic victory', rather it seeks to consider human life as it is actually experienced and felt. Nevertheless, like the notion of eschatological verification that we saw in chapter one, it must rely on the idea of human survival beyond death being coherent. Thus, our next task is to consider Hick's response to this issue.

Notes

1. Hick, 'Hick's Response to Critiques' in S. Davis, (ed.), *Encountering Evil*, p.68. Moreover, Hick describes *Evil and the God of Love* as 'a critical study of the two responses to the problem of evil that have been developed within Christian thought, and an attempt to formulate a theodicy for today'. *Evil and the God of Love*, p.3.
2. Augustine, *De Genesi ad litteram* 6.36. Cited in H. Bettenson, *The Later Christian Fathers*, p.194.
3. Augustine, *De Corruptione e gratia* 33,34. Cited in Ibid., p.195.
4. Hick, *Evil and the God of Love*, p.69.
5. Hick, Ibid., pp.62-63.
6. Hick, Ibid, p.220.
7. Hick, 'Critique [of S. Davis' theodicy] by John Hick' in S. Davis, op.cit., p.86.
8. Augustine, *On the Predestination of the Saints* ch.34, trans. Peter Holmes in *Nicene and Post-Nicene Fathers*, first series, Vol. V. Cited in Hick, *Evil and the God of Love*, p.67.
9. Hick, *Evil and the God of Love*, p.237. Further to this, Hick strongly asserts the need for an eschatology: 'I nevertheless do not see how any coherent theodicy can avoid dependence upon an eschatology.' J. Hick, 'An Irenaean Theodicy' in P. Badham, (ed.), *A John Hick Reader*, p.103. For a defence of an Augustinian approach against Hick, see R. Douglas Geivett, *Evil and the Evidence for God: The Challenge of John Hick's Theodicy*.
10. D.I. Trethowan takes exception to the idea that God is responsible for evil. This, for Trethowan, makes God the author of sin. He writes: 'The alternative [Hick's view], at this point, is to explain sin by referring to the conditions in which God has created us, and then the responsibility for it becomes not ours, but God's. This conclusion, from the Christian point of view is completely disastrous.' 'Dr. Hick and the Problem of Evil', p.408. However, independently of Trethowan's remarks, Hick does seem to respond to this issue when he writes: '...the ultimate divine responsibility for the existence of a "fallen" humanity does not cancel, or even diminish, our human moral responsibility. For this latter depends upon the fact that our actions flow from responsible choices. They are our actions and we must be judged by them.' *Evil and the God of Love*, p.360.
11. Julian of Norwich, *The Revelations of Divine Love*, p.92.
12. Hick, *Evil and the God of Love*, p.342.
13. Augustine, *Confessions,* book I, ch.1 Cited in Hick, *Death and Eternal Life*, p.251.
14. K. Chrzan states the problem of dysteleological (excessive) evil, 'Among theists inclined to combat the problem of evil with a greater good theodicy, aversion to

admitting the existence of gratuitous (superfluous, surd, unjustified, dysteleological or pointless) evil is almost universal. Greater good theodicies characteristically assert that all evils are such that greater goods require and outweigh them. In response, atheodicists cite instances of 'gratuitous' evil, evils unencompassed by a given greater good theodicy; the concept of gratuitousness is thus essentially dependent for its specifics upon the precise formulation of the given theodicy. Obviously a demonstrably gratuitous evil falsifies its respective theodicy by counter-example. Theodicists are understandably loath to admit the existence of evils that definitionally rupture their defenses.' 'When is gratuitous evil really gratuitous?', p. 87.

15. See R.Z. Friedman, 'Evil and Moral Agency'.
16. Ibid., p.6.
17. D.Z. Phillips, *The Concept of Prayer*, p.93.
18. F. Dostoevsky, *The Brothers Karamazov*, trans. C. Garnett, p.254.
19. Hick, *Evil and the God of Love*, p.386.
20. H.H.Farmer, *Towards Belief in God*, p.234. Cited in Ibid., p.336.
21. R. Puccetti, 'The Loving God, Some Observations on John Hick's "Evil and the God of Love"', p.266.
22. Ulf Gorman speaks of this when he says 'The apologist may be unable to give full explication of his conception of the evil in the world and its relation to the will of God. And he may argue for the acceptance of the Christian faith and the goodness of God in spite of the absence of such explanations. This would be a faith in spite of obscurity, on the confidence that evil can be explained, although he does not know how.' *A Good God?: A Logical and Semantical Analysis of the Problem of Evil*, p.21. However, Hick would probably not claim to be hiding behind 'mystery' as such, rather it is a *utility* to his theodicy.
23. Hick, 'Hick's Response to Critiques' in S. Davis, op.cit., p.68.
24. See Hick, *Evil and the God of Love*, pp.333-336.
25. Thus, it is important that suffering remains 'unjust and inexplicable, haphazard and cruelly excessive', Ibid., p.335.
26. William Rowe, 'Paradox and Promise: Hick's Solution to the Problem of Evil' in H.Hewitt, (ed.), *Problems in the Philosophy of Religion*, p.124. Similarly, Linda Zagzebski further elucidates this argument when she writes: 'if the soul-making hypothesis is true, it would be rational for us to believe that it is false. That is, it would be rational for us to believe that there is a great deal of excess evil beyond that needed for soul-making' , 'Critical Response' [in response to William Rowe], in Ibid., p.126.
27. A. Flew, 'Divine Omnipotence and Human Freedom', in A. Flew and A. MacIntyre, (eds.), *New Essays in Philosophical Theology*, p.151.
28. Ibid., p.152 (emphasis mine).
29. Ibid., p.153.
30. Hick, *Evil and the God of Love*, p.277.
31. Ibid., p.276.
32. See Ibid., pp.271-275.
33. Ibid., p.274.
34. Ibid., p.273.
35. Ibid., p.275.
36. Ibid., p.274.
37. Ibid., p.344.
38. See K. Ward, 'Freedom and the Irenaean Theodicy'.
39. Hick, 'Freedom and the Irenaean Theodicy Again', p.422.
40. Hick, *Death and Eternal Life*, p.252.
41. It could, of course, be maintained that this point is more effective with a *timelessly eternal view* of God than an 'everlasting' view. Thus, advocating the former view,

Anselm writes: 'You were not, therefore, yesterday, nor will You be tomorrow, but yesterday and today and tomorrow You *are.*' *Proslogion*, ch.19. Alternatively, some modern philosophers prefer the latter view that God is not *outside* of time but is, nonetheless, *everlasting*. See, for example, R. Swinburne, *The Coherence of Theism*. Nevertheless, even for a conscious Being who is everlasting and where time-spans are much greater than in the human consciousness, the point made about a 'million years and a day' may still have some force.

42. Ibid., p.127.
43. Doctrine Commission of the General Synod of the Church of England, *The Mystery of Salvation*, p.199.
44. T. Talbott, 'The Doctrine of Everlasting Punishment', p.37.
45. L. Zagzebski, op.cit., p.128.
46. R. Swinburne, 'A Theodicy of Heaven and Hell', p.49.
47. See Augustine, *De Civitate Dei*, XXII. 30.
48. L. Wittgenstein, *Culture and Value*, p.223.
49. J. Hick, 'Reply' [to Linda Zagzebski and William Rowe] in H. Hewitt, op.cit., pp.136-137.
50. J. Hick, 'An Irenaean Theodicy', in P. Badham, op.cit., p.92.
51. T. Penelhum, 'Reflections on the Ambiguity of the World' in A. Sharma, *God, Truth and Reality*, p.172.
52. C. Robert Mesle, *John Hick's Theodicy*, p.102.
53. G. Stanley Kane, 'Soul-Making Theodicy and Eschatology', pp.30-31.
54. Hick, *Faith and Knowledge*, p.186.
55. C.D. Broad talking to C. Wilson in C. Wilson, *Afterlife*, p.266.
56. G. Stanley Kane, op.cit., p.28.
57. See Hick, *Death and Eternal Life*, pp.250-259.
58. For example, M. Stocker writes about 'desiring the bad': 'The concept of selfishness may encompass the "metaphysical" egoist who believes that something is good only if it is good for, or good of, him/herself [...] That the believed good must attract is consistent with the metaphysically selfish, family-ish [...] Such people see no good elsewhere; nor therefore do they desire it elsewhere. But evaluative egoists, familists [...] do see value outside their area of concern. They simply may not be attracted to it.' 'Desiring the Bad: an essay in moral psychology', p.744.

Chapter Three

Death and Eternal Life

'Is there a life after death?' This is a question that is of great importance to many religious people and has inspired a significant amount of philosophical discussion. It is an important question for Hick too: If the cognitivity (or 'factual' integrity) of religious claims depends on eschatological verification, and a viable theodicy relies on the continuation of the human soul-making journey beyond death, then questions about the coherence of the concept of life after death are especially significant. Hick's contribution to the debate about such issues has been extensive and is chiefly to be found in *Death and Eternal Life* (1976). Nevertheless, it is an issue that he has sought to address right from the very start of his career, thus the idea of an 'exact replica' first appeared in an article entitled 'Theology and Verification', *Theology Today*, April, 1960. Moreover, Hick has returned to such issues in his later writings with, for example, a chapter entitled 'A Possible Conception of Life After Death' in his *Disputed Questions* (1996).

In this chapter we will be discussing some of the main aspects of Hick's speculations. Hick's work on death and eternal life has provoked a large amount of critical comment and response and we shall be considering these things in some detail. Moreover, this chapter will be largely looking at the coherence of the idea of survival beyond death. To begin, we will look at Hick's perspective on the various positions within the debates about the mind and brain. Next, we will look at his handling of some of the empirical evidence for the independence of mind from brain suggested by parapsychology. Then, we will briefly consider Hick's views about the nature of the disembodied life. Finally, we shall examine Hick's most famous contribution of all in this area - the interpretation of the resurrection body as an 'exact replica' of the person who dies. Hick's work is provocative, and so I have sought to explore some possibilities that stem from his thinking. Thus, we shall also explore a suggestion that we could view the resurrection body in light of the 'new physics'.

Dualism

In *Death and Eternal Life*, Hick wrote:

> I do not claim that a capacity of the mind to survive the decay of the body can
> be established by philosophical argument, but I claim that it cannot be
> excluded either by philosophical argument or by empirical evidence.
> Inspection of the notions of mind and body and evidence of mind/brain
> correlation, I shall argue, leave the door open, or at least unlocked, to a belief
> in the survival of the conscious self.[1]

Although, as we can see, Hick expresses a qualified scepticism about
dualism he decides, after critically analysing the mind/brain identity and the
epiphenomenalist theses, that dualism is his preferred option.

Mind/Brain Identity (Identity) Thesis

Hick argues that the only monistic view, it would seem, is the mind/brain
identity thesis, all the rest are, as Hick points out, dualist in one way or
another. According to the mind/brain identity theory, although the concepts
'mind' and 'brain' are generally understood in different senses, they
nevertheless refer to the same thing, namely the brain:

> As examples of such contingent identity, 'morning star' and 'evening star', or
> 'cloud' and 'mass of particles in suspension', or 'lightening' and 'motion of
> electrical charges', or 'volume of water' and 'collection of molecules each
> containing two atoms of hydrogen and one of oxygen', or 'heat' and
> 'molecular motion', are names and descriptions which pick out different
> characteristics of the same object or process.[2]

Thus, the mind/brain identity view argues that we should not differentiate
between events in the brain and events in the mind, but make both
synonymous.[3] With scientific advance there has been a progressive
identification of mental events with electro-chemical brain processes. That
is, for every mental event there is supposed to be a parallel brain event, thus
identifying the two as identical. However, Hick believes that such findings
only offer evidence for mind/brain correlation, not for identity. Or rather,
we might say that there is a correspondance between 'thoughts' and electro-
chemical reactions in the brain but this does not irrefutably demonstrate
that we must *identify* thoughts as being such chemical events. The crucial
point of making this distinction is that it allows us to say that even if there
is some future ability to correlate every mental event with a brain process,

this does not exclude a dualist option. To discover that such a correlation can be made would, as Hick says, be 'compatible with mind/brain identity, but it will be equally compatible with the other main theories in the philosophy of mind, namely epiphenomenalism and dualistic interaction'.[4]

Hick believes, overall, that the mind/brain identity thesis is the least plausible of the available options.[5] He argues that 'thoughts' and 'electro-chemical reactions' seem to be different realities. For example, an awestruck emotional/aesthetic response to the magnificent splendour of the night sky does not seem in the least 'like electro-chemical change in a bit of grey matter'.[6] Of course, in saying this Hick succeeds on an emotive level, but it does not seem that an Identity thesis supporter is unable to brush aside such observations and claim that the universe is perhaps more 'brutish' than Hick allows. In fact, he himself seems to implicitly acknowledge this when he concedes that 'what is subjectively the experience of seeing the night sky may be, objectively, a brain state or states. It must I think be granted that this is a conceptual possibility. To this extent the mind/brain identity theorists may be said to have made out their case'.[7]

Are there any empirical experiments that can be undertaken to resolve this issue? That is, can we apply a test to ascertain whether or not mental events take place within the brain's chemical processes? The problem here is that, (as Hick points out), looking for such data within the brain's processes merely begs the question. That is, by looking inside the skull we have assumed *a priori* that mental events are brain processes. And testing for thoughts in the brain is, as Norman Malcolm has said, a *further* test - it is logically independent from testing for brain processes.[8] Indeed, the oft-used analogies by the mind/brain identity theorists, also beg the question within themselves. For instance, comparing lightening with 'electro-chemical reactions', is to still operate within the physical universe. The analogies used by the Identity theorists presuppose that mind is brain, but that is just what is in question, so the analogies carry no real weight.[9] Thus Hick believes that there is not, and could not, be empirical evidence for mind/brain identity as opposed to mind/brain correlation.

All this, of course, still does not actually refute the mind/brain identity theory in itself, but it demonstrates that it is 'extremely rash to regard the mind/brain identity theory as being entitled to forbid the idea of the mind's surviving the death of the body'.[10] Hick therefore moves on to consider the various dualist theories.

Epiphenomenalism

Epiphenomenalism is the view that the mind is separate from the physical process of the brain, however the mind is entirely affected or caused by the brain; one could perhaps say that the brain *secretes* the mind. Despite the separation of mind from brain processes this is not an equal dualism. The mind arises out of brain processes and is therefore wholly determined by the brain.[11] However, it is this very entailment of determinism that Hick believes makes both epiphenomenalism and the Identity theories logically self-refuting. Hick states that in nature 'every constituent event is caused'.[12] In saying this, he is following a scientific tradition of Laplacean determinism. Assuming a deterministic model, Pierre Laplace was able to confidently write assert that if a Supreme Intelligence had at its disposal all the data in the universe concerning the motion and position of every atom and particle, it would be able to accurately predict the future states of the universe. Literally, 'both future and past would be present before its eyes'.[13]

Hick maintains that arguing that total determinism (in the context of mental events) is true is in fact 'logically suicidal, or self-refuting'.[14] The reason is that, at least according to the libertarian, rationality presupposes intellectual freedom, and if total determinism is true then there can be no *rational* argument for it at all, because all our thoughts and conclusions have been determined by past conditions. This kind of objection was first raised by Aquinas, who also believed that determinism 'overturns all the principles of moral philosophy'.[15] If as rational beings we inquire after truth, then we must believe we are free, otherwise our considered pronouncements are mere products of our determined nature. By 'logical contagion', Hick believes that both the Identity theory and epiphenomenalism are infected by the same 'epistemological contradiction'.[16] J.B.S. Haldane, stated the case very succinctly: 'If my mental processes are determined wholly by the motions of atoms in my brain, I have no reason to suppose that my beliefs are true...and hence I have no reason for supposing my brain to be composed of atoms.'[17] Hick would appear to agree.[18] Thus, 'mind is a reality of a different kind from matter'.[19]

Gerard Loughlin, a critic of Hick, is not convinced by this line of argument. He rightly points out that the rigid and deterministic Laplacean/Newtonian model of physics has been replaced by the more fluid dynamics of the 'new' physics. He writes:

> ...it is far from evident that the mind/brain identity theory necessarily implies determinism. For it is less than evident that the function of the brain is

appropriately modelled by Laplacean determinism. Indeed, the appropriateness and adequacy of determinist mechanics for modelling the natural world (at all levels) is disputed.[20]

However, although the revolutions in modern physics at the quantum level may seem to ease the problems of determinism in nature (and hence the 'natural' processes of the brain) for the Identity theorists, it is far from clear that the ambiguous and indeterministic model of quantum physics provides an attractive alternative. The popular scientific writer Paul Davies points that even if we assumed that an indeterministic quantum physics applied at all levels (especially the brain) then we would not necessarily have free will, instead we might have 'breakdown'. That is, if physical events were wholly erratic and unpredictable we would have no control over our actions. So, Davies comments that if your decision to 'raise your arm' was affected by 'a quantum fluctuation' then your leg might move instead. Thus he asks: 'Is that freedom? That is the fundamental problem of indeterminism: your actions may not be under your control because they are not determined, by you or anything else.'[21]

Davies' point serves as a proviso against the notion that freedom of thought requires indeterminism - (which seems to play a significant role in the dualist's argument for the immateriality of the mind). Finding myself unable to control actions due to indeterminism means that my 'choices' are meaningless and inconsequential. Going further, D.J.O'Connor argues that libertarians merely refute one type of determinism - physical, but then inevitably encounter another - mental.[22] If the 'causes' of our conclusions are to be no longer physical they will be mental. We may well emphasise freewill for rational choice, but we are only actually free to choose if the evidence is ambiguous or absent, 'but where the evidence is all in, we have no such option'.[23] O'Connor asks us to consider an example of an experiment where a person is faced with a number of switches and is asked to choose one. However, there is no further information given to the person, there is no indication as to what the experiment is for, or what the switches do. 'Having no reason to prefer one switch to another, I am indifferent to all of them and equally free, in consequence, to choose any'.[24] His point is that the range of choice is so large only because 'my degree of rational motivation is at a minimum'.[25] He sums up his argument tersely:

> ...he (the libertarian) wants to claim that it is rational estimation that is the standard case of free action. Capriciously irrational actions, however deliberate, do not meet his standards. Thus the libertarian's attempt to make freedom dependent on reason has failed. He has fallen from one kind of determinism to another, exchanging the whips of causal regularity for the scorpions of logical necessity.[26]

It would appear that even if there are stumbling-blocks for the Identity/epiphenomenalist theories on the basis of deterministic obstacles, then one cannot necessarily be convinced that this compels us to adopt the dualistic option. That is, if there are problems with combining our reasoning processes with determinism, there would seem to be equal problems arising from envisaging our mental processes being undetermined. Perhaps Hick was right, as we saw at the beginning of this chapter, to state *somewhat reservedly* that the door was 'unlocked' with regard to the survival of the mind rather than wide open.

Parapsychology

If the 'deterministic argument' cannot fully persuade us towards a dualist position, then it is possible that Hick succeeds by taking seriously the findings of parapsychology. That is, if phenomena like telepathy, near-death experiences and cross-correspondence are demonstrated to truly exist, and furthermore *cannot be accounted for by any materialistic model*, then such things can only be adequately described within a dualistic immaterial mind explanation. Keith Campbell makes an important observation (and a striking challenge): '...if even a single example of paranormal phenomena is genuine, Central State Materialism is false'.[27]

Hick considers the evidence from ESP to be impressive. He writes at the beginning of a section on this subject: 'The experimental evidence for ESP...is now very strong, and is probably well enough known for detailed description no longer to be necessary...'[28] The philosopher C.D. Broad, made a fascinating observation in his autobiography: 'So far as I can tell, I have no desire to survive the death of my present body, and I should be considerably relieved if I could feel much surer than I do that no kind of survival is possible.'[29] It is as if the evidence would appear to be strong enough to make Broad unsure about his hoped-for extinction. The implications of parapsychology on the materialist view of the mind are daunting. In an interview with Colin Wilson, Broad made an important statement: 'If these facts of psychical research are true, then clearly they are of immense importance - they literally alter everything.'[30] So, the evidence being marshalled within parapsychological research may turn out to be of significance, and offer good reasons for preferring a dualistic account of the human mind.

Nevertheless, is it possible that these very things upset Hick's finely balanced system of ambiguity that we have talked about in previous chapters? That is, does the evidence of parapsychology disrupt Hick's idea of the world being religiously ambiguous? What if further research into parapsychology demonstrates once and for all that Central State Materialism is false? D.M. Armstrong referred to parapsychological evidence as a 'small black cloud on the horizon of the materialist theory of mind';[31] but what if that small black cloud becomes an enormously insuperable obstacle for the materialist? C.D. Broad, as we have seen, thinks that if this became the case such facts would *literally alter everything*. Indeed, it might alter everything to the extent that the religious world view becomes more plausible than the naturalistic one. If we are forced by such empirical evidence to conclude that there is some kind of supernatural element in human beings (namely, the soul or immaterial mind), then this possibly serves as strong evidence against naturalism. Although there is no space to debate this issue at length, we might draw attention to some commentators who have felt compelled by parapsychological evidence and seek to endorse the view that something supernatural is happening in outstanding cases.[32] For example, Colin Wilson is able to say: 'It is not my purpose to try to convince anyone of the reality of life-after-death; only to draw attention to the impressive inner consistency of the evidence, and to point out that, in the light of that evidence, no one need feel ashamed of accepting the notion that human personality survives bodily death.'[33] Again, concerning the evidence from Near-Death experiences, Paul Badham - a leading thanatologist - writes that there is 'at least some evidence to support the belief in the immortality of the self through bodily death'.[34]

If there is at least some evidence to support the idea of immortality of the soul through bodily death, then does not this also serve as at least some empirical evidence for a non-naturalistic world view? Such an observation is of course open to the serious objection that there is as yet no unanimous opinion on the significance of the paranormal. It is certainly true that paranormal phenomena do not prove the survival hypothesis. Hick himself rightly says: 'Where then does the empirical research leave us? It leaves us at present in uncertainty.'[35] This being granted, Hick can argue that if there is no consensus of opinion about the significance of the paranormal, then his idea of a state of finely balanced ambiguity remains. Nevertheless, one of the peculiar side-effects of asserting mind-body dualism is to say that there is a *supernatural* presence in the world, namely the human mind. Presumably Hick believes that dualism is the most plausible option available because of logical and empirical considerations. Paradoxically, this means that Hick believes, at least, that a non-materialist account of the human being is more probable than not. The facts of parapsychology require further investigation, but for those who, (through religious faith or whatever), believe in the soul it is perhaps expected that paranormal phenomena will continue to baffle and frustrate the physicalist account of human existence. In addition, as a dualist, and one who maintains that the world is in a state of finely balanced ambiguity, Hick is in a paradoxical position with regard to his treatment of the evidence provided by parapsychology. It is possible that one may not be able to maintain ambiguity when such empirical evidence is presented to show that a dualistic and non-naturalistic interpretation of the human being is more likely. So we might want to question Hick's reasons for employing such evidence at all.

The Disembodied Life

Turning aside from such issues, let us take a step further and look at Hick's considerations of what it would mean to live a disembodied life. Firstly, we shall be looking at Hick's responses to the survival hypothesis proposed by the philosopher H.H. Price in his celebrated paper - 'Survival and the Idea of Another World'.[36] Then, we shall consider the points made by one critic, B.R. Reichenbach, who has sought to show that Hick's criticisms of Price's theory were not as strong as Hick thought.

Hick discerns three stages in Price's theory. First of all, Price envisages our post-mortem perceptions to be similar to that of dream perceptions. Such perceptions will be mind-dependent and will get their source from our pre-mortem embodied lives. These mental images:

> are not...imaginary at all. We do actually experience them, and they are no more imaginary than sensations....Indeed, to those who experienced it an image-world would be just as 'real' as this present world is; and perhaps so like it, that they would have considerable difficulty in realising that they were dead.[37]

Secondly, there would be real communication between minds by means of extra-sensory perception. 'There may be continual telepathic activity, producing visual and auditory images, so that the resulting experience is just like that of seeing other people and hearing them talk.'[38] Also, '...such a group of images might contain tactual images too. Similarly it might contain auditory images and smell images.'[39] In addition, this 'other' world may appear to be three-dimensional: 'It would be quite a satisfactory substitute for material objects which we perceive in this present life.'[40] Alternatively, there could be a number of worlds, Price writes:

> It is likely that there would still be many next worlds, a different one for each group of like-minded personalities. I admit I am not quite sure what might be meant by 'like-minded' and 'unlike-minded' in this connection. Perhaps we

could say that two personalities are like-minded if their memories or their characters are sufficiently similar. It might be that Nero and Marcus Aurelius do not have a world in common, but Socrates and Marcus Aurelius do.[41]

Thirdly, Price writes: 'Their memories and their desires would determine what sort of images they had. If I may put it so, the "stuff" or "material" of such a world would come in the end from one's memories, and the "form" of it from one's desires.'[42] That is, 'the next world will be fashioned by the power of our desires'.[43]

Responding, Hick feels that there is a problem between the first two of these sections. 'There is however in his theory a tension between the idea of the formation of a post-mortem world by the power of desire and the idea that such a world is common to many minds in virtue of telepathic links between them.'[44] He gives an analogy of a married couple on a beach, one desires a calm sea for bathing, the other desires tempestuous seas for surfing. Indeed, the wife would prefer to be in Paris rather than on the beach at all![45] These are contradictory states for the environment to be in, and if there can be no agreement between two individuals who are supposed to be harmoniously in union with each other, then how, argues Hick, can there be agreement amongst multitudes?

If we allow B.R. Reichenbach to intervene at this point, he argues that Hick's objections overlook Price's primary element: the status of this putative world as *mind-dependent*. He contends that Hick's portrayal of potentially incompatible states of affairs are still located within a physical, concrete situation, and not really within Price's non-physical, mind-induced environment. Reichenbach grants the force of Hick's criticisms if they are situated in a physical, concrete world where people's incompatible wishes would run up against each other. However, he points out that seeing that Price's world is mind-created and not properly physical one should allow for ostensibly incompatible wishes to be fulfilled.[46]

In short, Reichenbach claims that in a mental world persons could imagine contradictory states like a tempestuous sea as well as a calm one, and that this would not 'lead to interpersonal contradictory states';[47] but this would lead to contradictory states in a physical world: Hick's objection thus relates to the latter but not the former state.

Nevertheless, is such criticism valid? We have already seen that this mental world, according to Price, is a product of our memories and experiences whilst in this embodied life. The next world seems so real that people 'would have considerable difficulty in realising that they were dead'. Moreover, the next world is a mutually-created environment. Price writes that: '...an image-world such as I am describing would not be the product of one single mind only, nor would it be purely private. It would be the joint product of a group of telepathically interacting minds and public to all of them.'[48] Further, Reichenbach in emphasising the *mental* rather than the physical overlooks, I think, that such persons will be conjuring up 'physical' images that they recall from their pre-mortem life. A mental image 'is an actual entity, as real as anything can be'.[49] Given this, there can be contradictory states in the mental world if only because the images produced are based on the pre-mortem physical world, and such images are group-created environments. Hick interprets Price as meaning that the public world would be a 'coherent three-dimensional world which we inhabit jointly with other persons',[50] so he believes that contradictory conflicts of will between persons would arise. Reichenbach however, asks the question: 'But is not a world produced by paranormal communication different from the kind of world or environment envisioned by Hick in his objection? Price's public world is a world of communicated meanings, ideas and mental images, not of objects or things (physical).'[51] Again, it is possible that Reichenbach is mistaken: these 'communicated meanings' and ideas etc. are images of a physical world, and they are as 'real as anything can be'. Reichenbach seems to make the error of envisaging the mental as vague or fluid or, as Price says, 'thin and unsubstantial', but this is just what Price does not believe. To repeat, for him 'an image world would be just as real as this present world is...'. For Reichenbach, Price's image world means that mutually incompatible wishes of different people can be fulfilled simultaneously.[52] But, in a public arena it seems that such a world would have to be a very confused one, similar to a mass of cross-lines in a telephone network. Thus, it is possible that Hick's objection stands.

Hick's further objection is that Price's world would not serve as a suitable environment for person-making. His Irenaean theodicy would seem to entail an environment which was not a product of our wishes and desires, but which at times acts contrary to our wishes. That is, Hick believes that a world of challenge and difficulty is one which is more conducive to soul-making than one in which our wishes are easily fulfilled.[53] Therefore: 'All that a wish-fulfilment world would seem able to do in the way of character formation would be to refine and purify the structure of desires and dispositions that had already been developed on earth.'[54] This objection applies if Price's mind-dependent world is viewed as an everlasting condition. Nevertheless, it would be compatible with Hick's system as a temporary stage. And indeed, in Hick's pareschatology (see the next chapter) we see him embracing an idea of temporary disembodiment as a *bardo* stage before re-embodiment in another space to continue one's spiritual journey. Therefore, Hick may not have a problem here; the notion of a person re-evaluating and re-assessing their lives before moving onto the next stage seems to fit quite comfortably with his putative 'many lives in many worlds'.

Resurrection and Replicas

It is not so much his ideas on disembodied existence that Hick is famous for. Rather, it is his hypothesis concerning *re-embodiment* that has attracted a great deal of attention and debate. Hick's 'replica' theory is an attempt to describe the resurrection of the person in such a way that it is acceptable to the modern mind. He rejects the traditional 'patristic' view of resurrection (a re-collection of the original bodily particles), and points out that the accepted modern view is that the resurrection body will be a new and different body. It will be designed for its new environment in much the way that our present bodies are suited to our environment. Thus, the 'personality' is re-embodied by God elsewhere.[55] His own variation on this is famous: he suggests that the resurrection body be envisaged as an exact psycho-physical 'replica' of the deceased person.[56]

Hick elaborates his theory as follows:

> For example, at some learned gathering in London one of the company suddenly and inexplicably disappears and the next moment an exact "replica" of him suddenly and inexplicably appears at some comparable meeting in New York. The person who appears in New York is exactly similar, as to both bodily and mental characteristics, to the person who disappears in London. There is continuity of memory, complete similarity of bodily features, including fingerprints, hair and eye colouration and stomach contents, and also of beliefs, habits and mental propensities. In fact there is everything that would lead us to identify the one who appeared with the one who disappeared, except continuous occupancy of space.[57]

Hick then goes on to apply, or extend, this picture to a replica appearing not on this earth but following death in another space. Instead of the transference of the person to another place, we have to imagine a transportation to another *space*. Furthermore, this 'other' world would be one inhabited by other 'replicas' (that is, it would not be a private world), and such beings would recognise each other.[58]

The Identity of the Replica

There has been a great deal of critical exchange about the concept of the 'replica', and critics have focused on questions of identity and uniqueness in particular. Thus, there is a question that can be (and has been) asked. In fact, such a question might be phrased in number of ways: Is the 'replica' and the original person before death one and the same person? Or, does Hick's account of an exactly similar replica assure us that this replica is indeed the person who died? And, is the personal identity of that individual preserved? In response to these queries, the answer would seem to be that, for Hick, exact similarity *plus uniqueness* is sufficient for us to identify the 'replica' person as the person who has just died. Hick seeks to accentuate the notion of uniqueness by placing the word 'replica' in quotes. He writes concerning his reasoning:

> The quotes are intended to mark the difference between the normal concept of a replica and the more specialised concept in use here...If a putative "replica" did exist simultaneously with its original it would not be a "replica" but a replica; and if there were more than one they would not be "replicas" but replicas.[59]

The 'replica' would have to be unique to be fully identified with the original. Nevertheless, we should also acknowledge, thinks Hick, that our perceptions of the individual body has to alter from being a *fixed* set of particles towards a notion of the body as a pattern or *code*. This last point is corroborated by Hick's appeal to the work of Norbert Wiener the cyberneticist. Wiener writes (Hick quotes): 'The individuality of the body is that of a flame rather than that of a stone, of a form rather than a bit of substance.'[60] Thus, one could even consider transporting or transmitting

> the whole pattern of the human body, of the human brain with its memories and cross-connections, so that a hypothetical receiving instrument could re-embody these messages in appropriate matter, capable of continuing the processes already in the body and the mind, and of maintaining the integrity needed for this continuation by a process of homeostasis.[61]

Hick argues that, setting aside questions of practicality, the implications of Wiener's idea is that identity does not depend on numerical exactness (i.e. the original particles); rather it relies on the 'pattern' or 'code' of the original body being faithfully instantiated. It is the 'code' that is crucial rather than the particles which are used.[62] Hick thinks, therefore, that 'replica' persons could be confidently identified with the person who had died. Nevertheless, A. Flew and T. Penelhum find such a notion very problematic. Flew formulates what he calls the 'Replica Objection'. He contends that even to produce the most identical object to one that has been destroyed is not to produce the same thing but merely a 'copy'. Thus, Flew asks us to consider the morality of punishing a replica person at Judgement

Day for the sins committed by the original. This is surely as repugnant as punishing an 'identical twin' for actions performed by the other.[63] Flew's point is powerful, but it is a somewhat loaded appeal. First of all, Flew is *assuming* that the relationship of the replica to the original is comparable to the relationship that exists between identical twins. There is no reason why one should assume this, in fact it rather begs the question because this is really the point at issue. Secondly, Flew is using the question of punishment and justice in order to enhance the sense of discontinuity that he perceives to exist between replicas and their originals. It is surely the case that punishing twin B for twin A's crime is unjust, but again there are a number of assumptions going on here (such as the one we have just seen) that misfire if they are directed at Hick. We will return to this specific point in a moment, but it would be appropriate to bring in T. Penelhum's argument first.

Penelhum, differing somewhat from Flew, accepts that the 'replica' person could be identified as being the original person who died, but the decision as to whether it is in fact the original person is a subjective decision on the part of that person. He writes that 'it is possible for Smith to say that that person is not going to be, Smith, but someone very like him. If he says this he will say that it is unfair for that future person to be punished for anything that he, Smith, has done, however willing he is to accept the punishments'.[64] That is to say, Smith is not *obliged* to identify the 'replica' in the eschaton with himself. The only thing that would oblige Smith to say that the replica is he, would be if some disembodied self were to leave his body at death and enter the future 'replica'. However, Penelhum rejects the notion of disembodied existence, so to his mind, his objection still stands - Smith is not required to say that the 'replica' will be him. Needless to say, both the criticisms of Flew and Penelhum stem from a physicalist understanding of personal identity.

Frank Dilley, a sympathetic critic, has attempted to come to Hick's aid. Replying to Penelhum in particular, he writes:

> It is difficult to see how a matter of justice could turn on a linguistic decision as to how to regard the matter rather than as to what the facts are. Would the punishment of the putatively resurrected Smith be fair if Smith decided that he was the same self, and not fair if he decided that he was only a replica? That would make the fairness of the punishment dependent upon Smith's subjective decision about the matter, and that seems to be a strange way to determine fairness.[65]

In fact, as I said a moment ago, it is possible that both Flew's and Penelhum's objections misfire. This is because they are based on a different conception of punishment than that which Hick actually holds. If

Hick held to an Augustinian view of punishment, that is a retributivist type
of God punishing sin in order to balance evil with just punishment, then
their objections might be sound. However, this is just the sort of
punishment that Hick rejects, and indeed finds morally repugnant. Hick's
actual view of punishment is utilitarian (as we saw in chapter two), that is,
punishment is largely educative and person-building. Again, this is
something that Dilley points out: 'We should assume that Hick would
maintain that anyone who was exactly like Smith would be in exactly the
same need of "education" that Smith is.'[66]

Returning to Flew's analogy of 'identical twins' in connection to the
punishment of replicas, his argument does not really do justice to Hick's
conception of a 'replica' at all. Admittedly, twins can be genetically very
similar, but their minds are different, they are different people. Moreover,
such criticisms are not really successful because they seem in part to rely
on a perception of Hick's position (e.g. a retributivist view of punishment)
which is actually incorrect. If we reject Flew's 'twin' analogy and accept
that the 'replica' is the same person as the original then 'punishment' is
justified. Nevertheless, even if we consider that the replica is merely a
copy, then on a utilitarian view of punishment one would presumably feel,
(as Dilley maintains), that the replica would benefit (as the original would
also) from such remedial and corrective 'treatment'.[67]

In these arguments Dilley has been fairly successful in defending Hick.
However, there is a more serious objection to the replica theory which
proves far more troublesome. This objection has centred around the
problem of *multiple replicas*. In the journals major broadsides were fired at
Hick's replica theory by J.J. Clarke and J.J. Lipner, who consider the
problem of multiple replicas. Clarke proposes the following possibility:

> Let us suppose that God, since he is especially pleased with Hick, decides to
> reconstitute, not one, but two Hicks. Let us call the heavenly twins 'H2' and
> 'H3' respectively, reserving 'H1' for their earthly forebear. This presents no
> difficulty for God. Instead of one qualitatively identical body, he makes
> two.[68]

That is, to have the inherent possibility of two Hicks in the resurrection
world rather than one is an absurdity to the conception of a person's
uniqueness. Clarke affirms: 'In view of this it would be absurd to suppose
that H2 and H3 were the same person.'[69] Now, if Clarke thinks that his
question poses problems for Hick, Lipner believes that Clarke's criticism is
an irrefutable stumbling-block: 'Clarke has argued against the viability of
Hick's view on the basis of "multiple replication" in the same space, and

from within the framework of Hick's own premises, his objection appears to me irrefutable.'[70]

Hick recognises the consequences of multiplicity. He admits that if multiplication were to occur it might cause conceptual confusion with regard to our present understanding of uniqueness and identity. He writes: 'Our concept of the "same person" has not been developed to cope with such a situation.'[71] This is a tantalising statement by Hick because it appears to imply the possibility that an evolution of conceptual personhood would alleviate the problem. That is, we might presently perceive personhood in uniquely *single* terms, but if we 'developed' a different view - which could entail no more than an imaginative thought experiment - then we might, presumably, begin to accept the idea of multiple 'continuations' of a person.

Nevertheless, to return to the present argument, Clarke believes that the mere possibility of multiple replication is enough to show that even one replica could not be identified with the original Hick. I quote at length:

> It is not even necessary to suppose that God has actually created H3, for the mere possibility of his doing so is as much a threat to H2's identity as is H3's actual existence. If the actual existence of H3 alongside H2 obliges us to refrain from identifying H2 as Hick, then the mere possibility of H3 ought similarly to restrain us from conferring identity. This is pinpointed by the fact that if H3 became reconstituted some while after H2, one would have to say that for a while H2 could conceivably have been H1, but then on H3's arrival in the resurrection world this identification ceased to be possible. This is incoherent.[72]

Hick's response to Clarke's criticism was to say that none of all this prevents the possibility that God will in fact only recreate a single copy rather than multiples.[73] However, as Dilley points out, this cannot be an entirely successful reply - 'It cannot be right to give, as an answer to a point about logical possibility, a merely factual answer'.[74] What Clarke and Lipner are arguing about is the nature of and the possibilities within the concept of replication, not about what God will or will not do.[75] Dilley seems to accept the implications of multiple replication. He advances an interesting proposal. He believes that Hick should have acknowledged 'that every duplicate of the pattern which constitute a particular person is the same person as that person, since he embodies the same pattern as the original person'.[76] Thus, Dilley actually thinks that Hick is wrong to find problems with the concept of the person in conjunction with multiplicity. Furthermore, rather than speak of God creating single instances of things, one might speak of a divine intention to create an infinite variety of instances of perfected beings. Thus, he remarks in humorous fashion that there might be perfected instances of 'Hick the plumber and Hick the lawyer in addition to a perfected instance of Hick the philosopher'.[77] Presumably, individual people have *many* capacities, not all of which can be realised within a single person. Thus, multiple replicas in the afterlife might be employed to realise the many varieties of potential within a single individual.

Such a proposal may present bold possibilities, but are they easily accepted? If we reflect on the kind of God represented here, then we have a God who is more interested in functions, abilities and capacities rather than persons. It is a profoundly utilitarian suggestion which seems to undermine the integrity of personhood – something which is surely fundamental to a *Christian* vision. In fact, Dilley's suggestion reads like a recommendation from an advisory firm to increase efficiency and productivity on a factory line. In attempting to defend Hick, Dilley in his enthusiasm has exposed a disquieting weakness in the replica theory. Hick himself states that 'a person is by definition unique. There cannot be two people who are exactly the same, in every respect, including their consciousness and memories'.[78] If the full conceptual implications of the meaning of replication causes an inevitable logical possibility of multiplicity, then Hick's replica theory is inadequate if we also desire to affirm that each individual person is unique and precious in the sight of God. What would be our conclusion if Hick the plumber, Hick the lawyer etc., came together as a group? It must be the case that the group of Hicks would be comprised of different people, not the same person. Furthermore, as the multiple Hicks develop through time there would be a gradual divergence of identity. Gerard Loughlin elaborates thus:

> That they are different people will become more obvious with the passage of time, as new and differing experiences modify and change the psychological pattern of each Hick. Eventually, not even the criterion of psychological pattern will be met by the developing replica Hicks. Even if they were once the same person they will not remain so.[79]

Nevertheless, does this somewhat miss Dilley's point? Sameness, or uniqueness, of identity does not actually seem to be Dilley's concern; in fact, he appears happily content to extend possibilities and speak of, what might be called, 'diversity in the mould'.

Is there a possible route of escape for Hick with regard to the problem of multiplication? Ostensibly, an obvious solution might be the acknowledgement of an immaterial self which would be transferred from the original body and into the 'replica'. Hick could thereby overcome problems of continued personal identity, and the replica could be said to be the same as the original person. However, Hick does not employ the concept of soul transfer into the replica as a reply to Penelhum or Flew. Although Hick is in fact a dualist he sought in his replica theory to argue for life-after-death without employing dualism. Earlier in his career, Hick appeared to eschew dualism: 'much mid-twentieth century philosophy has come to see the human being as in the biblical writings, not as an eternal soul temporarily attached to a mortal body, but as a form of finite, mortal psychophysical life'.[80] However, later, when *Death and Eternal Life* was published, he claimed (as we have seen) that the philosopher H.H. Price had made dualism intelligible for the first time with his paper 'Survival and the Idea of "Another World"'.[81] Hick writes: 'The independent reality of the mind and brain, as mutually interacting entities or processes, is of course compatible both with the simultaneous persisting of both and with the mind surviving the death of the body'.[82] Thus, Hick would call himself a dualist: 'In rejecting mind/brain identity, then, we accept mind/brain dualism. We accept, that is, that mind is a reality of a different kind from matter.'[83]

In the present context, if Hick thinks he can accept dualism, it is perhaps appropriate for him to use the concept of a disembodied self to defend his 'replica' theory against the charges of discontinuity and multiplicity. Dilley affirms: 'With the possibility of soul transfer both problems are solved.'[84] Furthermore, as we shall see in the next chapter, Hick's pareschatology incorporates the Eastern/Buddhist *bardo* concept into a systematic framework of successive re-embodiments in many worlds. This bardo world represents the disembodied state in between each re-embodiment, a period of self-evaluation and self-purging. So it should seem clear that Hick does indeed have a notion of soul transfer even if it is not mentioned *explicitly* in defence of his replica theory.[85]

Nevertheless, perhaps the critics of the resurrection/replica survival hypothesis are overly concentrating on the mechanics of the problem rather than giving attention to wider theological intuitions? Such intuitions should not be deemed inappropriate because of the basic religious context of Hick's speculations. For example, we might seek to guarantee identity by bringing in the notion of divine will, or intention. Robert Herbert has argued that if there is any ambiguity about the identity of persons in the afterlife then it is surely resolved by the appeal that God *intends* that a resurrected person be the same as the original.[86] Similarly, Stephen Davis writes: 'My continuing identity through time as the person that I am, then, is based in the first instance not on my own properties but on the fact that God sustains and upholds me as that being by recognizing and calling me.'[87]

It is surely correct to consider the whole issue of survival beyond death within the context of a loving Creator who values each individual. In fact, we saw earlier that Hick argued that a loving God would not desire that individuals should perish before their potentialities had been allowed to fully develop. If this basic intuition is extended to the present discussion, then we might argue that from the divine perspective there is a desire, or even necessity, that the resurrected person is fully identified with the original. This is perhaps not a statement about divine omnipotence as such (as if we are appealing to the divine *ability* to authentically 'replicate' individuals), but more of a consideration about divine omniscience. Putting it provocatively, what might we say about the *beliefs* of a putatively omniscient Being about the resurrected person in question? If such a Being is able to meaningfully relate to a resurrected person *as a continuation of the person who died* than can we say that its beliefs are false?

Finally, we might return to Hick's point that the fact that the creation of multiple replicas is not impossible does not rule out the possibility that God will in fact create only one. Thus, the fact that replicas are in principle capable of multiplication is acknowledged. However, in this context, it is important to note that Hick is not trying to remove all possible doubt about the identity of future 'replica' individuals - if that were the demand then it is unlikely that anything could be firmly established. Rather, in verifying the identity of the 'replica' we are, perhaps, only seeking to remove rational doubt. The tone of Hick's original analogy, about the individual who vanishes from London and reappears in New York, is not one which seeks to remove all possible doubt, but rather is a suggestion about an open possibility. Moreover, in some of his later writings, Hick is happy to modify his thinking on this issue. Thus, he even speaks of embodied existences 'not necessarily in the matter or forms that we know.'[88] The reality, it seems, is not that he has presented something which he considers to be utterly watertight. It is rather a sort of challenge of the form 'do you really think that it is irrational that this person ('replica') be the same as the person who just died?' The decision is ours.

Resurrection as a Universal Transformation

Is it possible to suggest another interpretation of what we might mean by the original body being raised? Stemming from Hick's contribution let us briefly expand on some of the issues raised about the nature of the resurrection body in the context of the whole of nature being transformed in the eschaton. Perhaps we should reconsider the eschatological relationship between humanity and nature. Let us propose that we should envisage ourselves as being contained within the whole of physical reality in congruence with the insights put forward by the 'new physics'. Moreover, one suggestion might be that we talk not of our bodies being reconstituted from the original particles, but from 'their original source' which is to be identified within this spatio-temporal universe.

To begin, let us consider a criticism raised by Paul Badham that concentrates on the notion of Hick's 'replica' being *exact*. His criticisms proceed from a strictly literal interpretation of the word 'exact'. Simply, if the replica of a person is to be exact, then such a person must by logical necessity be replicated into this spatio-temporal universe and not another, otherwise the replication would not be exact.[89] This criticism would seem to have weight, because if Hick wants to talk about persons being replicated to the extent that details such as stomach contents are observed, then the replication can only take place in this universe. And yet Hick speaks of replication into many other worlds which are in different spatial zones than this one. Hick has run into logical difficulties if he wants to assert our resurrection into another space. It seems that Badham is victorious with this criticism.

To be clear, Hick describes the scenario as: 'The divine creation in another space of an exact psycho-physical "replica" of the deceased person.'[90] He maintains that it is possible for there to be two, or many more, spaces that exist alongside each other. Each of these spaces can be fully dimensional (or rather - 'spatial') but be invisible to the others, but there is no sense in talking of such spaces being a certain distance from each other because they are totally unrelated. From the point of view of someone living in another space, our particular space does not even exist, it is nowhere.[91] Badham believes that the concept of plural spaces is coherent and reasonable, but he does not feel that it can aid Hick's replica hypothesis. For Badham, Hick requires a space which physically interacts exactly like our own for talk of *exact* replicas to make coherent sense.[92] He goes further, 'though there may be any number of dimensions and any number of different spaces, there cannot be two space-time systems subject to the same physical laws for two such systems could not avoid being spatially related'.[93] Thus, crucially, Badham concludes that Hick must adjust his argument from talk of other spaces to other *places* instead.

We might highlight two points:

1. Hick's replicas are unrelated to the matter that once formed the environment of the deceased persons. They represent divine recreations in another space of such bodies, and they occupy a space that cannot be spatially related to this universe because, as has been suggested, plural spaces are totally unrelated to each other. Therefore, in Hick's replica

notion there can be no physical connection whatsoever between the material that once comprised the old body and that of the new.

2.   Can we speak of resurrection in terms of Hick's 'replica' and at the same time maintain the sense that it entails a 'conquering of death' (in the physical as well as the spiritual sense)?

Hick's replica is made up of particles that belong to another space, so, whatever else we can say about this replica, we must say that it has no relation with the particles of this space. Now alternatively, as a thought experiment, let us suppose that God will, in a sense, make a 'replica' of a person from the particles of this space. Ostensibly maybe, we are suggesting the same thing as Hick is (i.e. replication) but I want to suggest that we have in fact, as regards theological meaning, said something significantly different. The meaning of resurrection, at least in the Christian context, is about the resolution of death into life, the transformation of perishability into imperishability, mortality into immortality.

If someone were to say: 'These are my particles' we could in fact expand this sense of ownership not just to those particles *prima facie* located in their body, but quite legitimately to the particles of the whole universe. This would be a suggestion that is inspired by the 'new physics' with its talk of *relatedness*.

It could be argued that the problem of re-assembling the original bodies (a concern in patristic times) appears insuperable because it is envisaged that such bodies will be reconstituted by strictly sorting through infinite varieties of matter and then be extracted from this present environment and placed into another space (e.g. the 'heavenly world'). Thus, it is perhaps important in this scenario to insist that the same particles are involved. But, might it be suggested that resurrection bodies are not extracted from this spatial zone, rather, this whole spatial zone, of which such bodies are an intimate part, is transformed. Crudely, there is no question of one of a person's bodily particles being overlooked at 'the resurrection' because every particle that makes up the cosmos will be transformed. Nevertheless, it could be argued that this contradicts what I hinted at earlier about the importance of it being *this* body that was resurrected and that there should be no replicas? I do not think that this is necessarily so, but some sort of fuller explanation is required.

To begin with, the 'new physics' that would seem to be emerging in modern science has adopted a new holistic view of the universe. This new emphasis implies that every particle in this present universe is in some way interconnected and interrelated to another, regardless of spatial distance. For example, selecting a few soundbites, David Bohm believes that 'Life itself has to be regarded as belonging to a totality'.[94] The physicist Paul Davies writes: 'There is a unity to the universe which goes far deeper than a mere expression of uniformity. It is a unity which says that without everything you can have nothing.'[95] If we are truly physically related, in Davies' subatomic sense, to the whole universe then conversely it is related physically to us. Bede Griffiths puts it more mystically when he says: 'The whole universe is in every part. That is the principle. Just as the structure of the whole universe is present in each one of us and we become conscious of the physical structure of the universe of which we are a part'.[96] Further, such notions have long been present in Hindu thinking, for example the following extract from the *Chandogya Upanishad* is typical: 'As great as the infinite space beyond is the space within the lotus of the heart. Both heaven and earth are contained in that inner space, both fire and air, sun and moon, lightning and stars. Whether we know it in this world or know it not, everything is contained in that inner space.'[97]

One could make the claim that 'I am contained within the universe and it in me'. And it is possible, therefore, that this has a bearing on what one might respond to the question 'Where are the particles that once comprised the physical body on earth?' Expanding further, the emerging holism in physics provides a paradigm for a new understanding of 'the reconstitution of "original" bodily particles'. Newtonian physics with its mechanical, determinate and reductionist view of nature leads to the view that the reconstruction of bodies from the original particles must strictly involve a search for certain, particular particles as opposed to others. The new physics however envisages everything as belonging to, and resonating within, a single reality. Thus, we might imagine the resurrection of a person in this paradigm as an event which is simultaneously the transformation of the entire universe.

What has been suggested might be envisaged as a merging of the patristic view of resurrection and the accepted modern view. The patristic view wants to say that the original particles have been resurrected and death has been conquered - mortality has put on immortality. The modern view, however, 'maintains that the resurrection body is a different body given by God, but expressing the personality within its new environment as the physical body has expressed it on earth. This view accepts that when we die our physical bodies disintegrate and cannot be reconstituted'.[98] This view would appear to be accepted by the Church of England: 'in the life of the world to come the soul or spirit will still have its appropriate organ of expression and activity.'[99] My point, actually, is not to claim that such notions are necessarily incoherent but simply that the new physics has provided a resource by which the notion of the original body being transformed into a living body is upheld whilst at the same time de-emphasising the need in the Newtonian sense of recollecting the original particles.

Ownership, Identity and Mechanics

Consider the following formulations:

Hick's "Replica"

1. In this space a person dies.
2. An exact "replica" of this person appears in another space (whilst the old body remains in this space).
3. "Replica" dies again and the process is repeated throughout many lives and many worlds.

Traditional (Patristic) View

1. In this space a person dies.
2. In the eschaton the person's body is resurrected by collecting together the particles that once comprised the original body. (Identity is assured by either insisting that the same particles are involved or by soul transference – or both.)
3. The resurrected person inhabits a 'heavenly environment' (or otherwise) for ever with his/her *new* body.

Universal Transformation

1. In this space a person dies.
2. The Cosmos as a whole is transformed 'in the eschaton' together with all the 'matter' contained (and therefore, persons) within it.
3. The transformed (resurrected) persons live in the transformed universe (new heaven and new earth)

These three formulations attempt to show that the idea of 'universal transformation' offers some kind of harmonisation of the patristic view with Hick's modern replica theory. It maintains the *sense* of the idea of the original particles being involved, but reinterprets this as a 'replication' of the person using the inter-related matter of *this* space.

Having suggested all this, could it not be argued that a sense of particularity is lost in a universal transformation account of the resurrection of the original body? The traditionally familiar notion of the original body being raised to new life seems to require some sort of notion of the actual particles of my present body being reassembled and given a new and dynamic life-force. But, given the new physics, maybe this old view can be modified providing that we can retain some sense of the meaning behind that view. One is not seeking to alter our sense of a person's location or particularity within the universe, but one is trying to acknowledge that a new 'underlying layer' has recently emerged which changes the picture somewhat. It has been suggested that the meaning that should be preserved when we talk of resurrection is the notion that mortality has been clothed in immortality - that which has died is raised and not left in *unresolved* death. It is in *this* universe that the story of life and death has been told a billion times over. The new physics seems to suggest that our particles are interwoven in one huge tapestry. In a sub-atomic sense, a person's particles are locatable only in the sense that they are in this universe. Thus, in a sense, a person's *original* particles involve all the particles of this universe.

Alternatively, we still want to say that there is particularity in this universe, but let us say that underlying this particularity there is a profound unity (or generality?) in the physical universe to which all things belong and find their identity in everything else. It might be argued that we could tap this holistic resource when referring to original particles. We can keep our notion of particular individuals being raised to new life, but the bedrock from which they are raised is a unity.

A difficulty that was disputed in patristic times was a question of particle ownership. Might it be that a person's resurrected body may in fact made up of leftover particles from other peoples' bodies, thus the somewhat macabre question of particle ownership arises. That is, when Smith died his particles dispersed into the ground and into the air and one eventually found its way into my body to become one of my particles. But is it one of my particles? Or have I merely borrowed it from Smith (who perhaps borrowed it from someone else)? This, ostensibly, seems to be a very reasonable way of to describe things. But it is clearly indicative of a Newtonian mindset. The 'new' physics does not talk this way. Indeed, in the emerging (post)modern scientific worldview such a method of identifying matter is somewhat out-moded. Thus, although he is cautious about the implications of quantum physics, John Polkinghorne writes: 'Quantum entities exhibit a counterintuitive togetherness-in-separation, a power once they have interacted to influence each other however far they subsequently separate. Paradoxically, the atomic world is one that cannot be described atomistically.'[100] Coming to terms with such notions might mean reassessing our views of original particles in the resurrection context. I have suggested that we could perhaps adjust our perspective and say that our bodies have all passed through the same physical reality and that this reality is their original source.

Nevertheless, because what is essentially being suggested is a 'replication' of the person from the original source, the problems that were raised with regard to Hick's replica theory inevitably arise again. But is the situation different such that we can suggest solutions that are more satisfying?

Multiple and Random Resurrections

To begin, does not talk of resurrection involving the usage of the particles of this universe mean that someone could quite easily create another Smith right now from this matter and absurdly declare that Smith had, according to my criteria, been raised from the dead? In response, it must surely be the case that such haphazard replications of a living Smith cannot be regarded as a *resurrection* of Smith. One can (and this is indeed now possible, it seems, in contemporary science) say that Smith has been cloned. But two Smiths existing alongside each other would surely be different people. The mere usage of particles of this universe cannot be a yardstick to wholly verify the authentic and unique resurrection of a person. Moreover, utilising the notion that it is this universe that is involved, it might be possible to suggest that the narrative of a person's life, like the narratives of every individual of the human race, is bound up with the narrative of the entire universe. Each narrative will have affected, however infinitesimally, the way the universe is. Thus, choosing to say that Smith had been 'raised from the dead' with reference to the usage of particles (rather than, in this case, merely cloned) would only be properly meaningful in the context of the continuing stream of the physical processes in this universe. But the problem is compounded for Hick by the temporal-relation that is thought to exist between different spaces. A. Olding elucidates: 'To speak about the simultaneity of events in the two different worlds presupposes that bodies in the two different worlds might be temporally related even though they are not spatially related, and it is not clear that this is possible.'[101] He goes further: 'But now it seems to make no sense to say that the resurrection body appears at the same time as the physical body dies. No time elapses between the death of the physical body and the appearance of the resurrection body, not because the two events are simultaneous but because they are not temporally related.'[102]

If we acknowledge the coherence of Olding's criticism, the idea of resurrection as a transforming event *after* death is lost in this scheme of multiple, and unrelated, spaces. However, in the picture of the transformation occurring in *this* space, I tentatively suggest that such conundrums are resolved, and the meaning of resurrection is retained. The notion of having a real predecessor is actualised in the continuing story and stream of physical reality - you cannot resurrect a 'story' that is yet to be told. A person has a real past in this spatio-temporal world and the importance of that past is reinforced, to my mind, by transforming the reality in which a person's life had its context.

Another problem could be that two or more of the same person might be raised out of the original source material. Both would appear after my death and so could be regarded as a dual-resurrection. In response, let me offer the following suggestion: If we are saying that it is resurrection into *this* world that is important (because of various theological meanings that can be obtained), then can we not also assert that by making positive affirmations about the *context* of individuals we are also saying something about the 'conditions' which might be said to govern the authentic resurrection of unique individuals? D. Cockburn, when writing about the irreplaceability of persons in his book on personal identity *Other Human Beings*, says:

> What I think of when I think back is her smile on catching my eye, or the smile in response to a humorous absurdity of the particular kind which struck her. It would hardly be '*that* smile' if 'it' was a response to the sight of another's suffering. At any rate, the sight of that facial configuration in *those* circumstances, so far from being a joy to me, would be positively nightmarish. When, then, my distress focuses on the thought that I will never see that smile again what is at issue is not simply, as I put it, a particular "facial configuration" there is a reference to context which is crucial.[103]

For Cockburn, a smile is only *that* smile when a particular situation is in view. Presumably, if smiles were just facial configurations not requiring a particular context then such things would be capable of multiplication in a variety of contexts. But *that* smile only occurs in particular situations.

Now, what if we proposed that in *this* universe there is only one instance of *that* person? Alternatively, if we say that persons are just *self-contained* forms or patterns that can be reproduced anywhere (like facial configurations in contrast to *that* smile) then maybe they are capable of multiplication. But by asserting the transformation of this universe we may also be saying that it is this context that is important - and in this context there can only be one instance of a particular person. To explain, it is perhaps the reference to something akin to relational identity, or more precisely, the possession of *relational properties*, that is crucial.

When discussing the identity of resurrected persons, Stephen Davis outlines the arguments for identity in a relational context.[104] It will be instructive to attempt to summarise something of Davis' argument and then seek to apply the sense of the argument to the idea presently being considered.

Firstly, Davis maintains that there are some 'properties' that can be applied to a person which are non-relational. To use an example (different from the ones that Davis employs) of a non-relational property, take the statement 'x is a red-head'. This is a 'property' of x that does not rely on factors which are extrinsic to x. It is an instrinsic property. Secondly, there are properties which are relational. For example, 'x owns a walking stick'. The crucial difference here is that whereas the red-headedness of x is ascertained intrinsically, the fact that x owns a walking stick entails that the walking stick logically has the 'property' of *being owned by x*. Thus, in the second instance, there is what might be called a 'property relationship'. That is, with this particular property there are other 'property bearers' extrinsic to x that are part of the picture. Davis goes on to pose the question of whether 'x survives death' should be considered a relational property also and then apply this to the debate about unique identity of resurrected persons. But I wish to remain for a moment with what has been said so far. Let us take the following sentence:

'x is a person who lived in this universe'.

Can the above be considered as relational? If the answer is yes, then might we go on to apply this to the notion of the universal transformation of this universe which involves the resurrection of a person? Consider the following:

1. x is a person who lived in this universe.
2. *In this universe there lived* person x.
3. There was only one x in this universe.

If these are 'relational properties' then we might therefore conclude that for such relational criteria to be satisfied in a resurrection context then

4. In accordance with the relational properties between x and the universe there can therefore be only one *authentic* resurrected x.

That is, if resurrecting an individual involves the simultaneous transformation of this universe then perhaps it also follows that for a 'replica' to be truly identified with the original there cannot be multiple 'replicas'. That is, the *relational properties* that exist between *this* universe and *that* person mean that only one *true* 'replica' could exist. We are proposing, then, that individual persons belong in the context of the whole community of creation and they find their *individuation* in this context. We could, as I have said, describe a person as 'a pattern of psycho-physical characteristics' which can be extracted from this space and be transmitted many times to different spaces. Contrarily, if we assert relational considerations such that a person is someone with a past in a specific spatio-temporal environment, or else a belongingness in a specific community of creation then maybe it is this that prevents multiple resurrections of individuals. Here then, context is crucial.

Nevertheless, might it be counter-argued that we are trying to tie the universe and an individual's person's identity together too closely such that to resurrect Smith means that one must 'resurrect' the universe as well? But surely this cannot follow from the identification of relational properties alone? For example, following such logic one might say that 'x uses a walking stick' means that for x to be truly resurrected means that x's walking stick must be part of x's resurrection too! This is not what is actually being said. This might be clarified with another 'relational' statement: 'x is shorter than y'. Such a statement is relational (it involves two property bearers: x and y), but doesn't imply that x needs y to be around in the resurrection world to secure x's identity. All it is suggesting is that when x and y get together, x happens to be shorter than y. Similarly, and importantly, when this universe and x are placed together in an eschatological resurrection context then the relational properties that exist between the two mean that there can be only one *true* x that is part of that universe.

This is, of course, just one particular development of Hick's 'replica' idea. However, it could be argued that the discussion above misses an important point about *faith* and the future. That is, perhaps those who already have faith in the resurrection hope will not require sophisticated mechanical explanations. In this connection, Peter Geach offers a passionate observation:

> The traditional faith of Christianity, inherited from Judaism, is that at the end of this age Messiah will come and men will rise from their graves to die no more. That faith is not going to be shaken by inquiries about bodies burned to ashes or eaten by beasts; those who might well suffer just such death in martyrdom were those who were most confident of a glorious reward in the resurrection. One who shares that hope will hardly wish to take out an occultistic or philosophical insurance policy, to guarantee some sort of survival as an annuity, in case God's promise of resurrection should fail.[105]

Summary

As the idea of some kind of post-mortem existence is central to Hick's thinking on a variety of issues, he has sought to suggest possible ways in which the survival of the human person might be intelligible. Hick has written on this topic at various points throughout his career with *Death and*

Eternal Life (1976) representing his most detailed treatment. Because of the challenge that determinism poses for the idea of a purely material mind, and the evidence of parapsychology, we have seen that Hick argues in favour of a dualistic conception of the person. He also seems favourably disposed towards H.H. Price's hypothesis regarding the possibility of a mind-dependent world. However, as Hick believes that the world is a vale of soul-making the idea that we create our own worlds in the afterlife means, for Hick, that such a world would be plastic to our wishes and therefore unconducive to soul-making.

There is also a basic commitment to the idea that we are not naturally to be considered as 'souls', but as psycho-physical beings. Moreover, it becomes evident from Hick's proposed pareschatology, that one is not necessarily talking about a re-embodiment into a 'heavenly world', but into another world where our soul-making journeys continue. Thus, the next world is an embodied one where we face challenges probably similar (though we cannot say) to this one, that is - a world that is not self/mind-made.

Hick's famous 'replica' theory offers a rational modern portrayal of the resurrection of the person. This theory has provoked extensive discussion in academic journals; critics have focused on questions of personal identity and the problem of multiple replication. One of the suggestions made in this chapter is that it is possible to reconcile the more patristic view of resurrecting the 'original body' with Hick's replica idea. Drawing on the 'new physics', a possible conception of this has been outlined.

Nevertheless, Hick is not just concerned with the questions of logical coherence that have preoccupied us in this chapter. He has also presented a systematic picture of the development of the human spiritual journey once the threshold of death has been crossed. With this picture he draws together his thinking about soul-making and also begins to develop a pluralistic understanding of religions.

Notes

1. Hick, *Death and Eternal Life*, p.112.
2. Ibid., pp.112-113.
3. Hick quotes Herbert Feigl in this respect: 'instead of conceiving of two realms or two concomitant types of events, we have only one reality which is represented in two conceptual systems – on the one hand, that of physics and on the other hand, where applicable…that of phenomenological psychology'. Cited in Ibid., p.113.
4. Ibid., p.114.
5. Ibid.
6. Ibid., p.115.
7. Ibid., p.116.

8. Ibid.
9. Ibid.
10. Ibid.
11. Ibid.
12. Ibid.
13. Pierre Laplace quoted in Paul Davies, *Superforce*, p.112.
14. Hick, *Death and Eternal Life*, p.117.
15. St. Thomas Aquinas, *Quaestiones Disputatae: De Malo 6* cited in D.J. O'Connor, *Freewill*, p.23.
16. Hick, *Death and Eternal Life*, p.117.
17. J.B.S. Haldane, *Possible Worlds*, p.209.
18. Hick, *Death and Eternal Life*, p.119.
19. Ibid., p.120.
20. G. Loughlin, *Mirroring God's World - A Critique of John Hick's Speculative Theology*, p.202.
21. P. Davies, *God and the New Physics*, p.140.
22. D.J. O'Connor argues: 'Consider what is involved in a typical rational process, say, the proof of a theorem in geometry. Once you have understood a particular step in the proof and seen that it follows from the previous steps in accordance with the rules of inference, you have no choice about assenting to its truth. To see that the proposition follows logically from information already proved is to assent to its truth. You can no more understand the evidence and reject the conclusion than you can look up at a cloudless sky and consider whether you will agree that it is blue.' *Freewill*, pp.44, 45.
23. Ibid., p.45.
24. Ibid.
25. Ibid.
26. Ibid., p.46.
27. K. Campbell, *Body and Mind*, p.91, cited in Badham, *Christian Beliefs About Life After Death*, p.118.
28. Hick, *Death and Eternal Life*, p.121.
29. C. Wilson talking to C.D. Broad in *Afterlife*, p.266.
30. Ibid.
31. D.M. Armstrong, *Materialist Theory of Mind*, p.365. Cited in P. Badham, *Christian Beliefs About Life After Death*, p.117.
32. M. Welman in introduction to E.D. Mitchell, *Psychic Exploration*, p.47, cited in P. and L. Badham, *Immortality or Extinction?*, p.91.
33. C. Wilson, *Afterlife*, p.265.
34. P. and L. Badham, *Immortality or Extinction?*, p.89.
35. Hick, *Disputed Questions in the Philosophy of Religion*, p.187.
36. Hick writes about the significance of H.H. Price's theory in the following: 'The notion of the survival of the disembodied mind has long been in need of being turned into an intelligible hypothesis, and it is something of a scandal that it should have had to wait until the twentieth century for this to be done. However, it has now been done by the philosopher H.H. Price in a long and important paper, "Survival and the Idea of Another World"' , *Death and Eternal Life*, p.265.
37. H.H. Price, 'Survival and the Idea of "Another World".', p.25.
38. Hick, *Death and Eternal Life*, p.266.
39. Ibid.
40. H.H. Price, 'Survival and the Idea of "Another World".', p.26.
41. Ibid., p.37.
42. Ibid., p.38.
43. Ibid.

44. Hick, *Death and Eternal Life*, p.267.
45. See Ibid., pp.270-271.
46. See B.R. Reichenbach, 'Price, Hick and Disembodied Existence', p.318.
47. Ibid., p.319.
48. H.H. Price, 'Survival and the idea of "Another World"', p.37.
49. Ibid., p.25.
50. Hick, *Death and Eternal Life*, p.266.
51. Reichenbach, 'Price, Hick and Disembodied Existence', p.320.
52. Ibid., p.322.
53. Hick, *Death and Eternal Life*, p.273.
54. Ibid., p.274.
55. Ibid., p.186.
56. Ibid., p.280.
57. Ibid.
58. Ibid., p.285.
59. Ibid., p.283.
60. N. Wiener, *The Human Use of Human Beings*, p. 91. Cited in *Death and Eternal Life*, p.282.
61. Ibid.
62. Ibid., p.283.
63. Antony Flew, *The Presumption of Atheism*, p.107. Kai Nielsen follows very much the same line against the idea of replicas when he writes: 'Persons are such that they are unique. There can be only one instance of each person. A replica of Hans could not be Hans. (If this be a conventionalist sulk so be it).' Kai Nielsen, 'God, the Soul, and Coherence: A Response to Davis and Hick' in S. Davis, (ed.), *Death and Afterlife*, p.151.
64. Frank B. Dilley, 'Resurrection and the "Replica Objection"', p.463 (citing Penelhum).
65. Ibid.
66. Ibid., p.464.
67. Ibid., p.465.
68. J.J. Clarke, 'John Hick's Resurrection', p.18.
69. Ibid., p.19.
70. J.J. Lipner, 'Hick's Resurrection', p.31.
71. Hick, *Death and Eternal Life,* p.291. Hick's views have apparently changed since he wrote this. Here he thinks that the possibility of multiple replication does put his replica theory in jeopardy, and his solution admits the need for there to be only one replica of the original if our present conceptions of the uniqueness of the person are not to be undermined. However in the H. Hewitt, (ed.), *Problems in the Philosophy of Religion*, he suggests something quite different. For example: 'We can imagine a universe in which after death there are a plurality of psycho-physical replicas of each person. People would multiply into branching post-mortem successor selves who would begin by being identical but gradually develop along different lines in the different circumstances in which they live. Such a universe would need a different conceptual system, including a different notion of "person", from the one we have developed in our actual universe.' Hick, 'Reply' in H. Hewitt (ed.), *Problems in the Philosophy of Religion*, p.161.
72. Clarke, 'John Hick's Resurrection', p.20.
73. Hick, *Death and Eternal Life,* p.292.
74. Dilley, 'Resurrection and the Replica Objection', p.468.
75. Gerard Loughlin highlights the same criticism: 'Hick agreed that there could not be more than one replica of the same person without calling into question the identity of replica and original, but went on to argue that there could be one replica which was the

same person as the original. In this he entirely missed the point of Clarke's criticism. Clarke did not argue that because several replicas of one person would not contradict the concept of a replica, but would contradict the concept of a person's uniqueness, there cannot even be one replica of a person. He argued that because several replicas would not contradict the concept of replicas, but would contradict the concept of a person's uniqueness, we can see that even one replica would not be the same person. And this because a replica is by definition capable of multiplication and a person is not.' G. Loughlin, op.cit., p.197.

76. Dilley, 'Resurrection and the Replica Objection', p.472.
77. Ibid. See the likeness in Dilley's suggestion to Hick's in note 71.
78. Hick, *Death and Eternal Life*, p.292.
79. Loughlin, op.cit., p.198.
80. Hick, *Philosophy of Religion*, p.12.
81. Dilley writes, 'The turning-point on disembodied souls seems to have been an essay by his former professor, H.H. Price, whose piece on disembodied survival was included in an anthology which Hick published in 1970. In *Death and Eternal Life*, (1976) he devotes a whole chapter to it, crediting Price with turning the idea of disembodied survival into an "intelligible hypothesis". Price was the first person to have done that, Hick claims.' Dilley, 'Hick on the Self and Resurrection' in Hewitt (ed.), *Problems in the Philosophy of Religion*, p.154.
82. Hick, *Death and Eternal Life*, p.265.
83. Ibid.
84. Dilley, 'Resurrection and the Replica Objection' p.474.
85. Concerning Hick's 'pareschatology' see chapter 20 of *Death and Eternal Life*; also, with regard to the question of soul transfer see Hick's comments in 'Reply' in Hewitt (ed.), *Problems in the Philosophy of Religion*, p.160.
86. See R.T. Herbert, *Paradox and Identity in Theology*, pp.149-155.
87. Stephen Davis, *Risen Indeed*, p.120.
88. Hick, *The Fifth Dimension*, p.245.
89. See Badham, *Christian Beliefs About Life After Death*, p.76.
90. Hick, *Death and Eternal Life*, p.279.
91. Hick writes: 'In this context the possibility of two spaces is the possibility of two sets of extended objects such that each member of the same set is spatially related to each member of the same set but not spatially related to each member of the other set. Thus everything in the space in which I am is at a certain distance from me, and vice versa but if there is a second space, nothing in it is at any distance or in any direction from where I now am. In other words, from my point of view the other space is nowhere and therefore does not exist. But if there is a second space, un-observable by me, the objects in it are entirely real to an observer within that space, and our own world is to him nowhere - not at any distance nor in any direction - so that from his point of view it does not exist.' Ibid.
92. Badham, *Christian Beliefs About Life After Death*, p.68.
93. Ibid., p.69.
94. D. Bohm, *Wholeness and the Implicate Order*, cited in P. Davies, *God and the New Physics*, p.64.
95. P. Davies, *Superforce*, p.22.
96. B. Griffiths, *A New Vision of Reality*, p.263.
97. *Chandogya Upanishad*, ch.8:1.3 in E. Easwaran, (trans.), *The Upanishads*, p.191.
98. S. Travis, *Christian Hope and the Future of Man*, p.101.
99. *Doctrine of the Church of England*, p.209.
100. J. Polkinghorne, *Reason and Reality*, p.43.

101. A. Olding, 'Resurrection Bodies and Resurrection Worlds', p.584; cited in Hick, *Death and Eternal Life*, p.289.
102. Ibid., p.585.
103. D. Cockburn, *Other Human Beings*, p.157.
104. See S. Davis, *Risen Indeed*, pp.140-142.
105. Peter Geach, 'Immortality' in T. Penelhum (ed.), *Immortality*, p.21.

Chapter Four

The Universe of Faiths

Hick seeks to resolve many issues and problems in the philosophy of religion by making reference to a 'cosmic optimism'. Such optimism is not just selected because he prefers a happy ending, rather he is being consistent with the expectation of all religions in anticipating a 'limitlessly better possibility'.[1] He writes that the 'cosmic optimism of the post-axial religions is a vision of the ultimately benign character of the universe as it affects us human beings, and an anticipation in faith that the limitlessly good possibilities of existence will finally be realised'.[2] In this chapter we will see how Hick expanded on the idea of soul-making beyond death. Also, Hick's speculations on this matter exhibit the way in which his work has increasingly broadened out to include the expectations of other religions. 'Speculations' is both accurate and misleading, for whilst aptly characterising the boldness and visionary quality of Hick's work, it also conveys a sense of recklessness. Hick's 'speculations' are not reckless, but carefully constructed and worked out. We will begin by looking at Hick's methodology, and then proceed to examine Hick's pareschatological proposals. Following this we will consider possible criticisms of his ideas and also the consistency of his thinking on these matters. Finally, we shall briefly suggest the possibility of broadening Hick's vision to be inclusive of the non-human world.

The word 'pareschatology' denotes a period *in between* death and the final fulfilment of everything - the eschaton. As we indicated in the last chapter, Hick's classic work, *Death and Eternal Life* (1976), is also a speculative attempt to spell out a possible pareschatology. Hick decided to concentrate on pareschatology in particular because he argued that it would be unrealistic to try and elucidate about the eschaton itself - a situation far beyond human comprehension. Rather, 'if there is life after death there may be a better possibility of picturing its more proximate than its more ultimate phases'.[3]

There are perhaps two things that we ought to say about Hick's methodology. Firstly, we might say that Hick's work in this field is from a religious perspective (whilst quickly adding the proviso that this does not necessarily indicate his actual beliefs, rather it describes his approach). That is, Hick is concerned to work out the implications of the hopes and expectations of the various religions themselves. His is no purely naturalistic account, nor is he concerned to undertake a mainly historical, cultural or sociological study. Furthermore, Hick assumes that the various religious expectations have a *reality* to them, and this is consistent with his realist position with regard to religious language (see chapter one). Secondly, Hick's pareschatology is a global theology of death. His extended treatment of eschatological issues came at a time when he had already proposed a 'Copernican' revolution in theology. By this he meant that (using an analogy from the field of astronomy) Christianity should no longer be seen as a centre which other religions revolve around, rather it should take its place alongside other faiths in their orbits around ultimate reality. It is important that we recognise this basic orientation in Hick's thinking because it helps to shed light on his methodology. As Hick himself states, 'If one sees man's religious life in this "copernican" fashion, a global theology of death is at least a possible project.'[4] Moreover, as death is a universal phenomenon there is a warrant, thinks Hick, for drawing threads from among all the major faiths of the world rather than just one.

The methodology used for a global theology of death is one which attempts to use the different religious expectations 'as data for the construction of comprehensive religious theories'.[5] This is not to say that Hick has merely sought to underline possible similarities between the different religions and construct a systematic compilation of different religious perspectives. Rather, he has sought to assess 'their respective strengths and weaknesses'[6] and then formulate a constructive proposal based on discriminations and conclusions about those perspectives. That is, although Hick's scope is global, his intentions are not blindly syncretistic. Nevertheless, it seems clear from the outset that if one does not share Hick's Copernican ideals then one will have serious reservations about this kind of project.

We have already considered some of Hick's views on mind, body and resurrection in the previous chapter; in his pareschatological proposals he has sought to bring them together, he writes:

> In *Death and Eternal Life* I tried to put these two strands together - the ideas of replica-style resurrection and of mental life independently of the physical brain. They come together in the hypothesis of a disembodied *bardo* phase immediately after death, followed in due course by re-embodiment in another space-time, and indeed possibly a succession of such re-embodiments separated by a succession of *bardo* phases. In the *bardo* phase we create our own mind-dependent world, and seeing our desires (including our unconscious

desires) reflected in it we undergo a kind of psycho-analytic experience as a result of which our next embodiment becomes a relatively new start.[7]

However, as well as bringing together the strands of disembodied minds and resurrection, Hick's pareschatology represents an impressive synthesis of eastern and western religious traditions about the afterlife. Within it he includes both eastern (summarised for Hick in the *Bardo Thodol*, or *Tibetan Book of the Dead*) and western (western spiritualism and mediumship) conceptions of disembodied existence. And also, the particularly 'abrahamic' notion of bodily resurrection is echoed in his notion of re-embodiment in the next world(s). It is an impressive speculative venture that Hick has constructed. Nevertheless, it might be wondered why he has speculated in such detail about events that are beyond our present experience. Would it not have been a lot better to merely adopt a vague optimism and leave it at that? For example, take the phrase: 'all things will turn out fine in the end', this sounds a lot safer bet than worrying about "replicas" or reincarnated souls, intermediate states or future details about heavens and hells. But, when we settle for nice-sounding generalities it is difficult to actually ascertain the real meanings that are obscured by an over-comprehensiveness. For example, the above hope about things 'turning out fine' can mean a whole host of different things for different people. For some it might mean that everybody is 'saved' in the end, but Augustine would equally be able to assent to it and also believe that the majority of the human race was going to perish in eternal fire. Moreover, for the Abrahamic traditions of Islam, Judaism and Christianity, it might mean individuals enjoying eternal bliss with the Creator, but for eastern traditions like Hinduism or Buddhism it could mean something like a loss of individuation or ego and dissolution into the ultimate. Hick's point is that 'a doctrine which can mean anything means nothing. So long, then, as we refrain from spelling out our faith it must remain empty'.[8] For this reason, Hick thinks that it is profitable to offer some kind of analysis of different religious expectations - or the various vehicles (e.g. resurrection or reincarnation) they put forward - and offer conclusions concerning their viability.

Reincarnation and Rebirth

Strongly influencing Hick's pareschatology are eastern conceptions of reincarnation or rebirth. This is not to say that Hick accepts such notions in an uncritical form, in fact he critically analyses the ideas of reincarnation and rebirth in *Death and Eternal Life* and concludes that they are beset by conceptual difficulties. One of the interesting things that Hick points out is that the eastern ideas of reincarnation and rebirth are taken for granted by those brought up in a Hindu or Buddhist environment like India. So much so that western worldviews which restrict the human journey to just one life are viewed as morally repugnant or spiritually blind. How cruel to say that this is the only life we have when there is so much inequality in the world? Some are born into poverty, others wealth; some are beautiful, others ugly; some have opportunities poured into their laps, others seem beset by ill fortune. Further to this, if we say that irrevocable decisions about eternity are made within this single life then we have underlined such inequality in perpetuity. Thus, it seems self-evident to the eastern mind that this is not the only life we have, rather we have lived many times and will live many lives to come. Chance and fortune do not arbitrarily disadvantage particular individuals or groups, what judges our numerous rebirths are the actions in our previous lives: we get what we deserve.

> There is no arbitrariness, no randomness, no injustice in the inequalities of our human lot, but only cause and effect, the reaping now of what we have ourselves sown in the past. Our essential self continues from life to life, being repeatedly reborn or reincarnated, the state of its karma, or the qualitative sum of its volitional activity, determining the nature of its next earthly life.[9]

Ostensibly, this seems a more morally defensible account of human existence. The problem of evil and suffering appears a lot less acute with the possibility of unlimited lives. Nevertheless, in his criticisms of reincarnation and rebirth, Hick does not think that such notions are necessarily more morally satisfying than the western alternative of a single life, or that they resolve the issue of inequality. In fact, rather than solving the problem of inequality, Hick argues that the notion of reincarnation merely *postpones* it. That is, even if we can explain the various inequalities that presently exist in terms of cause and effect, or *karma*, we must inevitably ask about the origins of such variety – where did it all start? Hick explains this as follows:

> When we have traced present inequality and inequity back into a previous life it then either exists there as an original and unexplained fact or must be traced back into yet earlier life. And so long as this regression continues the problem is merely being postponed: it can no more be solved in this way than indebtedness can be abolished by paying a debt with money borrowed from one who must borrow it from another, who must borrow it from another...[10]

This is a strong point. Alternatively, it might be argued that it is only effective so long as we assume that things must have a beginning. With classical Hindu philosophies like *Advaita Vedanta*, it is held that there is no beginning, things are beginningless. But Hick thinks that stipulating no beginning at all does not actually make the problem any better: rather than postponing the problem to a definite point, 'the explanation of the inequalities of our present life is endlessly postponed and never achieved[....]The solution has not been produced but only postponed to infinity'.[11] In response, Arvind Sharma, when writing about the Advaitin perspective, believes that Hick is looking at the problem from the wrong angle. He writes that 'the Advaitin response here is that the doctrine of karma and reincarnation, far from *perpetually postponing* the explanation of inequality, *continually supplies* it'.[12] So, there is a matter of orientation. The complaints about postponement assume *within their logic* that things must have a beginning, and this might be merely a western preoccupation. It is this *sense* of a beginning that provokes Hick's argument. Whilst explicitly allowing that there need not be an actual beginning, we might say that his argument still retains the 'flavour' of a beginning. However, following Sharma's point, the Advaitin notion that things are beginningless calls for a different paradigm. That is, rather than understanding karma and reincarnation as emerging from some point in the distant primordial past and thus requiring explanation, one should see them as existing eternally - or else, they *are* reality. Of course, making a decisive judgement between the two views (beginning or beginningless) is extremely difficult because it takes us into the complexities of time and infinity and reflects fundamental differences in worldview.

The basic idea of reincarnation is that the self transmigrates from body to body. The body is like an outer garment which the self 'puts on' as it travels through time. But one of the noticeable weaknesses in this basic picture is the blunt fact that memories of previous lives are virtually absent from the human consciousness. In the overwhelming majority of cases, we simply do not have a recollection of existences that have preceded our own. However, such facts are not necessarily fatal for reincarnation. This is because the inability to remember an event in the past does not mean that the event did not happen or that one was not present at the time. For example, Hick asks us to consider the memories connecting a baby with the full adult person.[13] He points out that the differences, both physical and psychological, between the baby and its 'grown up' version are probably so immense that there is virtually no connection at all. The adult certainly doesn't look like the baby anymore (and the baby looks like every other baby). Furthermore, the adult cannot really remember anything at all from those very early stages of life. However, despite these facts, one is still content to see personal identity continuing from baby to adult because there is an unbroken (if evolving) connection between them. That is, there is at least a bodily criterion (and a 'developing' psychological continuity) for personal identity.

However, what about cases where we are not talking about connections of identity within a single life but between successive lives? Hick asks us to consider three criteria for personal identity:

1. Bodily continuity
2. Memory, and
3. 'the psychological continuity of a pattern of mental dispositions'.[14]

It seems that the first two are not sustained within the basic reincarnation hypothesis because neither bodily continuity or memory are present. There would also seem to be a discontinuity with regard to the transmission of the ego from one life to the next. That is, 'babies are not born with adult egos, as would be if they were direct continuations of egos which had died at the end of a normal life-span'.[15] Given this, the supporters of the reincarnation idea are led to make increasingly abstract accounts of the soul, or that part of us which somehow connects our different lives across time, so much so that the original idea of an ego being reincarnated again and again becomes obscured. This abstract account is described by the third criterion above and it is this third criterion that has to bear the weight of identity across rebirths. This is the particular set of psychological characteristics or dispositions that continue to exist after the individual has died and are re-embodied in another form. That is, rather than memories specific to a particular person or ego, it is dispositions or personality traits that continue: like kindness, courage, shyness, selfishness, musicality, artistry and so on. However, Hick's problem with this explanation is that it too broad. For these are characteristics that many human beings share, and so the criteria for a *particular* person and their continuity are generalised until only a vague conception remains. Nevertheless, Hick does think that some of the Hindu and Buddhist versions of reincarnation offer richer conceptions of the third criterion above which render it more acceptable. For example, the Hindu concept of *linga sharira* (spiritual or 'subtle' body) seems to provide a more *solid* account of the collective psychological, moral and spiritual characteristics of a person. Hick calls this the 'dispositional structure'. The dispositions of a person become established and reinforced over time such that they 'form relatively stable and enduring structures which constitute the basic character of the individual through whom they express themselves...'.[16] Hick argues that it is this dispositional structure that provides the vehicle for continued existence.

However, even if we are not impressed with the metaphysics of reincarnation, the moral meaning of *karma* and rebirth convey a sense of responsibility. There is a (Buddhist) sense that our actions do not take place in a vacuum but are interdependent with other beings and things. Thus, our actions do affect others, and Hick makes the point that even if it is difficult to wholly accept the literal truth of reincarnation, there is still the idea that *someone* is going to bear the consequences of our actions.[17] Could the idea of reincarnation be reconciled with Christian belief?[18] Hick acknowledges that reincarnation has never been part of Christian orthodoxy. Indeed, an Augustinian account which talks of a single earthly life in which to make eternal decisions cannot be easily compared with the slow progression of a human soul throughout many lifetimes. Moreover, the idea of grace (or God's merciful intervention in forgiveness and restoration) seems to have little affinity with the laws of karma and rebirth. Hick would respond to these difficulties by drawing attention to the Irenaean strand of thinking in the Christian faith.[19] As we saw in chapter two, he opted against Augustinian interpretations and favoured an Irenaean account, and it is once again this Irenaean preference that Hick draws on when seeking to find points of contact between reincarnation and Christian belief. So, for example, one does not have to view 'salvation' or 'grace' as events or experiences which occur within a single lifetime. Instead, 'It could be said that the response to God's love made flesh in Christ is the end for the sake of which men are born on earth, and that they go on being reborn until eventually they make that response'.[20] Thus, seen through Irenaean lenses, there is a longer time in order to make a response - a vast extension of future probation beyond death. Moreover, Hick argues that an Irenaean approach and the reincarnation idea agree on the basic notion of continued moral and personal development. Interestingly, he remarks that 'They differ only as to where this continued life takes place. The Christian belief (in the irenaean tradition) has been that it takes place in other worlds beyond this one. The indian belief has been that it takes place by means of repeated returns to this world'.[21] We shall return to this issue of 'other' worlds or 'this' world in a moment.

Many Lives in Many Worlds

What attracts Hick to the eastern view of reincarnation is the *framework* it presents for human growth and personal development in the life (or lives) to come. It is good for soul-making. Here again is Hick's Irenaean intuition.

Despite the eastern influences, Hick characterises his pareschatology as 'a christian contribution to global or human theology'.[22] Yet it seems clear that in formulating his overall pareschatology, Hick has constructed an understanding of the meaning of death which is more consistent with his

Irenaean preferences than that found in more Augustinian types of Christian interpretation. Indeed, this is a fact that Hick clearly admits when he claims that the 'Augustinian type of theology in which death is held to be the wages of sin should be replaced by an Irenaean type of theology which sees our mortality in relation to a positive divine purpose of love...'.[23] That is, according to Hick, death is not an enemy as such, but a helper; or as a sort of service station along the way throughout our many lives in many worlds. It would also seem that the death that awaits each of us at the end of our present lives is not the only death that we are going to have to experience until we reach the state of Reality-centredness.

Hick asks how we should view 'our total career'[24] which progresses towards the Ultimate. This is a question that is very significant for his pareschatology. We are faced with the choice between i) two phases of existence: a short earthly life followed by everlasting post-mortem existence; and ii) a multi-phased model of many lives, each bounded by death.[25] Hick takes a negative view of the former possibility and believes that, all things considered, the latter is more preferable.[26] He concedes that spiritual and moral growth can occur in the context of an immortal ego after death, but believes that the soul-making venture becomes more structured and effective within the notion of successive and divided stages.[27]

Hick's understanding of the meaning of death is the deciding factor in his preference for a series of mortal existences rather than a post-mortem existence of endless longevity. He writes:

> I do not say that we cannot conceive of loves and hates and purposes enduring through unending time; but I doubt whether they would be human loves and hates and purposes. It seems that if the boundary of death were removed, and we are faced with a limitlessly open future stretching to infinity, what we now know as human nature would be transformed out of existence. There would no longer be a basis for the familiar emotional stuff of human life, with its parameters of love and hate, hope and fear, self-sacrifice, achievement and failure, tragedy and nobility; and the distinctions between older and younger, between generation and generation, between epoch and epoch would disappear in a universal endless longevity.[28]

Thus, Hick concludes that if the human ego is to be considered everlasting then it is more fruitful to consider its continued existence in terms of successive limited phases rather than as one continuous stretch.[29] Death is a suitable boundary which gives a life its shape and meaning and context. In this, Hick is opposing, for example, a pessimistic view that death is ultimately meaningless and infects all other things with meaninglessness. Though he admits that death has its inevitable destructive quality, it also has a quality which bestows meaning upon life. 'Death is the end of a chapter but not of the book; or better, it is the end of the volume but not of the whole work.'[30] Hick draws an analogy from sleep, and believes that this illustrates the principle of division that occurs throughout life. He states: 'Even if we did not need this relapse into unconsciousness after every eighteen hours or so for the sake of physical rest we should still need it in order to divide life up into manageable sections.'[31] The pressure of life 'is relaxed every night by the disengagement of sleep, making it possible to begin afresh in the morning'.[32] Sleep is believed by Hick to be an apposite analogy for the function of death. Thus as we saw a moment ago, death is not an enemy at all in his thinking, rather it should be envisaged as a service station for travelling souls. Death's purpose is to: '...bracket a space within our immortal existence, making a limited span within which to live. Within this horizon there is the possibility of finite achievements and failures in finite situations, and consequently of the growth and development of character.'[33]

Yet despite this rather auspicious picture Hick lends to death's role, he still wishes to affirm the intense fear and dread that accompanies it. Death will always, Hick maintains, be confronted with 'awe and apprehension that engulfs our whole consciousness'.[34] Although Hick would like to affirm death in positive and negative terms, it is very difficult (considering the role that he gives to death in his pareschatology) to detect an equal balance between these two understandings. The darkness of death is somewhat overly tempered by Hick's sunny treatment of it. But, perhaps this is a rather Augustinian complaint, and we must remember that Hick is proceeding from an Irenaean standpoint. Such a standpoint or framework entails that many of the traditional (Augustinian) theological formulations that makes up death's composite meaning are rejected. For example, we saw in chapter two that Hick rejects the traditional concept of a Fall in the primordial past; that is, there was never a time in his Irenaean scheme when human beings became alienated from God and thus felt the *sting* of death.

Following death we enter the *bardo* stage. This is a period of disembodiment. As already alluded to, the bardo stage is a synthesis of the teachings of the *Bardo Thodol* (Tibetan Book of the Dead) in the Nyingma or old tradition of Buddhism, the evidence of western spiritualism, and the work of H.H. Price on the afterlife.

In their commentary on the *Bardo Thodol*, Fremantle and Trungpa write:

> The concept of bardo is based on the period between sanity and insanity, or the period between confusion and the confusion just about to be transformed into wisdom; and of course it could be said to be the experience which stands between death and birth. The past situation has just occurred and the future

situation has not yet manifested itself so there is a gap between the two. This is basically the bardo experience.[35]

The bardo experience is supposed to be 'part of our basic psychological make-up'.[36] That is, we experience visions and feelings that reflect our cultural upbringing and our spiritual condition at the time of death. Furthermore, the bardo stage is a period of unhindered reflection on our lives. The experiences in the bardo state are to be understood as projections of the mind, the individual may experience encounters with peaceful and wrathful deities but these should be perceived as reflective of the individual's karma. These experiences are to be faced openly, and not recoiled from, as they are instrumental in resolving the blockages within the individual that prevent the union with Reality. The nature of these subjective experiences in the bardo world are such that the visions of the individual will reflect their own religious culture or cultural tradition. Hick comments that 'released from the pressures and threats which sustain our self-image in this life, the mind realistically appraises itself in a kind of psychoanalytic experience and the outcome reaches consciousness in the imagery provided by one's own religious faith'.[37]

The similarities here between the teaching of the *Bardo Thodol* and Price's theories (which Hick would appear to be impressed with) about the afterlife are striking. If we remember, Price's afterlife is a kind of wish-fulfilment dream-world, a landscape of mental images. Hick notes that, from the point of view of some depth psychologists, dreams can be seen as wish-fulfilments. These can be either pleasant or unpleasant. Moreover, if our bodies were to be removed then we would be left with these unconscious experiences in all their intensity. Desires that are repressed in our waking moments would be fulfilled.[38]

Hick also refers us to the testimony of western spiritualism in formulating his view of the disembodied state. Although Hick cautiously acknowledges the ambiguity of such evidence from alleged mediumistic communications with the dead, he believes that 'since we cannot exclude the possibility that some [communications from the deceased] may come from full discarnate personalities, it seems right to take note of their contents'.[39] In such parapsychological evidence there can be seen real affinities with the teaching of the *Bardo Thodol*. Some of the examples, like the F.W.H. Myers case that Hick employs, show likenesses with the Buddhist conception of the bardo world as a place of spiritual development towards the Ultimate.[40] It is unnecessary for me to recount such case examples at the moment (besides, they are very numerous); however we shall look in a moment at some of the examples that Hick uses from western spiritualism; this will be for the purposes of seeing if such examples actually conflict with Hick's emphasis on ambiguity and epistemic distance amongst other issues.

The stage at which individuals emerge from this bardo realm is conditioned, it would seem, by their readiness (or restlessness) to move on. There will be factors, so Hick believes, that will cause a sense of yearning, or restlessness, for something different and new. Or else, there may be a feeling of anticipation for, or mystical glimpses of, higher or better possibilities ahead. Drawing attention to parapsychological evidence, Hick notes that 'the "dead" who profess to speak through mediums often refer to higher spheres to which people sooner or later gravitate'.[41]

Hick remains open-minded about the actual character of existence in the *post*-bardo stage, but, as we saw in the previous chapter, he suggests the possibility that the individual might receive a replica body in order to continue a psycho-physical life in the next world. Nevertheless, when it comes to his pareschatology he is actually agnostic about this, as the following reveals:

> We cannot say anything about the next world beyond the bardo state except that it will be a real spatio-temporal environment, functioning in accordance with its own laws, within which there will be real personal life - a world with its own concrete character, its own history, its own absorbing and urgent concerns, its own crises, perils, achievements, sacrifices, and its own terminus giving shape and meaning to existence within it.[42]

Finally, the story thus far will be repeated, says Hick, until the ultimate goal - transcendence of ego-centredness to Reality-centredness has been attained. Thus the amount of lives that an individual goes through is not of fixed quantity, it depends rather on the progress of the individual, and one can expect the length of time in each case to be unique.

Licentious Speculation?

Hick's pareschatology is, after all, a possible view of the afterlife, and the fact that it is possible needs to be stressed. Critics have often attacked the speculative character of Hick's work. For example, the German critic, K.R. Schmidt, in his comparative study of Hick with Karl Barth, expresses disappointment at the fact that Hick's proposals can at best be merely offered as possibilities. He laments that after all of Hick's work on death and eternal life he can come up with no more than a 'possibility'.[43] Moreover:

He does not contend that he has given any proof of his positions. Hick speculates quite freely upon his religious and scientific investigations. For someone to follow Hick will therefore require not an insignificant leap of faith or, as Hick would state it, leave one for considerable grounds for rational doubt. Since one of the expressed goals of Hick is to produce a credible global eschatology, the more the speculation and leap become apparent in Hick, the more incredible his thought will appear to modern man.[44]

However, why Hick's speculations and 'leaps' are incredible to modern man is far from clear. There are Bultmannian echoes here. Schmidt considers the implications of a statement made by Hick in *Faith and Knowledge*, 'to the believer faith is not a probability but a certainty...'.[45] Schmidt seeks to bring this statement to bear on the speculative nature of Hick's eschatology. That is, this statement by Hick in *Faith and Knowledge* would seem to rub against any notions of mere possibilities and speculations when viewing the future through the eyes of faith. Nevertheless, I think Schmidt's point is only true *prima facie*, for one might easily observe that the intermediate state and the precise nature of the eschaton is a matter of speculation even within fundamentalist Christian quarters! Perhaps what is supposed to be certain for the religious believer is that the eschaton is an ultimately good outcome that s/he anticipates; the process which leads to such an outcome (pareschatology) is not certain, and it is difficult to see how constructive speculation on the matter can be viewed as contrary to the certainty of faith that Schmidt protests is the case. In fact, Schmidt's criticism could conceivably be applied against any eschatological proposal which sought to elaborate on a basic theme. So, it is possible that Schmidt has neglected to distinguish between the Christian hope on the one hand and its many possible expositions on the other.

On the other hand, endorsing Schmidt's point, there is a potential problem which faces all attempts at a global (or, syncretistic) theology, and not just in the realm of eschatology. If one is faithful to one particular tradition then it is arguable that there is a certain degree of control in one's speculations (perhaps doctrinal boundaries for instance). There is surely validity in Schmidt's point that constructing a global eschatology, as Hick has sought to do, is very uncontrolled, that is, there would appear to be no yardstick to judge where speculation ought to cease. There are, perhaps, no doctrines to break other than that established by his Irenaean intuition that 'all shall be well'. Hick's motives in seeking a global outlook due to the obvious pressures of our growing awareness of the pluralistic society that we live in, are undoubtedly sincere. But is his methodology sound? In synthesising the various religions for a pareschatology Hick makes careful selections, like a bardo world (Tibetan Buddhism), a notion of re-embodiment (resurrection) and a plurality of lives (reincarnation). Indeed, when reviewing *Death and Eternal Life*, Terence Penelhum spoke of: 'A working principle that if there are two textually-supportable interpretations of one's own tradition, one should prefer that which makes it coincide with another (major) world religion, rather than one which clash with it. In other words a deliberate eclecticism.'[46] One might doubt whether the formation of a possible global pareschatology can be accomplished by finding seeming likenesses in the various world traditions, lifting them out of their contexts, and placing them into another context which has been created by natural induction. Similarly, when speaking in the context of Hindu-Christian dialogue, R. Panikkar says that, 'most of the existing common aspects are common only when they have been disconnected from the whole, and are mutually compared against an abstract and sterilised background which does not belong to either of them'.[47]

Further to this, is it possible to say that Hick is attempting to create a new pareschatology which is *better* than the previous pareschatologies that were peculiar to the separate religions? In this context we are using the word 'better' to describe a pareschatology which, by taking account of the global evidence, might be considered more comprehensive than *localised* accounts - that is, accounts which are peculiar to the separate religions. Those who are doubtful of a liberal, or universalising, project will have serious reservations about this. For example, take an analogy from the world of art. Let us say that we have five paintings, painted by five great painters of genius. Each of these paintings is different from the others, but it is possible to separate them into roughly two groups by likeness of style. On the one hand, we have the starkly Modern; on the other we have more Romantic types of style. Now suppose that various art critics had all generally agreed that each of the paintings had a particularly striking part to it - like a beautiful waterfall, or a foreboding sky, or a moody landscape, or a post-modern brightly coloured building. Some of the critics decided that they could form an even greater picture by cutting out these parts from each painting and arranging them together onto a completely new canvas. Instead of one genius, they would have five all rolled into one! The truth is that the resultant synthesis of the five pictures would not be better that the original separate five, because the parts that had been taken from each picture were only truly great, or possessive of their real meaning, when left in their original contexts.

According to the argument of this analogy, context is crucial. Alternatively, it rather depends on which analogy we choose, or how we present the analogy. For instance, reviewing the analogy above, if the painters were trying to convey, say, their visions of human destiny, then it might be argued (given the subject matter) that their *collective* vision would be more powerful than their individual contributions. Here, perhaps, a lot depends on intellectual taste.

Hick's eschatology is a somewhat 'natural' theological exercise. Those who are at pains to emphasize the importance of a revealed eschatology will, like Schmidt, find Hick's speculations unwarranted or unauthoritative. This is, perhaps, Duncan Forrester's point when he suggests that 'we can receive surer guidance from theologies which are at pains to check and develop the Christian projection as accurately as possible and lay it charitably and boldly alongside other projections which also claim to guide man in his pilgrimage'.[48] Yet, again, this is surely a matter of orientation? Hick's simple response might be to say that one can make one's mind up whether or not one wants to hold to Ptolemaic or Copernican views. Or rather, a choice between more 'tradition-specific' perspectives and a liberal universalism.

So, Hick's pareschatology has a distinctly natural theological cast. Although the obvious difference is that Hick is taking as his foundation the various revelations (though interpreted through the idea of experiencing-as) that exist within the major world faiths, he seems to be treating such testimony in a 'natural' way. This raises the question of how religious people might deal with Hick's suggestions. It seems that the different world traditions each contain within them a volitional response to what is believed to be their future hope; one might characterise this as first-order discourse. Dorothy Emmet wrote: '...faith is distinguished from the entertainment of a probable proposition by the fact that the latter can be a completely theoretic affair. Faith [...] is a volitional response which takes us out of the theoretic attitude.'[49] Hick's speculations (and their 'theoretic attitude') may be characterised as a second-order natural theological exercise. And so, we might ask how 'first-order commitment' deals with second-order discourse?[50] Or else, can a second-order speculative venture have any authority or purpose in this arena? Having said this, one might add the twist that Hick's constructions do not actually appear to be ideas without any intended substance, rather they are fleshed-out proposals. This means that they *make a difference* and, if accepted, imply that each of the religions' expectations would have to undergo alteration. Thus, to reverse things somewhat, can Hick's pareschatology be a second-order discourse after all? Does it demand the kind of allegiance that might be shown to one of the individual religions?

Given this, some might prefer to steer clear of Hick's speculative liberalism and adopt a greater faithfulness to the individual religious accounts. John Bowker, concerning the differences between the world religions concerning death, writes:

it remains clear that many of the propositions maintained by different religions, in relation to human nature and to death, cannot possibly all be true. They may all be false, but they cannot all be true, at least about putative matters of fact. It is not possible for both a Hindu and a Buddhist to be correct in terms of what they propose about human anthropology (what it is that constitutes human nature and appearance). It is not possible for both a Muslim and a Christian to be correct in terms of what they propose about the death and resurrection of Jesus.[51]

It seems from reading this that Bowker is expressing scepticism about there being some sort of underlying similarity between religions. He is right to point out the explicit differences that exist, particularly with the examples he gives. However, in response, it is possible that Bowker's comments do not allow enough for implicit parities between the various religious expectations. As we said a moment ago, Hick is not engaging in a blunt syncretism; he is also careful to distinguish what he sees as the different layers to a religion. That is, one should differentiate between the 'central affirmations concerning the nature of reality, including its affirmations about human destiny...' and the 'rich poetic elaborations and its concrete cultic expressions'.[52] Whereas one might ask questions of truth and falsity with regard to the former, one would not apply such categories so readily to the latter. This, in fact, may be another way of looking at the question of first and second-order discourse. That is, one might say that one is expressing (first-order) commitments to these 'central affirmations' rather than the 'poetic elaborations' or 'concrete cultic expressions' that embellish them. Thus, each of the religions is able to fully or strongly assent to the central affirmations that Hick has distilled even if the individual expressions are significantly modified. However, the issue hangs on whether we can actually distinguish between the 'layers' (mythological/cultic and 'ontological') so to speak. Is it possible to so readily separate out universal essences from their particular instances? If this cannot be done, if such layers are in fact inseparable, then perhaps Hick's global project is impossible. But, here again, we have returned to the debate between the Ptolemaics and the Copernicans.

Death and Many Lives

We have seen that Hick envisaged death in a distinctly positive light as a meaningful boundary that separates and gives shape to our many lives. Hick's view stems ultimately from a rejection of the Augustinian position which sees death as a direct resultant of sin. (That is, death is tied up with the doctrine of the Fall, and the tradition which says that had human beings not sinned they would never have died.) Hick points out the unhistorical character of the Fall in the Augustinian account, and concludes that the tradition about the origin of death is also unhistorical and therefore we must search for a different meaning behind death in light of what we know from modern evolutionary theory.[53]

Stating things from a traditional perspective, the conservative evangelical writer, R.S. Anderson writes: 'The death of human persons is the death of a relationship between persons and God. Death is a threat to personhood, not merely a fact of natural life. For animals, death is a fact of natural life; this is not true of humans, who were created to share in a relation with God as their creator and Lord.'[54] Given Hick's evolutionary or Irenaean perspective, it appears that such a distinctive characterisation of death is absent from his overall thesis. And yet, it may be that this creates a weakness in his argument in connection with his case for many lives rather than one immortal existence. So, if we conduct a thought experiment, let us imagine the lesson that the post-mortem person will learn from his/her experience of death. On finding themselves able to remember dying they will at once be struck by the fact that death was not nearly as awesome an event as they had been led to believe, this will seem to be the case purely because they are alive in another world; that is, death isn't final after all. Now, considering that (as Hick proposes) they will probably pass through a plurality of lives and deaths, they will remember their initial lesson, as it were, and death will become just another mundane fact - it will have lost its ability to cause profound awe. (Alternatively, with death occurring on a single occasion, it retains its fearsome quality). Hick writes:

> the facing of death is often an ordeal of doubt and fear when for perfect faith it would have the different character of a great transition, coloured by the sadness of parting but not evoking deep dread and terror. We can only say that in so far as the trust is real and operative it must take the final sting out of death, the sting of ultimate meaninglessness and vacuity, and must therefore deprive the grave of its victory over life.[55]

Here we see that Hick has associated fearlessness in the face of death with perfect faith or, as he says elsewhere, with 'a total trust in the love of God'.[56] Nevertheless, as I claimed above, the final sting of death is removed in Hick's pareschatology not by perfect faith but merely by the learning experience of surviving death many times; rather like a child who enters the room that he/she was once terrified of - the subject of wild nightmarish imagination, and learns that there was nothing to be afraid of. Interestingly, it is the mystery and apprehension of death, its cruel finality, that Hick believes is one of the reasons why the idea of successive lives for building character is more effective than the notion of an immortal ego.

However, it seems apparent that such mystery and apprehension disappears after the first few lives and deaths of an individual. Hick makes a point of arguing that:

> not only does the notion of human purposes and their success and failure, and of one's life as a complex of projects, seem to cohere best with our mortal condition, but many other aspects of human existence as we know it are likewise bound up with the fact of death - courage, which is ultimately courage in the face of death; fear, which is ultimately fear of annihilation; love and tenderness, which ultimately involve the possibility of mortal sacrifice for another; tragedy, which assumes the finitude of life and a terminus to hope...[57]

However, such a significance of death would only operate in a pareschatology under conditions where the individual did not consciously recall their previous lives (and consequently their deaths). But, as we saw earlier, this is just what Hick finds difficult in the eastern concept of reincarnation, he claims that 'a link of memory is essential to any theory which identifies individuals as being reincarnations of specific members of an earlier generation, and which thus speaks of a particular series as the successive lives of one and the same soul'.[58] One could therefore conclude that since an individual will remember his/her past lives and deaths this will: a) Remove the sting of death not by 'a total trust in the love of God', but by a natural learning experience; and b) Seriously undermine Hick's argument against an immortal ego in favour of successive mortal existences, because the removal of death's 'sting' due to the learning experience will also weaken the significance of death as a crucial boundary for meaningful life. Thus, it seems that for the purposes of spiritual and moral development there are no compelling reasons to adopt Hick's 'many lives in many worlds' model in favour of one continuous post-mortem lifespan. Nevertheless, reasons to prefer such a model may be that one is trying to be inclusive of Hindu and Buddhist perspectives; that is, it is the project of constructing a global theology of death that is the important factor.

When defending the idea of everlasting life against some of its critics, Keith Ward writes:

> Is 'forever' not too long to be the same person? To think that it is, is to judge by the standards of earthbound experience, for which time can stretch ahead as a blank space, needing to be filled with ultimately futile diversions. One should rather seek to conceive of an experience which is in itself of supreme value, so that it fills the moment with happiness and a sense of fulfilment.[59]

Here Ward is speaking of everlasting life as a transformation of existence and believes that it is unwisely compared to our earthly experience. Ward's vision is of a heavenly experience (in the presence of the Creator) which is so fulfilling and complete that everlasting existence is both meaningful, 'developing' and creative. That is, there can be further meaningful development of persons when life is everlasting. However, Ward's perspectives are different from those of Hick. Ward is speaking of a life in the presence of God; that is, he is speaking of a heavenly existence - one has already arrived into this 'presence', so to speak. Alternatively, Hick's picture is of further journeying and development in a religiously ambiguous environment. Perhaps such an evolutionary vision is poorly served by an everlasting existence following death? The real choice, then, is not necessarily between many lives or one everlasting life, but between Hick's Irenaean, developmental construction and those pictures which emphasise the arrival into a heavenly existence immediately following death.

Re-embodiment and Many Lives

In the previous chapter, we asked whether Hick's replica theory could be accepted within Christian theology as an adequate view of the meaning of resurrection. This question, it might be suggested, is accentuated by the real differences of meaning that exist between reincarnation and Christian resurrection. Hick believes that the doctrines of reincarnation and resurrection are in agreement:

> in their view of man as a psycho-physical unity, so that life after death must be in a body, and a body which expresses the inner character of the individual...If he is 'reincarnated' he is thereby resurrected (brought back) to a new embodied life; if he is 'resurrected' he is thereby reincarnated, i.e. incarnated (enfleshed) again....Thus considered as pareschatologies, reincarnation and the resurrection of the body are superficially different but more fundamentally in agreement. For the reincarnation doctrine affirms repeated resurrections of a particular kind.[60]

Nevertheless, there is surely more to the meaning of resurrection in the Christian sense than mere re-embodiment? The likeness between the doctrines of reincarnation and resurrection on the grounds that both somewhat reject a notion of immortality of the soul as sufficient for continued meaningful existence is granted, but the doctrine of resurrection is saying more than merely that humans are psycho-physical beings. When Hick claims that 'reincarnation and the resurrection of the body are superficially different but more fundamentally in agreement', one might be tempted to reverse this statement and say that the two doctrines are fundamentally different but superficially in agreement. The basic reason for this is because of an understanding of resurrection to mean 'victory over death', a conquering of death such that *death is no more*. Resurrection is thus the tangible evidence that death is a past reality, and that life has overcome its old enemy. Resurrection stands in stark contrast to death, it is resurrection that gives death its positive meaning in the sense (Pauline) that unless something first die it cannot be raised to new life. Resurrection has bound up in its meaning the glorified existence in the age to come, it speaks of transformation to a higher mode of life. Moreover, it is this very meaning behind resurrection in the New Testament that has allowed some theologians to perceive the existential significance of resurrection - that is 'resurrection' not in the sense of an afterlife, but in terms of this present life. Thus Moltmann (although not to be placed into a reductionist camp) interprets resurrection in this life as 'a wholehearted, unrestricted and unreserved assent to life, to the body and to the world.'[61] Similarly, H.A. Williams,[62] P. Selby,[63] H.J. Richards,[64] and P. Tillich[65] (and to some extent K. Barth) all interpret the meaning of resurrection in qualitative terms and describe it as a transformation of life for the better, that is, a quality of existence which envisages a realising of life in all its fullness. For example, 'The good news', writes H.J. Richards, 'is not that resurrection of the body is a guaranteed future bonus, but that it is a present reality.'[66] Therefore, it seems possible that the doctrine of resurrection (with all these meanings attached) is not sufficiently described as merely asserting that we are psycho-physical beings; the interpreters above show that there is a much deeper understanding of resurrection to be grasped, and although I am one who would accord with Hick in rejecting a model that entirely reduces talk of resurrection to a quality of existence in the here and now, we must not dispose of the meaning that those who advocate this idea have found in the resurrection message.

Thus, it may be difficult to uphold a commitment to such meaning in resurrection and wholeheartedly assent to Hick's pareschatology at the same time. Simply, if resurrection is a victorious transforming event, (victorious because death has not succeeded, and transforming because it is the taking of the old life into a new and glorious life) then the notion that the resurrected person will face a series of more deaths (many lives in many worlds) in the afterlife appears to nullify such a distinctive perspective.

Related to these issues, we spoke in the last chapter about the problem of 'multiple replicas' of the same individual. Frank Dilley, a sympathetic critic, viewed things positively and suggested such an idea that might allow all the different avenues in a person's character to be brought to fruition, so that there might be 'perfected instances of Hick the plumber and Hick the lawyer in addition to a perfected instance of Hick the philosopher'.[67] In *Death and Eternal Life*, Hick admitted that such views would be outside our conceptual scope of what we presently view a 'person' to be. Hick then thought that: '[A] person is by definition unique. There cannot be two people who are exactly the same, in every respect, including their consciousness and memories.'[68]

However, it seems that a later Hick was willing to accept such a notion. In 1991 he wrote concerning multiple replication in a way that resembles Dilley's suggestion:

> We can imagine a universe in which after death there are a plurality of psycho-physical replicas of each person. People would multiply into branching post-mortem successor selves who would begin by being identical but gradually develop along different lines in the different circumstances in which they live. Such a universe would need a different conceptual system, including a different notion of "person", from the one we have developed in our actual universe.[69]

If Hick feels that he is willing to speculate beyond our present conceptions of personhood, then it is possible that he has removed the foundation of his argument against the immortal ego that 'with a limitlessly open future stretching to infinity, what we now know as human nature would be *transformed out of existence*'.[70] Hick, as shown above, believed that successive deaths were required in order to give life its distinctly 'human' quality; but it seems that if the notion of multiple replica persons in the afterlife is rendered acceptable, he cannot use the kind of argumentation that he does against the concept of an immortal ego. That is, Hick's preference for a series of mortal existences in the pareschaton instead of an immortal one is based on our this-worldly conceptions of the nature of human existence and what is required in order to identify it as human as opposed to 'angelic'. But, if he now thinks that present conceptual frameworks may not be adequate yardsticks to speculate on the pareschaton, then he is rubbing against such an argument for successive mortal lives.

The Consistency of Hick with Himself

In the previous chapters we have seen that one of the central tenets in Hick's system is *epistemic distance*, or religious ambiguity. Revisiting the questions raised in those chapters, one might ask whether or not this conflicts with the realities of the pareschatological world he has suggested. For, in Hick's construction, the spiritual growth of human beings is not just something reserved for this life only, it is something that takes place throughout many lives in many worlds. As religious ambiguity is a crucial part of the free development of persons, then it could be argued that this epistemic state of affairs must continue throughout the pareschaton. Now, put bluntly, is the mere existence of an afterlife enough to remove a significant amount of uncertainty with regard to the plausibility of, say, the theistic worldview? Moreover, in chapter one we saw that Hick proposed an eschatological verification of religious claims to render them cognitively significant. So, it seems that we have a possible clash between two of Hick's building blocks: epistemic distance (or religious ambiguity) and eschatological verification. Perhaps Hick's eschatological verification would be realised too early on and thus upset his vision of free uncoerced personal development?

We can see this possible contradiction even more explicitly when we look at the empirical evidence that Hick includes. For example, let us consider the actual content of the western spiritualist and mediumship evidence that he employs to complement his pareschatology. To be clear, Hick expresses caution about the authenticity of such testimony, but if he is going to use such data to build up his pareschatological picture then his critics have the right to tackle him on it. One thing that is particularly intriguing is that many of the 'communicants' from beyond the grave that Hick quotes seem to be remarkably clear and understanding about the *overall purpose* behind everything. For example, one such communicant says (Hick quotes):

> You know there are many different spheres in this world, many of them far higher than the one I and those of my family and yours are now living on. These spheres are all much more beautiful than even this one and those who live there are all more highly evolved spiritually than we who have only recently come into this world.[71]

And take one communication from the deceased F.W.H. Myers (again Hick quotes):

> The purpose of the sixth plane of being might be described as "The assimilation of the many-in-one," the unifying of all those mind-units I have called souls, within the spirit. When this aim has been achieved, the spirit which contains this strange individualised life passes out Yonder and enters into the Mystery, thereby fulfilling the final purpose, the evolution of the Supreme Mind.[72]

Such testimony from those who are allegedly communicating from beyond the grave is very striking in that it comes close to what Hick is suggesting in his pareschatology. But looking closer at such testimony, it seems that these communicants sound remarkably well informed! Notice that in the first quote, the communicant says at the end that he/she has only 'recently come into this world'; and yet, even at this stage they seem to have seen all the things that are ahead of them: the higher levels, and spiritual evolution etc. The basic point I am making is 'where is the ambiguity here?' These communicators from beyond the grave seem to tell us the destiny of humankind in the eschaton in such a matter-of-fact way, that one must seriously question whether any epistemic distance or ambiguity exists in the next life. It does seem that Hick's postulate of an epistemic distance is fraught with practical difficulties. As an idea it works pretty well in this present life, but what happens when the threshold of death is crossed? Once this barrier has been crossed, it is possible that the universe will appear to be far less religiously ambiguous than it is now. Hick has sought to counter this argument by proposing that an afterlife: '[W]ould not necessarily be a state of affairs which is manifestly incompatible with the non-existence of God. It might be taken as a surprising natural fact.'[73] However, the issue as to whether or not this is a realistic possibility hangs on the nature of the afterlife that is being proposed. In relation to the evidence of near-death experiences, a leading thanatologist, Paul Badham says: 'On an atheistic presumption, near-death experiences might encourage belief in a temporary survival for human personality, but they could not guarantee an eternal destiny.'[74] This suggests that the atheist may be able to find room within his/her schema for the temporary continuance of some kind of consciousness after death. But, rejecting a concept of an immaterial or 'spiritual' Cartesian mind (which it seems the atheist is virtually compelled to do), the nature of the afterlife in an atheistic framework would surely have to be no more than a kind of psychic remnant in a quantum ocean. The nature of the afterlife proposed by Hick is one where fully conscious replication occurs in another world; for a post-mortem atheist to remain a committed atheist in such circumstances seems to require credulity on his/her part of quite implausible proportions.

Nevertheless, is all this being fair to Hick? We saw in chapter one that when talking about the classic proofs for the existence of God, Hick noted that: 'In many persons - indeed taking Mankind as a whole, in the great majority the effect of a theistic proof, even when no logical flaw is found in it, would be virtually nil!'[75] Further, '...a verbal proof of God's existence cannot by itself break down our human freedom; it can only lead to a notional assent which has little or no positive religious value or substance.'[76] Now, let us imagine a situation where God's existence is rationally proved beyond a shadow of a doubt: if this by itself 'cannot break down human freedom' then there would appear to be little need of *total* ambiguity. Perhaps, the existence of God could be rationally proved and this would not actually upset the epistemic distance that human beings *experience*. However, the limitation with this is that we are not talking at the merely rational level. In fact, the afterlife is surely a kind of *experiential* confirmation which takes us out of a purely notional sense; and it is the experiential corroboration of pure notions that *does* change lives and perspectives. Thus, the inescapable conclusion still seems to be that the afterlife experience would shatter epistemic distance.

However, in Hick's defence it is possible that this kind of criticism is too simplistic and takes no account of the later directions that his thinking took. Firstly, religious ambiguity is not simply described as being a neutral state of affairs. In fact, it might be better described as a *complex* state of affairs, in the sense that people living in a religiously ambiguous environment do not *experience* neutrality, instead they feel that their different perspectives are wholly justified by the evidence and thus express deep commitment to them. That is, the environment facilitates contradictory stances. Secondly, to characterise religious ambiguity as a choice between theism and naturalism looks anachronistic anyway in light of the pluralistic hypothesis that was developed in Hick's later work. In the first case, as we have said, we suggested in the first chapter that religious ambiguity did not necessarily mean that the world appeared neutral, rather it meant that the world was capable of sustaining religious (or non-religious) commitments of various kinds. That is, people can feel thoroughly convinced of different (and, perhaps, contradictory) things. In the second case, Hick's pluralistic view entails that all religions constitute equally valid responses to the Real (ultimate reality). This means that, according to Hick, no one religion is going to be verified, or seem the more 'likely' account, in the hereafter. Or else, it may seem, from the point of view of the followers of the different faiths - or none, that each of their expectations has been realised. This is roughly the same kind of experience as found in this world - deeply felt, but contradictory stances, or else *religious ambiguity*. Thus, in the pareschaton we might say that the situation is epistemically complex, and given the plurality of faiths, such complexity is likely to continue for many lives in many worlds.

In chapter two we also drew attention to a further difficulty - the confidence shown by Hick that there will be a final consummation of all things which he envisages as the universal salvation of humankind. Why the confidence? Given human freedom and divine *non*-coercion, it would appear that this eschatological outcome is brought into being not by divine stipulation, but if and when humanity decides, individually and collectively, to conform to Reality-centredness. Thus, Hick's optimism that there will be a situation in the eschaton which is 'a limitlessly good fulfilment of the project of human existence' becomes an enormous statement of faith in the human conscience. Indeed, there is perhaps a hint of nineteenth century liberal optimism here. (Having said this, Hick can reply that his optimism is not from himself, rather it is derived from the 'cosmic optimism' of the religions themselves. Thus he has the collective optimism of the various religions as his authority on this matter.) Nevertheless, perhaps it could be suggested that the experience of the afterlife, with the possible erosion of ambiguity that this brings, provides the impetus for change and movement towards the final consummation?

In this connection, when commenting on liberal optimism, Brian Hebblethwaite remarks that '*structural* change, as well as that of individual attitudes'[77] is required for the realisation of the Kingdom of God. Now, in the context of the present discussion, could we say that just such a 'structural change' is in fact envisaged in the experience of an afterlife? That is, in the afterlife ambiguity is critically ruptured and this provides the structural conditions necessary for change. Indeed, the conception of 'changes' and crisis points might not be entirely alien to Hick's own speculations on human progress throughout the pareschaton. We have seen that he argues for 'many lives' on the basis that death marks an ideal boundary for meaningful spiritual growth. ('Death is the end of a chapter but not of the book; or better, it is the end of the volume but not the whole work.')[78] Even though we have questioned Hick's idea of many lives (and thus many 'deaths') for nurturing spiritual growth, the notion that some kind of change or 'boundary' is required to bring persons to a point of 'crisis' is, nonetheless, very promising. Might we say that the notion of ambiguity, or epistemic distance, is a *theme* which belongs to this present chapter in life? Thus the next chapter of life contains a different theme - the unambiguous confirmation of the religious world view?

However, once again, even if this is constructive thinking it is anachronistic in light of Hick's later pluralistic hypothesis. In fact, perhaps all our criticisms about the alleged 'shattering' of epistemic distance in the afterlife have to be revised as a result. For, if Hick maintains that all religions (including atheistic Buddhism and non-personal *Advaita*) are equally valid responses to ultimate reality, then we have the question of what, exactly, 'confirming the religious worldview' constitutes? Given this, perhaps Hick does not have to worry that epistemic distance will be shattered. For, as we have said, according to this pluralistic picture we are no longer faced with a simple choice between Christian theism and atheism, instead we are faced with a rich and complex picture in keeping with the plurality of the religious landscape.

Broadening the Vision - Other Worlds or This World?

In *Death and Eternal Life*, Hick wrote:

> Our eschatological speculation terminates in the idea of the unity of mankind
> in a state in which the ego-aspect of the individual consciousness has been left
> behind and the relational aspect has developed into a total community which is
> one-in-many and many-in-one existing in a state which is probably not
> embodied and probably not in time. [79]

It seems, that in the ultimate outcome of Hick's eschatology humankind is
distilled out of this spatio-temporal universe and proceeds to become
increasingly unified in an environment which becomes more and more
'mystified' or abstract. The future is focused upon the destiny of the human
individual as s/he progresses towards Reality. Thus, one question might ask
why Hick's eschatological vision concentrates on primarily human
progress and does not appear to mention the non-human world as well?
Indeed, Hick might have said more about this. Is it possible to suggest an
eschatological picture which is more universal in its basic orientation and
yet following the form of Hick's proposals? That is, an eschatology which
includes the whole of reality in its vision, not just human beings. Here one
is not just seeking to work out the eschatological implications of a Christian
doctrine of creation; but one is also, in Hickian style, seeking to be
inclusive of the mystical holism (or monism) that is found in the eastern
perspectives. This latter concern is perhaps something which would have
affinities with Hick's overall project for a global theology of death. In fact,
in his book *The Fifth Dimension*, it is possible that Hick himself may be
beginning to entertain the possibility of what might be called universal or
'cosmic' eschatology. For example, when talking of many lives in many
worlds he seems to be speaking of possibilities in this universe as opposed
to another:

> The astronomers tell us that in the vastness of the universe there may be other,
> and if so probably many other, planets sustaining life. It is possible then that
> there are other worlds in which personal-spiritual life is lived.[...]All we can
> say at present is that the idea of multiple embodied lives, whether in this or
> other worlds, is an open possibility. [80]

Given this, it could be suggested that an eschatological proposal which
takes full account of a cosmic vision might actually suit Hick's
eschatological schema. Some Christian scholars are persuaded that the
sense that the whole of reality - the physical universe and the spiritual
world (to impose a dualistic language) - is involved in the future needs to

be recaptured in theological/eschatological speculation. For example, Moltmann in his book, *The Coming of God*, would appear to have affinities with such a suggestion when he says:

> Christian eschatology must be broadened out into a cosmic eschatology, for otherwise it becomes a gnostic doctrine of redemption, and is bound to teach, no longer the redemption of the world but a redemption from the world, no longer the redemption of the body but a deliverance of the soul from the body.[81]

Moreover, a number of theologians have pointed out the somewhat anthropocentric concerns of much theological reflection. For example, in the introduction to their jointly edited text, *Cosmology and Theology*, N. Lash and D. Tracy write: 'Contemporary theology is in danger of developing interpretations of God and self (including the social self in society and history) while quietly dropping the traditional third category of world and cosmos.'[82] In his book, *Theology of Nature*, G.S. Hendry argues that there is a decline in the theological world of a 'complete' understanding of the significance of nature and its relationship to human beings. He claims that such issues have 'been virtually ignored for the past two hundred years nature has been dropped from the agenda of theology, which has been preoccupied with other themes, and, in consequence, has failed to develop resources to deal with it'.[83]

Hendry traces the cause of such a decline back to the devastating criticism of natural theology at the hands of Hume and Kant. Hume's *Dialogues Concerning Natural Religion* contained a challenge to the assumptions of natural theology, it was a 'thorough examination and critique of the whole enterprise of natural theology...'.[84] Also, Kant rejected the practice of natural theology and exhorted us to look at the 'moral law within'.[85] It may well be that such critiques of natural theology provided necessary correctives, but the effect was that theological reflection took a turn towards the inner human self and away from the cosmos as a whole. Hendry sees many theologians taking their cue from Kant, like Ritschl and Schleiermacher, Bultmann and Tillich, (and of course Hick himself owes much of his epistemology to Kant as well). If the theologies of such thinkers have any affinities at all Hendry claims that it is that 'they relate the thought of God, not to the world of nature, but to certain aspects of the experience of self'.[86]

In urging a re-orientation towards a universal eschatology, might one argue in Hickian fashion that such a concentration on humanity is merely a residue of the pre-Copernican old cosmology? That is, the old cosmology which envisaged the earth as the supremely central and most important body in the universe, all other bodies were considered secondary and lesser. Perhaps it is time for a Copernican revolution in eschatology? We must extend our eschatological vision beyond humanity and towards a cosmic hope. That is, a 'hope for a new heaven and a new earth and an entirely renewed natural order'. 'This', writes Macquarrie, 'is the grandest of all eschatological visions, and perhaps more than any other would deserve to be called a "total hope".'[87]

Following from this, then, a possible criticism of Hick's eschatology is that it limits itself to the developing of the moral law within (Kant). Hick's speculations are almost exclusively about human souls facing a challenging (soul-making) passage throughout many lives and many worlds until they emerge into a unitive state of 'Reality-centredness'. This comes close to a private eschatology. The transformation that takes place is concealed deep in the human heart and mind - it is a story of personal, moral, ethical and spiritual growth towards some final end when all souls will be united with the Ultimate. Let us call this kind of eschatology an *introverted* eschatology. Introverted eschatology is hardly a grand affair. If one compares an eschatology which concentrates on the soterio-ethical progression of the human person with the 'clamour of nature' evidenced in Psalm 148, for example, then it becomes clear that such an anthropocentric eschatology seems to be lacking:

> *Praise him, sun and moon, praise him, all you shining stars!*
> *Praise him, you highest heavens, and you waters above the heavens!*
> *[....]*
> *Praise the Lord from the earth, you sea monsters and all deeps, fire and hail,*
> *snow and frost, stormy wind fulfilling his command!*
> *Mountains and all hills, fruit trees and all cedars! Beasts and all cattle,*
> *Creeping things and flying birds!* (Ps. 148: 3,4; 7-10) RSV

To my mind, the vision here compels one to talk of, what might be called, an extroverted eschatology. Individual spiritual development is important, but this is set in the framework, and involvement, of the whole community of creation - and not just the community of humanity. The picture presented by the Psalmist is not a 'celebration of man' or a transformation of the *soul*, but a monumental cacophony of the whole creation being brought into fulfilment. There is far more meaning to be found in eschatology than just soterio-ethical matters - life *in all its fullness* amounts to more than moral purging and human refinement.

In *Evil and the God of Love*, (thus writing in the mid-1960s before the 'Copernican Revolution'), Hick made the following important and tantalising comment:

...we should perhaps rather stress man's solidarity as an embodied being with the whole natural order in which he is embedded. For man is organic to the world all his acts and thoughts and imaginations are conditioned by space and time and in abstraction from nature he would cease to be human. We may, then, say that the beauties and sublimities and powers, the microscopic intricacies and macroscopic vastnesses, the wonders and the terrors of the natural world and the life that pulses through it, are willed and valued by their Maker in a creative act that embraces man together with nature. By means of matter and living flesh God builds a path and weaves a veil between Himself and the creature made in His image. *Nature thus has a permanent significance* for God has set man in a creaturely environment, and the final fulfilment of our nature in relation to God will accordingly take the form of an embodied life within "a new heaven and a new earth".[88]

Nevertheless, Hick wants to qualify this because 'however fully we thus acknowledge the permanent significance and value of the natural order, we must still insist upon man's special character as a personal creature made in the image of God...'.[89] Thus Hick backs away from making explicit a possible eschatological application. This is even more clear when we look at Hick's later ideas (quoted at the beginning of this chapter) in *Death and Eternal Life*: 'Our eschatological speculation terminates in the idea of a unity of mankind...existing in a state which is probably not embodied and probably not in time.'[90] (Notice the development of his thinking from his earlier view just quoted from *Evil and the God of Love*: '...the final fulfilment...will accordingly take the form of an embodied life within "a new heaven and a new earth".') Clearly, an insistence that humanity is uniquely special from the divine perspective does not mean that all other things must be brushed aside. If Hick said that nature has a permanent value and significance then what did he mean by this? Perhaps that it will be 'eternally remembered' as being the instrument for our soul-making years? But this kind of explanation would be out-of-character with Hick's critical realism because when he refers to human beings as having a 'permanent value and significance' he is seeking to argue for a literal life-after-death. In Hick's scheme it seems that nature's chief utility resides in its function as a value-neutral environment for souls to grow to maturity. This is not necessarily an erroneous notion, but if this is the only purpose of nature then ultimately it is an anthropocentric view. It appears that whilst Hick insists on the permanent significance and value of the non-human world, he is *ultimately* content to overlook it. Moreover, in recognising that humanity is organic to the world he has decided not to follow this through eschatologically.[91]

It is interesting that one of the reasons why Hick shows a preference for many lives in many worlds (as opposed to one continuous post-mortem existence) is that it seems to give shape to distinctively 'human' development. But there are other things that preserve our humanity, and one such thing, for Hick, is that we are 'organic to the world'. Indeed, he has said that 'in abstraction from nature he [humankind] would cease to be human'.[92] So, with a universal eschatology we are being inclusive of an important aspect which contributes to human life - our setting. However, in this universalist picture, we are perhaps envisaging the moment of resurrection to be a transformation upwards to an immortal life.[93] Thus, it might be more accurate to say that a transformed universe is not strictly a pareschatological state in the Hickian sense of punctuated development towards the Ultimate.

These ideas, together with the suggestions about the resurrection body in the last chapter, are only bare sketches that should be developed elsewhere. However, the basic point is that rather than just talk about the progression of humanity throughout many world's, this progression might involve everything else as well.

Summary

With the publication of *Death and Eternal Life* in 1976, Hick produced a landmark study of the different perspectives (covering a vast scope: from the origins of humankind until the contemporary scene) on death and possible human destinies. This chapter has not conveyed the wide breadth of that work, but has concentrated more on the actual possibilities that Hick proposes in its final chapters for the pareschatological journey.

From the outset, Hick has approached the issues from what might be called a Copernican and an Irenaean standpoint. This means, firstly, that Hick is committed to seeing all religions, including Christianity, as revolving around Ultimate Reality (rather than religions revolving around Christianity); and, secondly, that he is committed to a non-Augustinian, somewhat evolutionary account of human existence and progression. Given these basic starting points, Hick has sought to investigate the possibilities for a global theology of death that draws on all the available evidence with regard to the future life. He is committed to the idea that the different religions point towards, 'a common conception of human destiny'.[94]

Criticisms have focused on Hick's methodology and on the actual mechanisms or structures that Hick constructs in his speculations. So, for example, is a methodology that seems to adopt, in the words of one critic, a 'deliberate eclecticism' (Penelhum), a valid approach? And, is it realistic to handle the religions as data on a universal playing field rather than as self-contained units? Nonetheless, it should be noticed that such criticisms reflect a particular intellectual standpoint that eschews the possibility of a liberal universalism. Therefore, it may well be that these kinds of criticisms only represent a preference that may or may not carry weight depending on the current climate of opinion.

Hick's distinctive contribution to thought about the future life can be sloganised under the heading 'many lives in many worlds'. This is in fact Hick's own invention and constitutes an impressive synthesis of eastern and western conceptions of the afterlife. Hick favours the framework of many lives rather than one continuous life because of the shape that it gives to personal development. That is, successive lives - each bounded by their own deaths - provide a meaningful structure and challenge for the making of souls. Here Hick reveals his Irenaean preference, and those within the Christian tradition who choose a more Augustinian account will not warm to Hick's universal 'evolutionary' scope. Also, there is the question of whether or not the different religions can recognise their particular expectations in Hick's global account. That is, in seeking to incorporate the different religious accounts of the future life, has Hick done justice to any of them? However, again, it is arguable that the demand that each of the religions' expectations should be represented in exact accordance with their different historical traditions is unrealistic and out of spirit with the project of a global theology of death. Finally, given Hick's 'Copernican revolution' in theology which sought to present a more pluralistic picture of the universe of faiths, perhaps Hick might actually apply such a revolution more literally? That is, a conception of eschatology which includes not just humankind but the whole of nature in its scope.

Many of these issues and controversies surrounding Hick's global project are to be found more explicitly in the debate surrounding the plurality of faiths. Hick's 'Copernican' revolution of the 1970s was to find its fullest expression in the next major work following *Death and Eternal Life*, perhaps his greatest work - *An Interpretation of Religion* (1989)

Notes

1.   Hick, *An Interpretation of Religion*, p.56.
2.   Ibid., p.57.
3.   Hick, *Death and Eternal Life*, p.22.
4.   Ibid., p.33.
5.   Ibid., p.30.
6.   Ibid., p.24.
7.   Hick, 'Reply' [to F. Dilley and S. Davis] in H. Hewitt, (ed.), *Problems in the Philosophy of Religion*, p.160.
8.   Hick, *Death and Eternal Life*, p.24.
9.   Ibid., p.301.

10. Ibid., p.391.
11. Hick, *The Philosophy of Religion*, p.139.
12. A. Sharma, *The Philosophy of Religion and Advaita Vedanta*, p.207.
13. See Hick, *Death and Eternal Life*, p.303; or Hick, *Philosophy of Religion*, pp.132-133.
14. Hick, *Death and Eternal Life*, p.307.
15. Ibid., p.363.
16. Hick, *The Fifth Dimension*, p.246. For an extended discussion of reincarnation see *Death and Eternal Life*, pp.297-398.
17. See Ibid, p.358.
18. For a defence of the compatibility of reincarnation with Christian belief, see G. MacGregor, *Reincarnation as a Christian Hope*.
19. For Hick's discussion of this see Hick, *Death and Eternal Life*, pp.365-373.
20. Ibid., p.372.
21. Ibid., p.371.
22. Ibid., p.27.
23. Hick, *God and the Universe of Faiths*, p.197.
24. Hick, *Death and Eternal Life*, p.408.
25. Ibid.
26. Ibid.
27. Hick weighs the balance between immortal and successive existences: 'No doubt within an eternal existence there could be relatively distinct phases in which particular purposes, and hence personal growth, are possible. But what is thus vaguely adumbrated is made more concrete and emphatic in the picture of a series of limited existences each lived out within its own world (or, in the vedantic and Buddhist versions, within different stages of the history of this world).' Ibid., pp.412-413.
28. Ibid., p.413.
29. Ibid., pp.413-414.
30. Hick, *God and the Universe of Faiths*, p.195.
31. Ibid.
32. Ibid., p.196.
33. Ibid.
34. Ibid., p.197.
35. F. Fremantle and C. Trungpa, *The Tibetan Book of the Dead*, pp.10-11.
36. Ibid., p.1.
37. Hick, *Death and Eternal Life*, p.403.
38. H.H. Price, *Essays in the Philosophy of Religion*, pp.116-117.
39. Hick, *Death and Eternal Life*, p.403.
40. See Ibid., pp.405-407.
41. Ibid, pp.416-417.
42. Ibid, p.418.
43. K.R.Schmidt, *Death and Afterlife in the Theologies of Karl Barth and John Hick: A Comparative Study*, p.169. Schmidt shows a preference for Barth's eschatological programme because Barth's eschatology exhibits a focal point of certainty which is Jesus Christ. The results, thinks Schmidt, in there being 'less speculation in the thought of Barth than one might anticipate, while there is much more in Hick than he initially want to exhibit'. Ibid.
44. Ibid.
45. Ibid.
46. T. Penelhum, 'Review and Critique of Death and Eternal Life', p.152.
47. R. Panikkar, *The Unknown Christ of Hinduism*, p.6.
48. D. Forrester, 'Prof. Hick and the Universe of Faiths', p.69.

49. D.E. Emmett, *The Nature of Metaphysical Thinking*, p.140. Cited in Hick, *Faith and Knowledge*, p.32.

50. Forrester argues that Hick's interpretations will be no more acceptable to the non-Christian faiths: 'And there is surely reason to believe that the recasting which Professor Hick's position would involve for other faiths would be in no way more acceptable to them.' op.cit, p.72.

51. J. Bowker, *Meanings of Death*, p.209.

52. Hick, *Death and Eternal Life*, p.29.

53. See *God and the Universe of Faiths*, pp.189-191.

54. R.S. Anderson, *Theology, Death and Dying*, p.46. Linking up with this, again Anderson notes: 'One's natural death as biological creature must be placed within the context of divine promise and hope for the continuation of life for death itself to be robbed of its power to destroy life. This promise and hope, of course, is the content of a Christian theology of death.' Ibid, p.50.

55. Hick, *God and Universe of Faiths*, p.197.

56. Ibid.

57. Hick, *Death and Eternal Life*, p.413.

58. Ibid., p.390. However, we should draw attention to the fact that Hick modifies his thinking in later writings in ways that have the effect of revising his earlier assertions. Thus, in this case, he argues that the 'culture-bound personality' with its 'time-bound memories' will fade away between death and re-embodiment. See *Disputed Questions*, p.193.

59. K. Ward, *Religion and Human Nature*, p.311.

60. Hick, *Death and Eternal Life*, p.372.

61. J. Moltmann, *Theology of Hope*, p.210.

62. See H.A. Williams, *True Resurrection*.

63. See P. Selby, *Look for the Living*.

64. See H.J. Richards, *Death and After*.

65. See P. Tillich, *Systematic Theology*, Vol. III.

66. H.J. Richards, op.cit., p.38.

67. F. Dilley, 'Resurrection and the "Replica" Objection', p.472.

68. Hick, *Death and Eternal Life*, p.292.

69. Hick, 'Reply' [to F. Dilley and S. Davis] in H. Hewitt, op.cit., p.161.

70. Hick, *Death and Eternal Life*, p.413.

71. See G. Rosher, *Beyond the Horizon*, p.28. Cited in Hick, *Death and Eternal Life*, p.406.

72. See G. Cummins, *The Road to Immortality*, p.71. Cited in Ibid, p.407.

73. Hick, *Faith and Knowledge*, p.186.

74. P. and L. Badham, *Immortality or Extinction?*, p.120.

75. Hick, 'Rational Theistic Beliefs Without Proofs' in P. Badham, (ed.), *A John Hick Reader*, p.54.

76. Ibid., p.55.

77. B. Hebblethwaite, *The Christian Hope*, pp.129-130.

78. Hick, *God and the Universe of Faiths*, p.195.

79. Hick, *Death and Eternal Life*, p.464.

80. Hick, *The Fifth Dimension*, p.245.

81. J. Moltmann, *The Coming of God*, p.259.

82. N. Lash and D. Tracy, (eds.), *Cosmology and Theology*, p.89.

83. G.S. Hendry, *Theology of Nature*, pp.11-12.

84. L. Urban, *A Short History of Christian Thought*, p.168.

85. Ibid., p.157.

86. G.S. Hendry, op.cit., p.16.

87. J. Macquarrie, *The Christian Hope*, p.106.

88. Hick, *Evil and the God of Love*, p.260.
89. Ibid., p.261.
90. Hick, *Death and Eternal Life*, p.464.
91. Having said this, Hick means 'organic' in the sense that it is a challenging environment in which human beings are *embedded* for the purpose of soul-making rather than physically attached to.
92. Again see Hick, *Evil and the God of Love*, p.260. (Quoted in 90 above.)
93. This somewhat connects with the suggestion, made in the last chapter, that the resurrection of humanity in the eschaton could, in fact, involve a universal transformation of nature.
94. Hick, *Death and Eternal Life*, p.34.

Chapter Five

Religious Pluralism

Probably Hick's greatest contribution is his philosophy of religious pluralism. The summation of a lifetime's scholarship and philosophical reflection is contained in his *magnum opus*, *An Interpretation of Religion* (1989). Hick follows Mircea Eliade in seeking to offer a 'religious interpretation'[1] of religion. He quotes Eliade when he wrote:

> a religious phenomenon will only be recognised as such if it is grasped at its own level, that is to say, if it is studied *as* something religious. To try to grasp the essence of such a phenomenon by means of physiology, psychology, sociology, economics, linguistics, art or any other study is false; it misses the one unique and irreducible element in it – the element of the sacred.[2]

This is not to say that Hick adopts a confessional approach, he still uses empirical tools in his methodology and subjects religious beliefs to critical scrutiny. As well as offering a comprehensive interpretation of religion, *An Interpretation of Religion* includes a highly developed and refined argument for seeing all the world religions as valid responses to a single transcendent reality. One of the reasons for leaving the topic of religious pluralism until now, is because it has the effect of changing the perspective of his thinking on the previous topics we have been discussing. We can now 'look back', as it were, and consider this.

Hick has emerged from his Judeo-Christian framework to formulate a comprehensive hypothesis that seeks to construct a global philosophy of religion. However, such a phrase - though indicative of Hick's vision - can be misleading with regard to the actual content of his hypothesis. For example, his hypothesis does not actually intend to merge religions into one (like a melting pot). Also, he is not proposing a new global religion. In fact, Hick would be very uncomfortable with the idea that 'we are all the same really'. Instead, his pluralistic hypothesis is a meta-theory (intended as a second-order philosophical exercise); it is an *explanation* of religious pluralism.[3] The fact that it is a meta-theory is so that it can stand beyond (though not in a superior sense), and allow people to be different. This means that Hick actually *affirms* difference in religion rather than seeking to bulldoze religions into the image of a 'first-order' pluralistic religion. Whether this is actually realistic or not is a moot point. But more about this later.

As we said in the introduction to this book, Hick has not always been a pluralist, indeed, as he himself points out, one of his earlier articles involved a criticism of D.M. Baillie's book *God Was In Christ* for not being orthodox enough.[4] Much of the reason for Hick's shift towards a more pluralistic perspective was experiential. This began when he moved in 1967 to the H.G. Wood Chair in Theology at the University of Birmingham. Birmingham's multi-cultural setting meant that Hick encountered people of a variety of different faiths, and such experiences were amplified when Hick travelled to India and Sri Lanka on a number of study visits.

Resulting from experience, then, Hick observes that 'people of other faiths are not on average noticeably better human beings than Christians, but nor on the other hand are they on average noticeably worse human beings'.[5] Further to this, he makes the point that if there is some kind of soteriological parity between different religions (that is, if a Buddhist monk seems to be as 'spiritually' or ethically advanced as a Christian monk) then can we so easily draw a stark distinction between 'saved' and 'lost', to use Christian parlance? Maybe there is a kind of Barthian reason for some people being in the light and others in darkness.[6] Alternatively, if the rule is 'By their fruits you shall know them',[7] then can we honestly say, asks Hick, that fruits such as generosity, kindness, non-violence, gentleness, selflessness and so on, are not present in abundance in all faiths? And if these practical expressions of faith are seen, in their own way, as human responses to some sort of higher reality, then is it not likely that such examples (being so similar) should be seen as *equally veridical* responses to that higher reality?

Popularly, one can identify three basic positions (largely within Christian theology) with regard to religious diversity: exclusivism, inclusivism and pluralism.[8] Hick, although aware of criticisms of this paradigm, believes that such distinctions are helpful in identifying and clarifying the issues with regard to attitudes towards other religions.[9]

Briefly, the *exclusivist* view can be described as a position that holds that there is no truth outside of its own discourse. So, for example, there is no truth outside of Christianity. In terms of salvation, this therefore means that in order to be saved one must become a Christian. But one of the implications of this, Hick argues, is that salvation becomes purely a matter of luck; put simply, it depends on where we are born. And, returning to the point made above, if we speak of salvation in terms of the actual effects on peoples' lives - or their 'fruits' - it is difficult, says Hick, to make a clear distinction between Christians and followers of other religions. Furthermore, if we attach significance to the effects that these different religions have on their followers - 'by their fruits you shall *know them*' - and, further, it is conceded that the effects are roughly similar, then is this not a good indication of truth present in these religions? Widening the scope, the *inclusivist* position (one version) might be characterised as saying that truth is to be found only in Christianity but that one can be saved in other religions because Christ is secretly at work in them. Nevertheless, despite such a position appearing to be more 'open' than exclusivism, Hick would not feel contented within such a position. In a sense, the problem is not only concerned with the eternal destiny of those 'outside' the true faith, but whether or not we think we can say that the 'outside faiths' contain no authentic religious experience of Reality *according to their own traditions*. And if we acknowledge that such religious experience does occur in other faiths, then should we label such experience (with Karl Rahner) as anonymously Christian?[10] If we adopt the strategies of some inclusivist theologians and say that Christ is hidden (or anonymous) within other religions one is forced into abstracting the historical Jesus into a 'cosmic Christ' or universal *logos*.[11] However, if we are going to use such abstractions then what is to stop us from abstracting even further and drop such inclusivist pretensions? Hick thinks that the only viable or realistic option is a full-blown pluralism.

In *God and the Universe of Faiths* (1973) Hick drew an analogy from the influence of Copernicus on astronomy and applied it to the theology of religions.[12] Copernicus radically altered prevailing thinking that the earth was at the centre of the solar system. This was replaced by the view that it was the sun that was at the centre and that the earth, together with the other planets, revolved around it. Using this as an analogy, Hick proposes that there should be a 'Copernican' revolution in theology. He argues that Christians must 'shift from the dogma that Christianity is at the centre to the realisation that it is God who is at the centre, and that all religions...serve and revolve around him'.[13] Here, Hick is still using 'personal' references to the divine, but later in 1989 Hick published *An Interpretation Of Religion* and the nature of the divine was elevated far beyond personal or impersonal terms. That is, Hick in his later writings refers to the Transcendent as 'the Real' which he sees as *transcategorial*.[14] One critic, Gavin D'Costa, has said that Hick has travelled from Christocentrism (his pre-Copernican days) to Theocentrism and, finally, to Realocentrism.[15] This does not reflect a fickle change of mind by Hick but indicates a gradual maturing and development of his thought.

Hick's theory is complex, and it is a mistake for critics to focus on one aspect of his thinking and pursue it as if it is the only thing that he has to say on the matter. Firstly, Hick sees religions as culturally conditioned, soterio-pragmatic systems which provide meaningful narratives and forms of life which lead to a transformation of the self (as defined by that particular system). Thus, there is a focus on the practice of religion and its transformative effect on the adherents rather than on metaphysical beliefs or doctrines. Nevertheless, if we left it at this we might conclude that Hick was committed to some kind of anti-realist account of religious life: that is, the view that although religious discourse and practice bestows meaning and effects beneficial transformation, it does not correspond with something 'out there' (e.g. an actually existing God). However, Hick *is* committed to the idea of an actually existing ultimate referent. So, even though he believes that the various religions are culturally-constructed systems, he nonetheless believes that there is an ontologically real higher reality to which these different systems refer. These two aspects are held together in Hick's hypothesis, and much critical discussion has centred around the coherence of him being able to do so.

In order to address this issue, Hick has incorporated a Kantian-influenced epistemology into his pluralistic hypothesis. Kant drew the distinction between the perceived world (*phenomena*), and the world as it is (*noumena*). That is, the objective world is beyond our direct knowledge, but it is known through the conceptual apparatus that our minds impose on reality. So if we picture a scene where twelve people are looking at a table, we might say (Kantian style) that there is a table *in reality* and then there are twelve different *perceptions* of that table. Applying this model to our knowledge about a higher or transcendent reality, Hick draws the distinction between the 'noumenal' Real and the 'phenomenal' Real. That is, there is the noumenal Real (higher reality) - which is beyond human conception - and then there are the various phenomenological conceptions/apprehensions of the Real evidenced in the world's wide variety of religious experience. He writes that the 'great world faiths embody different perceptions and conceptions of, and correspondingly different responses to, the Real';[16] and again they 'constitute different ways in which the same ultimate Reality has impinged upon human life'.[17] Thus, to clarify further, in Hick's view religion is a mix of culturally conditioned responses to a higher reality and the universal *impingement* of the Real. Hick uses the word 'impinged' because he is trying to capture a sense of the Real's activity (rather than passivity) in human religion without using loaded terms such as 'revelation' which would favour one religion's discourse above another. However, it is also important to remember that the Real's *activity* should not be understood according to our human comprehension. The noumenal Real, or the Real *in itself*, is beyond our comprehension, so concepts like activity or non-activity are transcended.

Furthermore, because Hick's Real occupies a place beyond the various religious descriptions of it (it/him/her), it is no longer valid to apply literal predicates to it. Hick writes in this connection:

> It follows from this distinction between the Real as it is in itself and as it is thought and experienced through our religious concepts that we cannot apply to the Real *an sich* [in itself] the characteristics encountered in its *personae* and *impersonae*. Thus it cannot be said to be one or many, person or thing, substance or process, good or evil, purposive or non-purposive...For whereas the phenomenal world is structured by our own conceptual frameworks, its noumenal ground is not.[18]

It may seem impossible to conceive of something holding together incompatible things within itself. So, for example, how can the Real in itself be both personal and impersonal? Firstly, in response, the idea of something possessing two incompatible characteristics at the same time is not uncommon. Such a baffling contradiction is seemingly observed in physics when light can be seen as a wave or a particle - it depends on the observer.[19] Or there is the psychologist Jastrow's celebrated 'duck-rabbit' picture (a picture that can appear like a rabbit or a duck depending on how you look at it).[20] Both ways of looking at the picture (duck or rabbit) are entirely valid, but they are different. Secondly, as we have just said, the Real in itself *transcends* the distinction between impersonality and personality, thus the seeming contradiction of both these characteristics being present in the same thing occurs not in the Real in itself but in the *human comprehension* of the Real. However, some critics have questioned Hick's apparent agnosticism on these issues and feel that he has to come down on the side of personality or impersonality. We shall consider some of these issues shortly.

Such ambiguity with regard to the *noumenal* Real reveals Hick's intention to affirm differences between religions rather than cause all religions to conform to a homogenising agenda. Although Hick postulates an ultimate referent called 'the Real' he does not wish to say anything concrete about it. If he chose to indicate that it was either personal or impersonal he would effectively be insisting that one religious claim about reality was more valid than another (e.g. either Christian theism or Buddhist atheism). Instead, Hick remains deliberately silent on this issue so as to render his hypothesis as comprehensive as possible. Moreover, being a 'second-order' philosophical explanatory (meta)theory means that Hick seems to be intending his pluralistic hypothesis to have a somewhat 'ghostly' character. That is, Hick is not endorsing the convergence of religions into a new pluralistic religion (designed by him). Rather his view of religions is 'complementary': he intends people to see the different religions as rich, legitimate and effective responses to the Real, each of which contains within itself well developed appropriate myths which can transform their followers. People should therefore stay in whatever religion they have 'received' or embraced; but they might also acknowledge the validity of the paths sincerely followed by others, and those other paths can contain insights or practices that could complement their own.

So, the various religious responses to the Real are not concrete pictures of the Real in itself, but they are nevertheless legitimate and valid responses to it. That is, under Hick's pluralistic system, various religious propositions from the wide spectrum of beliefs become *mythologically* true rather than being literally true.[21] This, it would seem, is how Hick circumvents the problem of incompatible truth-claims. That is, by saying that religious truth-claims are mythologically true of the Real in itself, he has cushioned or softened the incompatibilities that would perhaps be insuperable if one asserted that such truth-claims were literally true of the Real in itself. Things appear to be incompatible from the phenomenal level, but they are not at the noumenal level.

Being mythologically true rather than literally true does not undermine, thinks Hick, the importance and legitimacy of such religious propositions. Western scientific rationality may be impatient with 'myths', viewing them as untrue fantasies with no factual validity. However, myths can also be stories of profound meaning that have a tremendous guiding impact on human lives. For example, the stories of 'the good Samaritan' (Christianity) or 'Rama and Sita' (Hinduism) do not have any historical or factual basis, but they nonetheless can effect deep life-long changes in the moral attitudes of people. For Hick, the value of myth lies in its utility towards creating the appropriate attitude to the Real, and the impetus to grow away from ego-centredness towards Reality-centredness. Thus he writes: 'Given the postulate of the Real *an sich* [in itself],[...]we can identify the various systems of religious thought as complex myths whose truth or untruth consists in the appropriateness or inappropriateness of the practical dispositions which they tend to evoke.'[22] Again, he expands on this in another place:

> They [religious propositions/beliefs] are literally or analogically true or false (analogy being a stretched literality) of the manifestation of the Real which is their intentional object - for example, the Christian Trinity, the Allah of Islam, the Brahman of Hindu thought. And, in so far as they are literally (or analogically) true of a manifestation of the Real, they are mythologically true of the Real in itself. They are 'mythologically true' in so far as the dispositional response which they tend to evoke is appropriate to an authentic manifestation of the Real, and so to the Real in itself. For that such a

manifestation is authentic means that it is in 'soteriological alignment' with the Real.[23]

As Hick sees it, the main function of religion is to bring about the salvation/enlightenment/liberation of its adherents. Thus, the criterion for identifying a religion as true is the extent to which the religion in question facilitates 'good fruit'. *By their fruits you shall know them.* Thus, Satanism or extreme cults - by encouraging destructive (even murderous) or delusory behaviour - do not satisfy this criterion.[24] To clarify further, Hick thinks that a religion is true not because its various propositions or truth-claims are literally accurate concerning reality, but because such things engender an 'appropriate disposition' (or good behaviour) in the individual and community. But this is not a criterion that Hick thinks he is imposing on the religions 'from above', rather it represents the consensus of the moral teachings in the great world religions themselves. So, Hick has evaded the problem of incompatibility between the numerous religious truth-claims by emphasising their soteriological function. Or else, it might be said that Hick has characterised 'truth' *ethically* rather than metaphysically. He believes that for all the differences that exist, the essential commonality in the vast majority of religious beliefs is the soteriological character that they all possess. Again, to speak of commonality is not to speak of 'sameness'. To repeat, Hick does not think that religions are 'all the same'. But religions, in their various ways, facilitate people towards their own salvation or liberation or enlightenment - in their religions people journey towards a limitlessly better possibility for their lives. Thus, he argues that the great world religions:

> are fundamentally alike in exhibiting a soteriological structure. That is to say, they are all concerned with salvation / liberation / enlightenment / fulfilment ... Along each path the great transition is from the sin and error of self-enclosed existence to the liberation and bliss of Reality-centredness.[25]

Pluralism and Eschatology

Applying Hick's pluralistic explorations to the eschatological 'experience', it appears that in the initial stages of postmortem life, the adherents to the major world faiths will encounter the religious objects of their various expectations. As we saw in the previous chapter, this takes place in the *bardo* phase that Hick thinks will immediately follow death. He writes:

> It is possible, for example, that in an immediately post-mortem phase the different expectations generated by the different traditions will each to some

extent be fulfilled in different individuals' mind-dependent bardo worlds; but beyond this there are other phases whose nature we cannot presently imagine.[26]

Despite each of the different expectations of different faiths being somewhat verified in the immediate post-mortem world, Hick clearly believes that in the long term a very much wider picture will emerge far beyond present religious conceptions. He writes of the various religions that 'each of them will almost certainly turn out to be extremely inadequate as an account of what actually happens, so that all of these pictures will probably have to undergo considerable amendment, or radical reconstruction, in the light of future post-mortem experience'.[27]

This is not to say that Hick thinks that all traditions will definitely be found to have considerably missed the mark where eschatological expectation is concerned. It remains possible that a particular religious tradition will be shown to have been closer to the truth about Reality than some others. Again he writes: 'It does, of course, remain logically possible that some present set of dogmas (Catholic or Protestant, Mormon or Seventh Day Adventist, Sunni or Shia, Theravada or Mahayana, advaitist or visistadvaitist) will turn out to correspond precisely with reality...'[28] Nevertheless, Hick wants to qualify this, '..but in view of the manifest human cultural contributions to all of these sets of ideas it seems more likely that all of them will, in varying degrees, have to undergo correction or enlargement or transformation of the light of fuller experience'.[29]

Thus, following the logic outlined earlier, Hick defines the various eschatologies evidenced in the world's religions as *mythologically* true, not literally true. All specific expectations 'are forms of eschatological mythology, imaginative pictures of the ultimate state, produced to meet our need, a need from which the Buddha sought to free us - for something to which our minds can cling as we contemplate our own finitude'.[30] Furthermore, the different eschatological mythologies are alike in the sense that they serve the same soteriological function.[31] Hick synthesises (not in a reductionist sense but as a meta-explanation) all eschatological expectations into the basic proposition that there will be 'a limitlessly good fulfilment of the project of human existence'.[32] Again he qualifies this last statement: '"Good" here means good from our human point of view, bearing in mind, however, that this point of view may itself develop through time in harmony with increasing insight and wisdom - perhaps even to the point at which separate ego identity is no longer valued.'[33]

Talking About 'The Real'

It would seem that a common criticism of Hick's hypothesis springs from his own premises for establishing the cognitivity of religious statements: eschatological verification. We saw in chapter one that Hick's proposal was in response to the verificationist (logical positivist) challenge in the 1950s: that is, in order for a given statement to have a factual significance we must be able to be say what *difference* it makes. Is the statement 'verifiable' or 'falsifiable'? If a statement makes no difference either way then the statement can have no cognitive value - it is merely poetry. Hick, in order to make religious claims cognitive, postulated that there would be a situation in the eschaton which would serve to verify the eschatological expectations of theistic propositions, thus rendering such propositions meaningful. With his pluralistic hypothesis, Hick has expanded beyond his earlier thinking, and some critics think that such new thinking should re-classify him as a *non-realist*. One critic, Gavin D'Costa, says that there are 'tensions generated in Hick's post-Copernican position between the idea that the Real cannot be known in itself, and his claim that religions make cognitive claims about the Real that are in principle eschatologically verifiable'.[34] If we cannot say what the Real actually is, then how can we know what would serve to verify religious (in particular, theistic) expectations?

Since Hick first proposed eschatological verification as a way of making theistic statements cognitive, his thinking has obviously developed. No longer does he talk in *literally* Christian, or even theistic, terms. To reiterate, in his pluralistic hypothesis he has sought to embrace non-theistic traditions (e.g. Buddhism) as well, and, moreover, Hick now thinks that none of the different religions' claims are in fact claims about the (*noumenal*) Real in itself but about the Real's various phenomenological manifestations. That is, although religious statements can be said to be literally true of the Real within its different manifestations (i.e. different religions), such statements are in fact *mythologically*, rather than literally, true of the Real in itself. As a result, D'Costa maintains that the cognitivity of religious statements is put in serious jeopardy. In fact, all religious eschatological expectations have been summarised by Hick under the general heading: 'a limitlessly good fulfilment of the project of human existence'.[35] Thus there is a drift into agnosticism regarding the factual nature of particular religious claims; claims which D'Costa feels are rendered 'no longer significant'[36] in Hick's system. This is because they do not await a literal fulfilment, they are merely allegories for a 'better future'. Furthermore, there is such a vagueness, or vacuity, associated with 'the Real' that D'Costa calls it 'transcendental agnosticism'.[37] He writes:

Transcendental agnosticism affirms the *transcendent* divine Reality over against *naturalistic* positions, while refusing to state that the eschaton may eventually be theistic rather than non-theistic, in however minimalist a sense. The transcendental agnostic prefers to remain agnostic on this question – and, by implication, *agnostic* as to the *ultimate nature* of the transcendent reality.[38]

Is this a fair criticism? In response one might say that there is a difference between being agnostic (i.e. undecided) about whether something is characterised one way or another (e.g. impersonal or personal, good or evil); and saying that something is 'beyond description'. Hick places the Real in the second category when he says that the Real is *trans-categorial*, or beyond description. It simply occupies a conceptual space beyond human comprehension. That is, 'personal' or 'impersonal', 'purposive' or 'non-purposive', 'good' or 'evil' are not predicates of the Real in itself. Neither is the Real correctly understood as a mixture of these things. It is not that Hick is agnostic with regard to saying clearly whether the Real is one kind of thing and not another, rather it is just that he *cannot* say anything about something that is not humanly comprehensible! So, is it accurate to label Hick as an *agnostic*? Hick draws attention to many great religious thinkers who have said similar things about divine ineffability from within their own specific religious traditions. For example, St. Thomas Aquinas wrote that 'by its immensity the divine substance surpasses every form that our intellect reaches';[39] and within the Hindu tradition, the Upanishads say of the divine reality: 'Thou art formless: thy only form is our knowledge of thee.'[40] Again, in the Taoist scriptures it is written: 'The Tao that can be expressed is not the eternal Tao.'[41] Admittedly, the thinkers behind these writings were not seeking to relate such statements to an abstract Reality within a pluralistic hypothesis like Hick's, but were making statements within their own traditions. However, to reply to Hick that such writers are writing within their own traditions is somewhat irrelevant. It seems difficult to get round the fact that the basic point being made by such religious thinkers is that the religions' ultimate referent is *beyond comprehension*; that is - beyond human conceptual abilities and thus beyond even their own traditions. Are these thinkers being transcendentally agnostic, or are they being *mystical*? Hick sees himself as merely affirming such mystical statements in a wider pluralistic context.

Nevertheless, D'Costa also argues that the vacuity of Hick's Real leaves theism bereft of anything to say against naturalism. Originally, the eschatological verification of theistic expectations was meant to verify the truth of such expectations against the claims of naturalism. Put crudely, the atheistic worldview would be shown to be wrong by the eschatological experience of God. But Hick includes Theravadin Buddhism (non-theistic), or non-theistic Advaita in his pluralistic scope.[42] Thus, effectively, the Real encompasses naturalistic perspectives within its umbrella - which would mean that both theistic and naturalistic accounts of reality are to be verified in the eschaton. This serves to show some of the difficulties of trying to include contradictory beliefs in a far-reaching comprehensive theory.

Staying with the theme of eschatological verification, S. Mark Heim also pursues the question of Hick's views of the cognitive status of religion in connection with his pluralistic hypothesis. He throws down the gauntlet to Hick by saying that the 'assertion that a single, noumenal Real impinges in all religion and is the source of human transformation to a limitlessly better future must make its own way as a cognitive claim'.[43] But, Heim points out that Hick's pluralistic hypothesis is in fact cognitively empty. This is because, *according to its own premises*, it is impossible to imagine a situation in the eschaton which would serve to verify the truth that there is a single noumenal Real behind the various religious traditions.[44] Heim comments that:

> Hick's hypothesis implies there are some conditions in which it would be verified by an experience of the noumenal Real, i.e. *experience of what cannot be experienced*. It is not a matter here of doubting that a given eschatological scenario will come to pass, but of a religious claim that corresponds to no differentiated set of circumstances at all. The failure of Hick's pluralistic hypothesis to specify any such set puts its own cognitive status in jeopardy.[45]

The prediction that there will be a 'limitlessly good fulfilment of the project of human existence', is something that any one of the religious eschatological expectations could fulfil on their own. That is, it is not a state of affairs that is only predicted in Hick's pluralistic hypothesis. It is an expectation that most religions in the world can assent to. Thus, to reach a state of affairs in the distant eschaton when there is a 'limitlessly good fulfilment of the project of human existence' is not peculiar to Hick's hypothesis and so does not verify the truth of Hick's hypothesis in particular. Heim takes this point further:

> His [Hick's] hypothesis states a condition that would have to be additionally true beyond any realisation of the hopes of a single religious tradition or any combination of traditions: namely that it will prove to be the case that a single noumenal Real, beyond description by any of the religious traditions, is operative in each of them to bring about one limitlessly better religious end for all humanity.[46]

Heim is making the point that according to the requirements of eschatological verification there needs to be an experience or situation in the eschaton that verifies Hick's hypothesis of an Ultimate Real working behind all the various pictures of it, otherwise his theory is non-cognitive according to his own premises. But according to Hick, we do not experience the noumenal Real - in fact the noumenal Real cannot by definition be experienced because it is inexperiencable. If we cannot even give a description of what kind of experience would serve to verify Hick's Real then it is in principle neither verifiable or falsifiable, and therefore cognitively meaningless. Hick has ceased to be a realist and has joined the non-realist camp.

Nevertheless, are we imposing unreasonable requirements on Hick's hypothesis? In a sense, the demand that he must specify exactly what the noumenal Real is like (in order for us to be able to verify its existence or not) is too simplistic and naïve. Hick distinguishes between two kinds of verification: direct and indirect.[47] Take the statement: 'the car is in the garage'. This is capable of direct verification (or falsification) by merely taking a look in the garage. However, what about the statement: 'Jones is an honest man'?[48] This is far more complex. To verify or falsify the truth of such a statement one would have to be with Jones for some time and observe his behaviour. Even then, the criteria used to judge Jones' honesty might contain elements of subjectivity. Nevertheless, despite this, it is reasonable to suppose that there would be a cumulative experience which would gradually yield a meaningful verdict on the statement. This is a kind of indirect verification. Honesty is not something we can directly point to (like a car in a garage). But one can experience its symptoms.

Similarly, the concept of God contains a vast range of additional ideas like 'God is love', 'God is all-knowing', 'God's purposes are good'. Thus, to verify the existence of God is not a simple or direct exercise; rather, it is an indirect, cumulative and experiential affair. Hick thinks that the verification or falsification of his pluralistic hypothesis with its noumenal Real is merely an extension of such indirect methods. So, as the human journey proceeds towards the eschaton and the 'bigger pluralistic picture' emerges, the pluralistic vision will seem to be increasingly and cumulatively verified. Conversely, in a remark of black humour, Hick points out that one would be able to indirectly falsify the pluralistic hypothesis if it turned out that (in accordance with Augustine's expectations) all non-Christians ended up in hell![49]

However, the whole issue of the alleged vacuity of the Real has caused some to question what might be called the *religious* validity of Hick's ontology. For instance, J. Kellenberger, when commenting on the question of 'transcendental agnosticism', asks us to consider the example of the biblical figure of Job.[50] He notes that Hick seems to be asking that all religious believers face up to the possibility of their own truth-claims being fallible and the validity of alternative world-views; but then compares this with Job's utterance of faith 'I know that my Redeemer liveth'. Kellenberger notes that it is like causing Job to cry instead: 'I know that my Redeemer liveth, but I may be mistaken!'[51] Of course, all great religious figures have wrestled with doubt without John Hick and his pluralistic hypothesis being around! Job was surrounded by confusing and exasperating circumstances - his faith was being tested; but Job remained adamant in his beliefs. Nevertheless, the question is: 'Is such religious steadfastness *in contrast* with Hick's deliberate unwillingness to say anything concrete about the Real?'

In seeking to answer this, it is important to understand what Hick thinks about the integrity of particular religions. At the beginning of this chapter, I said that Hick's pluralistic hypothesis is intended as a second-order philosophical exercise rather than a first order discourse. By this is meant that Hick's pluralism is not meant to be a new religion in its own right. Thus, we do not respond directly to the Real itself but with one of its many manifestations. That is, we do not worship, or respond directly to, or steadfastly affirm our allegiance (like Job) to the Real *in itself*, the Real remains the unfathomable ground of all religious experience. In this sense, Hick's pluralistic hypothesis leaves religions as they are; that is, his pluralism is an explanatory hypothesis rather than a reductionist exercise. To explain further, if he was proposing a new first-order discourse or religion - with a 'Real' to be worshipped - then we might want to know (like Job) what this Real was like; and such first-order claims would compete with other religions like any other conflicting religious truth claim. That is, in entering the sphere of first-order discourse, Hick's pluralism would have a reductionist affect with regard to other religions' self-interpretations. However, he is not seeking to talk like this, instead he wants to suggest a second-order philosophical explanation of the diversity of religions. Thus, Hick might reply that there is nothing illegitimate about the firm faith commitment exemplified by Job (or anybody else). Job is expressing his faith in accordance with the way in which the Real has impinged on his life. Job's response to the Real is one of the multitude of valid human responses to the Transcendent; just because Hick wants to suggest a much bigger picture in no way undermines Job's convictions. Job's convictions are *literally* true of his picture of God as defined in his tradition and experience, and mythologically true of the noumenal Real that is its ground. We shall return to issues concerning religious certainty and commitment presently, but let us look a little more closely at the nature of the Real in itself.

Even though we have distinguished between the Real in itself and the Real in its phenomenological manifestations, can we say nothing at all about the nature of Real in itself? For example, can we say whether or not the ultimate is personal or impersonal? As we have seen, Hick thinks that the Real in itself transcends such distinctions. So, with his pluralistic hypothesis it even seems that calling the Real 'personal' is either inappropriate, inaccurate or incomplete. Such ascriptions belong only to the Real in its phenomenal manifestations. However, another critic, J. Lipner, argues that Hick's Real must be personal;[52] that is, it cannot be indefinable - occupying some nebulous region beyond personality and impersonality.

Firstly, Lipner notes Hick's claim that 'all authentic religious awareness is a response to the *circumambient presence and prevenient pressure of the divine Reality*'.[53] To this Lipner asks the question: 'Does it make sense to speak of a response to the Transcendent without implying some sort of initiative on the part of the Transcendent in the first place?'[54] He proceeds: 'Well now, speaking properly, it only makes sense to talk of persons taking the initiative, does it not? Doesn't Hick thereby covertly imply by his terminology that the Real behind the various personae and impersonae is basically personal?'[55]

Secondly, Lipner also argues that in order for real spiritual transformation to take place among human beings, a two-way personal relationship between the person and a personal Real is more effective. He writes, 'Surely those who respond to the Transcendent within the parameters of an interpersonal relationship are in closer touch with the core of the Real than those who do not, and, being thus closer, grow the more perfectly into full personhood?'[56] Hick replies to this second point by saying that spiritual transformation does not necessarily require a personal universe because such transformation evidently seems to take place in all religions, theistic or non-theistic.[57]

Hick may be correct in saying that roughly similar kinds of transformation seem to occur in non-theistic as well as theistic religions, and so Lipner's point about a personal conception of the divine being a more effective vehicle for spiritual transformation somewhat misfires. However, Lipner's first point is more interesting. This is the question that relates to divine activity. If we are 'responding' to the Transcendent then is it not a response to some initial 'act' of communication by the Transcendent in the first place? And does it not seem to be the case that only 'persons' (rather than things) can be seen as 'taking the initiative'? Furthermore, a more fundamental question might be: 'What is the *impulse* of the Real to desire to bring about the transformation of human beings?' Surely such impulses involve concepts of love, desire for the well-being of humanity and so on, and these concepts only make sense by envisaging the

Real as ultimately personal? Take, for example, Hick's arguments against
Flew and Mackie (who, as we saw in chapter two, argue that God could
have created human beings to freely choose to do the right), where he said
that from God's point of view it was more valuable that creatures respond
to him freely whilst there remains the contingent possibility that they might
reject him.[58] (In this connection, note especially his analogy of the
hypnotist and his patient.)[59] Again, there is his parental analogy (the
'parent' symbolising God) which he employs to tackle how a loving God
could allow pain and suffering in this world.[60]

Hick has altered the status of his Irenaean soul-making theodicy from
literal meaning to mythological meaning. He writes that: 'Such a theodicy
is mythological in the sense that the language in which it speaks about the
Real, as a personal being carrying out intentions through time, cannot apply
to the ultimate transcendent Reality in itself.'[61] Hick thinks that his
theodicy represents 'a true myth in so far as the practical attitudes which it
tends to evoke amid the evils of human life are appropriate to our present
existence in relation to the Real'.[62] Here he turns away from discussing the
character of the Real itself and prefers to concentrate on the problem from
the human soteriological level. Hick expresses this very well in connection
with the 'goodness' of the Real:

> [...]the sense in which the Real is good, benign, gracious is analogous to that
> in which the sun is, from our point of view, good, friendly, life-giving. (Poets
> have spoken, for example, of 'the blessed sun himself' and how 'the sun
> shines sweetly on'). The life-giving warmth of the sun is the ground, or the
> *sine qua non*, of our existence and our flourishing. Likewise, the Real is the
> necessary condition of our existence and our highest good. It is in this sense
> that we can speak of the Real as being, in relation to us, good, benign,
> gracious.[63]

But the problem of theodicy is surely located in harmonising the presence
of evil with a God of love, or a question of why God chose to create the
world the way it is? That is, we are asking questions not about the
pragmatic effect of a given theodicy on our attitudes towards the
Transcendent, but the motivations of the Transcendent *towards us*.
Moreover, this is not really a matter of how we apprehend the Real in one
of its manifestations but a question about the Real *in itself*. It is the picture
of the divine as loving and personal that makes the question of evil and
suffering a religious issue at all. In this case, why do we need a theodicy if
the Real in itself should be described as neither '...one or many, person or
thing, substance or process, good or evil, purposive or non-purposive'? In
light of this is it really satisfactory to speak of 'true myths'? In fact, should
not Hick just throw up his hands and claim that evil and suffering are

mysteries without explanation. The strength and power of Hick's theodicy rests, in my view, on the notion of a personal divine being choosing the best and most authentic way (an ambiguous, free, and objective soul-making environment) to bring free, autonomous beings into full personhood. Surely, the *soul-making* world is a creation of a personal Real? And, further, if theists are ever challenged to give some account about the possible meaning of evil, are they endeavouring to give *real* replies or merely content to tell tales (or myths)? Perhaps there are no straightforward or satisfactory answers to these questions, but the process theologian, David Griffin, identifies the real reason (to my mind) behind the necessity (or desire) for total freedom in Hick's soul-making world: '[I]t is for God's sake, not ours.'[64]

Should we therefore conclude that Hick's theodicy requires a 'personal' Real? Firstly, it would not be true to say that Hick thinks that the Real is impersonal either. As we have seen, Hick wants to say that the Real transcends personality and impersonality ('transcategorial' being Hick's preferred term). Secondly, Hick will respond by saying that the statement 'God desires that we all fulfil our potential' is something that may be literally true of the Real in its theistic manifestation but mythologically true of the Real *in itself*. Hick can therefore maintain that the Real is simply beyond our own comprehension, that it is false to anthropomorphise the Real, and erroneous to insist on a fully comprehensible substance to the Real's 'personality'.

However, it still seems that the reasons that Hick gives for the way the universe is appear to derive from the notion that *from the divine perspective* it is better to have a free, soul-making universe than not, or better to preserve human beings who have not yet fulfilled their potential and so on. Admittedly, such reasons date back to 1966 and *Evil and the God of Love,* but we are still entitled to ask if these are *real* reasons why we live in a soul-making universe or mythological ones. To illustrate this, take the statement: 'God values persons and seeks their development and fulfilment' - does this have any literal significance or is it merely mythologically 'appropriate'? If it is mythological then what about the additional statement: 'God desires that people do not perish but that they continue after death until they reach a limitlessly good outcome to their existence.' Does *this* have any literal significance? If not, then can we use the argument that is expressed by this statement when seeking to persuade for a literal understanding of life after death?

Christology and Pluralism

Hick's Christology is not directly connected to his pluralism, but it should come as no surprise that his pluralistic views have a profound effect on his Christology. Or rather, it is slightly misleading to make reference to his Christological thinking in sole connection with his pluralistic hypothesis because much of his writing in this area reflects other concerns. Nevertheless, the driving force behind his revision of traditional formulations is the existence of other religions. Looking at his Christology provides us with an example of the effect of his pluralism on traditional formulations within Christian belief.

There are roughly three areas that are of concern to Hick: The first two represent concerns other than religious plurality, whilst the third is directly relevant. More specifically, the first concerns what the historical Jesus actually said and claimed; the second addresses the logical problems associated with 'literal-metaphysical' approaches; and the third, as we have said, is about the existence of other religions. It is important to appreciate that Hick has sought to be constructive with his Christology. His is no reductionist exercise for the sake of it (or for the sake of notoriety), he is genuinely concerned to formulate a Christology that has meaning for us in the contemporary world. Hick is famous for a book which he edited called *The Myth of God Incarnate* (1977). This book provoked a tremendous reaction at the time of its publication, and it may be one his most well known books. More than a decade later he published another book called *The Metaphor of God Incarnate* (1993) which provides a more extended treatment of his thinking.

Drawing on the conclusions of what he sees as the consensus of New Testament scholarship, Hick thinks that the historical Jesus did not claim to be God.[65] Such claims express the developing theology of the early Church rather than the words of Jesus himself. But this is not to say that the Christian faith is one big hoax. Instead, Hick thinks that Jesus was an exceptional man who exhibited such a spirit-filled life that 'a close encounter with Jesus in first-century Palestine would be a conversion experience'.[66] Furthermore, because Jesus was so open to the presence of God, 'the divine creativity flowed through his hands in bodily healing and was present in his personal impact upon people, with challenging and re-creating power'.[67] It is this picture of an historical Jesus completely filled with the Spirit of God, or *agape*, that Hick is impressed with. The metaphysical doctrines relating to Jesus' two-natures (divine and human) owed themselves more to the later influences of Greek philosophy on the Church's thinking than to the actual Jesus of history. Thus, in adopting an 'inspiration' Christology (referring to Jesus' intensely inspired relationship with God), Hick thinks that we are getting back to a more authentic picture of things. Moreover, he thinks that such a picture is not in conflict with much recent New Testament criticism, and it is more helpful in light of religious pluralism.

Secondly, can we make sense of the doctrine of the Incarnation as traditionally understood? Hick thinks not.[68] This is because it is impossible to explain coherently the actual meaning behind the notion that an individual is both fully divine and fully human. For example, how can a finite man embody or contain *infinite* qualities? How can an omniscient being also express ignorance about something, or an all-powerful being be vulnerable and weak? In short, arguing in Greek fashion about Jesus being of one 'substance' with God only leads us into numerous insoluble conundrums that, despite immense intellectual effort over the centuries, has never been satisfyingly resolved. It is a mistake, thinks Hick, to approach the meaning of incarnation using 'literal-metaphysical' rather than metaphorical or mythological modes of discourse. The whole idea of an individual being both fully divine and fully human at the same time is rather like trying to visualise a square circle, that is, it is a ludicrous proposition.[69] Moreover, such descriptions of 'substance' are static, immovable conceptions which are preoccupied with abstract metaphysical questions of Being.

Nevertheless, a possible criticism is that Hick is tending to define the problem in ways that create a deliberately constricted atmosphere. For example, the 'square-circle' complaint deals with the matter as if it were a case of a simple geometrical contradiction. It is precisely this kind of approach that the theologian Maurice Wiles, for example, expresses reservations about. Wiles comments that: 'It is much harder to plot the borderline between sense and nonsense in talking about the mystery of God.'[70] If this is the case, then perhaps the language of incarnation should not necessarily be taken to imply clear-cut, humanly-comprehensible distinctions. Nevertheless, to make these kinds of points is actually to fall into Hick's hands. For it is precisely an admission of the inadequacy of the 'literal-metaphysical' language that leads Hick to recommend his mythological approach! However, he hasn't really shown why the choice is between the language of substance in Greek philosophy on the one hand, and the complete mythologisation of the Incarnation on the other. Instead there could be an appeal to mystery (something which is a frank admission by innumerable theologians throughout history) which nonetheless upholds the *metaphysical* sense as important.

As well as finding difficulties with the classical substance Christologies, Hick is also unimpressed by other interpretations such as the idea of divine kenosis (self-emptying).[71] This idea centres on the claim that

Christ's divinity was deliberately concealed or laid aside when he took human form (however, he still retained his divine status). Hick's observation about kenotic interpretations is that, despite often being used as an apologetic for traditional doctrine, they do not actually seem to do justice to the traditional picture of Jesus as fully God and fully human. Or rather, in seeking to find a philosophically coherent model of incarnation, the kenoticists have emptied the doctrine of its religious value.[72] Nevertheless, Hick thinks that the idea of kenosis or self-emptying serves as a 'vivid metaphor' of the divine love, but one should not seek to turn a good metaphor into 'bad metaphysics'.[73] Hick prefers a more fluid and non-metaphysical view of incarnation; and furthermore a view which he feels that human beings living in the contemporary world can connect with. So instead of speaking the outdated metaphysical language of Chalcedon we might instead portray Jesus as an outstanding individual who 'incarnated', in a metaphorical sense, the divine, and inspires us to realise our potential to be fully spirit-filled. Thus, in doing God's will, *God was acting* through Jesus; Jesus *exemplified* the life led in openness to God, and he finitely incarnated the infinite *agape* love of God. Jesus embodied these things to such an extent that people who came into contact with him sensed the presence of God.[74]

   The third, and most important, problem of asserting the Incarnation in its traditional form (i.e. the pre-existent divine Son descending from heaven to atone for the sins of the world and then returning to the eternal Trinity) is that it implies the superiority of the Christian faith above other faiths. That is, if Jesus is *the* incarnation of God, then it suggests that 'the Christian religion, alone among the religions of the world, was founded by God in person...'.[75] This is incompatible with the pluralistic picture that Hick wishes to present of Christianity being just one salvific religion amongst many. Hick is recommending that the development of Christian doctrine (and Christology in particular) be undertaken not just within its own community, but with reference to the existence (and teachings) of the world religions. Taking such a broad perspective means that Jesus is one amongst many outstanding individuals like Gautama, Guru Nanak, Mohammed and Moses. Thus, the alternative to the traditionally 'superior' Christian rhetoric is:

> a Christian faith which takes Jesus as our supreme (but not necessarily only) spiritual guide; as our personal and communal lord, leader, guru, exemplar, and teacher, but not as literally himself God; and which sees Christianity as one authentic context of salvation/liberation amongst others, not opposing but interacting in mutually creative ways with the other great paths.[76]

Consistent with his pluralistic perspective, Hick is hinting at a broadening out of the notion of incarnation which emphasises the 'salvific efficacy of the variety of ways formed around the different incarnations that have occurred throughout human history'.[77] Such plural notions of 'incarnation' have been criticised by more conservative scholars. For example, Brian Hebblethwaite thinks that a multiple picture is impossible. He argues that Hick has confused the notion of incarnating an *expression* of divinity with incarnating the actual divine *identity*. The former idea may be consistent with the concept of *avatar* within Hindu thought, but not with the idea that a *specific person* within the Trinity has become flesh and dwelt among us. Thus, Hebblethwaite argues that there is a crucial difference between many individuals manifesting general divine characteristics and God coming 'in person'.[78] However, Hick thinks that this kind of emphasis on the unitary nature of God's identity is chiefly motivated by 'Christian absolutism', and that such a conceptual framework inevitably colours Hebblethwaite's views of the meaning of incarnation.[79] Nevertheless, there must also be a question of whether Hick's re-interpretations of incarnation are likely to be accepted as genuine reflections within a Christian framework at all. That is, is Hick reforming Christian thought from within or is he imposing an external pluralist agenda?

Hick's views on the person of Christ have been controversial, and so one might expect that he has been heavily criticised for them. When looking back on the impact of *The Myth of God Incarnate*, Hick draws attention to how 'frenetically polemical'[80] the subsequent debate was. This is hardly surprising given the sensitive and important subject matter. With regard to logical difficulties, Hebblethwaite argues that the 'logic' of the Incarnation is something that is intentionally paradoxical in order to draw us into 'thought of the transcendent'.[81] He writes, 'The paradoxes are a sign that we have to stop thinking anthropomorphically; and they are a tool for thinking theologically about the one who cannot be comprehended with clear-cut univocal terms.'[82] Perhaps it is interesting to note that whereas Hick seems to dismiss as nonsensical (as a metaphysical assertion) the idea of Jesus being simultaneously fully human and fully divine, he is nonetheless able to conceive of 'the Real' which transcends such polarities as 'personal or impersonal', 'good or evil', 'purposive or non-purposive'. When referring to the Real, Hick comments that it/he/she simply occupies a conceptual space that is transcategorial and beyond our comprehension. If Hick is prepared to attempt things like reconciling contradictory religious ultimates by making reference to a transcategorial noumenal level, then why could he not adopt a similar posture towards the Incarnation?[83] Perhaps this is a clue to the *overriding* concern for Hick. That is, the crucial issue is not really one of *logicality*, but a matter of making reference to global religious diversity.

Evil and Religious Pluralism: Comparative Solutions

Recalling Job's defiant declaration of faith that we briefly discussed a moment ago, we might extend the discussion with regard to the *religious* validity of Hick's pluralistic hypothesis.

When Flew in the 1950s declared that religious assertions died 'a death of a thousand qualifications' (see chapter one), he was expressing frustration in the face of a dogged refusal by theologians to relinquish cherished beliefs.[84] No matter what conundrum the atheist camp hurled at the theists, they found (to their considerable consternation) that the theologians had moved the goalposts just that little further away. Although the debate following Flew's comments addressed crucial questions concerning the meaningfulness of religious statements, it also highlighted, in my view, the durability and resilience of religious beliefs and assertions in the mind of the believer. Flew's point was that religious believers, despite being surrounded by confusing and contradictory evidence, refuse to give up their notions and convictions concerning the divine. It is this resilience in the face of cognitive and experiential difficulties (exemplified by Job) that we might discuss further.

We will briefly look at Hick's treatment of the problem of evil and compare this with his response to the problems of religious diversity. The purpose for such a comparison is not to provide an exhaustive study of these separate issues in relation to each other. However, it will hopefully show how differently Hick has treated both problems and lead into a consideration of how the eschatological dimension of his thinking can result in a different 'solution' to the question of religious diversity. I will argue that it is possible to treat both questions in similar ways because of one highly significant feature common to them both - the possibility of further opportunities beyond death.

Let us begin by suggesting that Hick's solution to the problem of evil is dissimilar to his solution to the problem of religious diversity. In the former he identifies (properly to my mind) that the solution to the problem of evil is closely related to the challenge given by Hume in his *Dialogues Concerning Natural Religion*: 'Is he [God] willing to prevent evil, but not able? then he is impotent. Is he able, but not willing? then he is malevolent. Is he both able and willing? Whence then is evil?'[85]

Here the challenge would seem to be 'can you keep your view of God intact in relation to the existence of evil?'; 'Is God really omnipotent, omniscient and omni-benevolent if evil exists?' Thus, the questions of theodicy are concerned with the necessity to assert all such predications about God whilst acknowledging the existence and full horror of evil. Of course, not all theologians have been equally concerned to maintain the classical picture of the divine in the face of evil and suffering. Process theology, for example, seems to tackle the conundrum of evil by denying the problem as posed by Hume. That is, from the process perspective, God is not wholly 'ultimate' but contigent and is struggling for self-disclosure. A notable exponent of process theology who was mentioned a moment ago, David Griffin, has argued that God is limited in the sense that he is seeking to 'persuade' the creation towards the good purposes that he desires to see actualised.[86] Griffin's theodicy proceeds from a method which looks at the situation in reality and then uses such observations to construct a particular conception of God. Or rather, Griffin is not seeking to 'defend' the concept of a wholly omnipotent, all-loving, personal God, but rather, he is allowing his own perception of the realities of existence to dictate his picture of God. Following such a methodology means that we have effectively dissolved the problem of evil by adjusting our view of the divine in order to make God a co-sufferer in the universe. Nevertheless, it does appear that such views only affirm the strength of Hume's challenge and succumb to it simply because one has adjusted one's view of God in honour of Hume's victory.

Alternatively, as we saw in chapter two, Hick undertakes a different strategy and prefers to uphold the view that God is limitlessly good and limitlessly powerful. Hick's theodicy has a significant starting point. He writes:

> Much depends, in the formation and criticism of theodicies, upon whether one starts from the pressing fact of evil in its many forms, and proceeds from this to develop a conception of God; or starts from a conviction as to the reality and goodness of God, derived from the stream of religious experience of which one is a part, and then asks whether the grim reality of evil is compatible with this.[87]

Hick prefers the latter approach. But if he upholds the view that God is limitlessly good and powerful he cannot, he thinks, construct an adequate theodicy whilst restricting the human story to a single lifetime on earth. If he wanted to do that then perhaps he would have to somehow postulate a limit to divine fiat. So, in order to uphold the view that God is limitlessly good and powerful, we have seen that he opts for the only strategy that he sees as open to him - to extend the human journey beyond death.

As we saw in chapter two, he suggests that God has created a world in which there is authentic freedom which facilitates an environment where souls can proceed freely towards salvation. This world is a 'vale of soul-making' where the various evils and afflictions that beset life are seen as somehow perfecting and moulding souls into God's likeness (*similitudo dei*). However, this perfecting process is rarely completed in a single lifetime. Thus, Hick suggests an eschatological resolution. He proposes that the human journey continues after death where there are further experiences and opportunities to be had which eventually bear good fruit and culminate in an experience of a limitlessly good end which renders all the preceding suffering to be justified.[88] Unlike other contemporary thinkers, Hick is committed to a realist conception of life after death which means that he is not restricted to this present life when seeking out solutions to the theological problems of existence.

Now, let us turn to the problem of religious diversity. Firstly, let me employ the *form* of Hume's challenge in this context:

> Is the divine 'Christian' only? then what about other religions? Has the divine revealed itself only in Christianity? then what about comparable religious experience elsewhere? If there are other religions and religious experiences comparable to the Christian experience then the divine cannot only be 'Christian' and in fact the Christian God as traditionally conceived does not realistically exist.

This problem is addressed in a different manner by Hick. He feels that he can no longer say that the Christian conception of God is literally true and has revised and extended his picture of ultimate reality. Furthermore, as we alluded to earlier, Hick suggests that as people progress beyond death towards union with Reality they will become increasingly aware that the divine was very inadequately represented by the particular tradition that they had followed.[89]

So, there is, I suggest, a *prima facie* difference in the way Hick has approached evil and the way he has tackled religious pluralism. In the former, he did not tamper with traditional images of God and in fact sought to preserve them. In the latter, he has pressed us to make adjustments to our assumptions concerning the particularity of the Christian revelation about God. The basic point is that he has not played his eschatological trump-card in the same way. But here is the core of the issue: We saw above that Hick rejected an approach to evil which sought first to evaluate and assess the realities of existence and then proceed to construct a conception of God. Instead, he preferred to follow a methodology which first assumed a particular conception of God and then sought to compatibilise the realities of our world with that conception. The reverse is true when he deals with the reality of religious diversity. That is, Hick's pluralistic hypothesis has not resulted from him receiving divine revelation as to its truth (the hypothesis itself does not allow this), rather, his hypothesis has stemmed from the cognitive and experiential pressures of a religiously diverse world. The point made a moment ago was that the problem of evil is only a problem if there is some ultimately good and powerful being to be reconciled with evil in the world. It ceases to be a problem if we shrink the divine down to a contingent size. Of course, it is important to note that we are not denying that evil and suffering are terrible things, but that the *problem* of evil is usually framed in the context of trying to compatibilise the notion of an all-loving, all-powerful God with the existence of evil. Similarly, despite the seeming affirmation of the diversity of religions within the structure of Hick's hypothesis, it appears that these diversities are overlooked by the hypothesis with its basic proposal that all religions are in fact equally in communion with the same absolute, there is no real diversity at the most fundamental levels (even if we grant that rich diversity exists at the phenomenal level). Although we have to be careful about oversimplifying the issues, it appears that it is no longer a question of trying to reconcile the truth-claims of a particular faith with the fact of religious diversity, but a denial that such truth-claims (which seem to constitute the real differences) have any significant weight or *depth* to them.

One obvious complaint against this procedure here would be to say that one is unfairly moulding the problem of religious diversity into the image of the problem of evil in order to make a critical point. There is a difference in Hick's treatment in these spheres simply because they are different problems. However, is this clearly the case? There are a number of likenesses that might lead us to adopt a similar methodology. If we look at both problems we can see that they are equally capable of presenting very searching and serious questions to faith. The two problems are in fact very much alike in the sense that they both level the charge that there are experiential and cognitive difficulties against holding certain beliefs. The presence of evil and suffering represents a profound challenge to our assumptions about the nature of God, it disquiets us whenever we come to meditate on the goodness of God or God's alleged benevolent purposes for humankind. Moreover, it can facilitate a prevention or undermining of faith in the sense that it initiates deep confusions and uncertainties. However, the challenge - 'In light of these contradictory phenomena, can you keep your view of God intact?'- is not only applicable in the area of evil and suffering; it surely covers all areas that seem to put in jeopardy a total commitment to one's faith.[90] After being firmly committed to the revelation of one particular faith (like Job), the person is made uneasy by conflicting claims from other traditions. Such things threaten to undermine the conviction that something with universal and decisive finality has been directly touched within the revelation of one's faith. A prominent researcher into religious experience, David Hay, made the following interesting empirical observations about religious experience: '...religious experience is not the same thing as pious uplift or emotional self-indulgence or, I would add, beautiful rhetoric; *it is much more like a direct confrontation with reality.*'[91] Given this, is it possible that the existence of other religions with alternative claims about reality present just as powerful a critique of 'totally committed faith' as does the existence of starving children?

W. Cantwell Smith, although persuaded by a pluralistic ideal similar to Hick's, said that 'religious diversity poses a general human problem because it disrupts community'.[92] However, it does much more than that. It does not just impinge at the social level but penetrates into the individual. It can be a religious crisis for the individual and disrupts certainty in faith. It raises questions that go deeper than the problems of social harmony within diversity; it intrudes at the deepest level - the human thirst for the absolute. So, it may be that the phenomenon of religious diversity presents difficulties for those people who have accepted a 'total life-stance.'[93] For people who place a high premium on their faith being somewhat more than *mythologically* true, the present pluralistic situation represents nothing less than a crisis. In this connection, C. Gillis asks: 'Yet is it not important for the believer to consider definitive or absolute the revelation known to him or her, in order to be capable of total commitment?'[94] If the answer to Gillis' query is Yes, then a world which contains a plurality of incompatible truth-claims possesses the real potential to challenge the very roots of such total commitment. Thus, is it possible to argue that the fact of conflicting truth-claims is all part of the deep uncertainty and confusion that *assails* faith in our world? P. Tillich wrote that 'the deep things must concern us always, because it matters infinitely whether we are grasped by them or not'.[95] This evokes something unconditional, or something that concerns us ultimately. In a theistic context, J.V. Taylor is speaking similarly when he writes: 'Every profoundly convincing encounter with God is with a jealous God...the meaning of things conveyed by such an experience is of such moment that it must be seen to have universal relevance, and to deny this is to be false to the experience itself.'[96]

Flew railed against the seemingly incomprehensible stubbornness of religious belief. Unfortunately, Flew might have to live with such irritations because it is this *stubbornness* that may authentically characterise the human religious experience when it is sincerely felt that something absolutely real has been encountered. In the context of religious pluralism, by seeking to overrule such stubbornness because of a pluralistic agenda we may be denying some of the most striking qualities of the religious quest.

So, despite its careful accommodation of different religious pictures, is it possible that Hick's pluralistic hypothesis can result in a kind of religious disappointment? Let me offer an analogy. Imagine a young child who writes a letter to the British Queen and receives a reply. She is overwhelmed and awestruck that Her Majesty has seen fit to reply to her letter and proudly shows all her family and friends. However, her parents break the news to her that the reply was in fact written by a Lady-in-Waiting, and not by the Queen personally. There follows the inevitable disappointment on the child's part who genuinely hoped and believed that she had actually corresponded with the Queen herself.

Similarly, imagine the effect on the person who, fully committed to his/her faith, is informed by Hick's hypothesis that s/he is not in direct communion with Reality but with one of its many faces. The pluralistic hypothesis maintains that people are unable to enter into unmediated communion with the divine but can only project their own cultural image upon it. My point is that such assertions lead to a feeling of spiritual disappointment. Here, once again, there are echoes of Tillich when he wrote: 'Why have men always asked for the truth? Is it because they have been disappointed with the surfaces, and have known that the truth which does not disappoint dwells below the surfaces in the depth?'[97] So, it could be suggested that the actual existence of a religiously diverse world threatens the need that something absolute and *definitive* with universal (rather than 'local') significance can be contacted by an individual.

Take the following statement: 'I have trouble believing that God is good because of all the suffering and evil in the world.' What if we replied to this statement like this: 'Indeed, you have good cause for concern. Such things evident in our world should persuade us towards broadening our view of the divine as "good" but also possessive of occasional psychotic tendencies.' In what way would we have been sympathetic to such fears? In summary, it is possible that saying

> I have trouble holding fast to my particular faith because of the claims of other religions.

is qualitatively the same kind of thing as saying:

> I have trouble believing that God is good because of all the evil and suffering in the world.

That is, they are both statements stemming from a deep anxiety regarding our convictions about God because of seemingly contradictory data. More importantly, it seems possible that in both cases the challenge is to tackle the problem whilst keeping a particular conception of God intact.

So, what if Hick had followed the same methodology as he did with the problem of evil? That is, how could he keep a particular conception of God 'intact' in light of conflicting truth-claims and yet still retain some kind of moral coherence? It is possible that there is a door open if we return to the notion of eschatological resolution. Here we can recall Hick and his idea of further opportunities beyond death. What might be proposed is that following death it will become apparent that, say, one particular faith (not necessarily Christianity) was the most faithful representation of ultimate reality. But, utilising Hick's idea of further development beyond death, we could say that such vindication of that particular faith will not serve as a kind of indictment against people who held different beliefs during this present existence. This is perhaps the advantage of rejecting the reductionist view which denies the continuity of the person beyond death. Given the existence of an afterlife there are thus many more opportunities to solve problems that cannot be adequately addressed if we say that this present life is the only one.

Looking at things eschatologically, it is not easy to detect much experiential difference between Hick's eschatological proposals and my suggestions. Focusing on such experiential considerations, let us remember from chapter four the actual experiences of people, of a variety of faiths, in Hick's pareschaton. He argues that in the immediate post-mortem world, persons from the various faiths may encounter the figures or experiences of their different eschatological expectations. However, as their journey proceeds, they will become aware of a much bigger picture; that is, they will recognise that behind their religious conceptions there is a common Reality which has manifested itself through these conceptions.[98] What are their impressions upon realising this? Maybe they will feel that they were mistaken in their beliefs, particularly if they believed that their religion was normative - that is, it possessed the real, all-encompassing truth about reality; only to realise that theirs is just a part of a much larger and more comprehensive whole. So there is the possible sense that they will be found to be wrong, and that they must somehow come to terms with something which widely differs from their expectations. Now, the question I pose is: is this possible scenario any different, in effect, if one says that eventually it will be found that just one tradition was right and the others considerably mistaken? If Hick's pluralistic hypothesis says that all adherents to the various religions will eventually come to acknowledge something different from their own individual expectations, then the idea that just one of the great faiths will turn out to be a truer picture of reality suggests, in effect or *experience*, nothing substantially different from it.[99] As I see it, the only real difference is that the nature of Reality will have been found to be faithfully represented by just one of the traditions, rather than by something that transcends them all. The notion of there being further opportunities beyond death means that a large part of humanity do not get passed over. So, if this is the case, does not this important feature go a long way to providing a satisfactory outcome? Is it really *experientially* different from Hick's proposals after all?

Should Hick's Pluralistic Hypothesis Become a 'First-Order Discourse'?

Some recent criticisms of Hick's pluralistic hypothesis have stemmed from postmodernist perspectives.[100] Is Hick's pluralism a product of the European Enlightenment, or rather is it 'liberal modern' thinking? The dominating feature of Enlightenment thinking was its tendency to eschew particularities and seek to find the universals behind them. For example, Kant argued that behind all the different religions there was a universal (true) religion based on reason. It is this confidence in a universal human reason that many postmodernists have identified to be at the root of Western intellectual imperialism in the modern world. *Post*-modernists seek to eliminate what they see as the tyranny of western 'reason', or what is generically called the *grand metanarrative*, and re-affirm the multitude of different discourses (or 'ways of being') in the world. Thus, there are many truths set in different contexts rather than one overall 'truth' that encompasses all contexts.

Ostensibly, it might seem that Hick's theory sounds pretty postmodern in that it also affirms the validity (on a mythological level) of the various 'truths' within the different religions. Moreover, the idea that the various religious truth-claims might be envisaged as 'relative', or contextually formed and influenced, is certainly something that Hick seems to espouse. On the other hand, Hick's pluralism is not really postmodern because it does seek to provide an *overall* explanation and hypothesis concerning religious diversity. In this sense, Hick is providing his own grand metanarrative (which is terribly *un*-postmodern!). So, Hick finds himself caught between critics who accuse him of denying the possibility of absolute religious claims and reducing them all down to a relative status, and (postmodern) critics who accuse him of proposing a modernist or absolutist metanarrative that eliminates real diversity, relativity and difference!

There is, what might be called, a postmodern 'hermeneutic of suspicion' which perceives all *global* endeavours as a western homogenising imposition on the rest of the world. One critic, Kenneth Surin, uses McDonald's hamburger as a symbol of the effects of globalisation which is associated with vast international corporations, global media and powerful image-makers who are sweeping the globe and bringing about global conformity at the service of capitalist magnates.[101] Religious pluralism can be seen to be a part of a 'global ideology' which reinforces the homogenising effects of globalisation, it sweeps away differences and 'local' traditions in favour of a theological or philosophical universalism.

It is certainly true that Hick's religious pluralism takes a global perspective. His preferred methodology is one which does not restrict theological reflection to one tradition alone, but rather seeks to draw resources and inspiration from all traditions across the globe. His interpretation of religion endeavours to take into consideration all the varieties of religious thought and experience and thus present a global hypothesis or framework. However, to portray Hick's pluralism as being a co-conspirator with globalising multinationals is a little far-fetched! It may be that his pluralism has been developed at roughly the same time that powerful forces are influencing the entire globe, but it is important to remember that the reasons (or intentions) for their emergence are different. Hick's interpretation of religion is a 'religious [rather than naturalistic, scientific or political] interpretation',[102] that is, one might say that its realm of discourse is within the concerns of religions themselves. Hick is not motivated by the same ideals as 'western intellectual imperialism'. Rather, arising from the experience of encounter, he has asked honest questions about the co-existence of different religious claims and sought to provide an explanatory hypothesis in response.

Nevertheless, even if Hick's intentions are honourable, some critics have suggested that his hypothesis has the effect of overriding the self-interpretations of the religions themselves. That is, there is another agenda - a pluralistic one - that is being superimposed on the various religions. For example, H. Netland writes:

> Hick's treatment of various beliefs is frequently reductionistic and he freely reinterprets troublesome doctrines so as to accommodate them within his theory. But to the extent that major religious traditions do not find their beliefs - as they are understood within the respective traditions - adequately accounted for on Hick's analysis, his theory is called into question.[103]

Netland's point certainly appears to be well-made when we take the Christian idea of Jesus as God incarnate into account. We saw a moment ago that Hick's reflections on religious plurality have played an important role in him reinterpreting this doctrine and its significance. However, a defender of Hick, S. Twiss, has pointed out that Netland's criticism fails to properly recognise Hick's hypothesis as an explanatory hypothesis rather than a reductionist one.[104] That is, Hick is actually seeking to leave religions as they are (their various discourses constitute *true myths* which orientate us appropriately towards the Real). His overall pluralistic perspective is, as we have said, a *meta*-theory which seeks to provide a second-order explanatory hypothesis. Nevertheless, his pluralistic views obviously do reduce the universal scope of the different religions. No longer are they pictures of the Real in itself, but are different *localised* pictures of the Real in its various manifestations. So, in the end Hick does admit that some change in the religions' self-interpretations is inevitable, he writes: 'we really do have to make a choice between a one-tradition absolutism and a genuinely pluralistic interpretation of the global religious situation'.[105]

Paradoxically, this last point raises questions about the nature of Hick's hypothesis itself. Is his hypothesis a 'genuinely pluralistic interpretation' at all? Or is it an absolutising 'tradition' itself? This is another way of putting the postmodernist questions. The point is that Hick cannot claim that his hypothesis is an *overall* explanation of the data, because he himself is bound by a perspective. Again, Gavin D'Costa claims that Hick's hypothesis, far from being the neutral exercise it pretends to be, is a liberal western discourse in disguise. It is a direct descendent of the totalising agenda of the European Enlightenment. In fact, all the positions we take are 'tradition-specific', no one steps into a realm of neutrality; or else, no one is truly pluralistic - we are all exclusivists really, says D'Costa.[106] We might add that it seems that Hick is claiming to be able to see the whole picture (whilst the individual religions' cannot), and yet his hypothesis itself suggests that we cannot see things as they really are (*noumena*), but only as they appear to us (*phenomena*). Surely his hypothesis is also bound by such restrictions and therefore, by self-definition, cannot be genuinely pluralistic - no one sees the overall picture (things as they really are).

It is important to note that Hick does not see his pluralistic hypothesis as speaking from some neutral vantage point. He does not claim to sit on a mountain top overlooking the various religions. For example, if we look at the salvation/liberation criterion of his hypothesis, we might suppose that Hick had arrived at some neutral ethical ground and then sought to superimpose it on the world's religions; but this is just the kind of methodology that he claims *not* to have followed. Instead he has reflected from the ground upwards, so to speak; that is, he has sought to look (as a Christian) at the world's religious experience and has extrapolated from it. Thus the salvation/liberation criterion:

is a basic moral insight which Christians have received from Christian teachings, Hindus from Hindu teachings, Buddhists from Buddhist teachings, and so on. And within the terms of the pluralistic hypothesis this criterion represents the basic moral consensus of all the great world faiths.[107]

Nevertheless, in referring to his hypothesis as a 'second-order' philosophical exercise or a meta-theory, there is a sense that Hick is trying to give his hypothesis a certain immunity, and this suggests that by being a meta-theory one is occupying some sterile region which is somewhat indicative of a 'neutral vantage point' after all. But, laying this aside, is Hick's description of his pluralistic hypothesis as a second-order philosophical hypothesis *religiously* satisfactory? Might it be suggested that his hypothesis could be more effective if it fully acknowledged itself as a first-order discourse? That is, if Hick's hypothesis is to have any effect in the religious sphere it must surely talk the same kind of language: there must be some kind of passionate concern rather than an aloof abstraction?

What could an appropriate attitude be towards the pluralistic landscape? Or else, is there an authentically religious attitude that we might identify? This seeking for an appropriate attitude is comparatively paralleled in B. Williams' discussion of morality in his little book, *Morality* (1972). When speaking critically about relativistic morality, Williams calls attention to the concessionary-type arguments that are often presented for adopting a relativist, or neutral, point of view in ethics and claims that they have little affinity with the nature of moral impulses. He argues that moral arguments are unlike, say, scientific or historical arguments. For example, two distinguished scientists may disagree about the explanation of a particular phenomenon and as they respect each other's achievements and abilities they may conclude that the matter is uncertain and therefore a final judgement should be suspended until further evidence is uncovered. Similarly, an ethical relativist might argue that where two people (or cultures) disagree on an ethical point one should suspend judgement as to the 'truth'. But this attitude, claims Williams, does not lend itself to morality:

> [F]or the vital difference is that the disagreement in *morality* [as opposed to factual knowledge] involves what should be done, and involves, on each side, caring about what happens; and once you see this difference, you see equally that it could not possibly be a requirement of rationality that you should stop caring about those things because someone disagrees with you.[108]

Notice that Williams is suggesting a degree of feeling (care) in ethics that removes it from a purely rational (or scientific) arena. It is possible that religious *cares* are made of similar stuff, that is - 'I care what I believe.' Moreover, because there is a 'care' about such things they cannot be classified as merely 'notional' assents; as with morality, we cannot cease to care about what we believe because there are other people who believe (and care about) quite contrary things. However, what those others could do - and perhaps this is the only really viable methodology - is to somehow get me to care about what they believe. Perhaps this is a more appropriately *religious* attitude towards interreligious dialogue? And there is something further: the necessity to passionately engage others in your religious perspective surely applies to the pluralist also? That is, the pluralist must somehow get us to care about his/her vision; the pluralist vision must appeal at the deepest level of religious experience. However, if we conclude that such an 'involved' approach to the pluralistic landscape is desirable, then there arises the paradoxical question of whether it engenders an attitude which is (or should be) contrary to the pluralist's (and Hick's in particular) disposition.

Hick's interpretation of religion is a religious (as opposed to naturalistic) interpretation. Given this religious concern, perhaps he could allow his pluralistic hypothesis to make what might be called a first-order religious appeal. For example, he might speak *religiously* of a sense of the 'numinous' in all faiths. Perhaps, some of the following statements seem to contain elements which illustrate this 'sense' or concern. With regard to an emerging new religious consciousness, E. Cousins writes: 'Many, especially the younger generations, are beginning to feel their primary relatedness not to their nation or culture, but to the human community as a whole.'[109] In somewhat more complex language, W. Nicholls suggests that the effect of living in a multicultural society is giving rise to an 'awareness' of global unity when he writes: '[T]he modern recognition of cultural relativity may serve to open the door for a transcendental awareness of one's own relativity.'[110] Again, Cousins encourages us not to underestimate the importance of this new global 'feel' in present society for: 'There is reason to think that the creative development of global spirituality, through interreligious dialogue, is the distinctive spiritual journey of our time.'[111] What is noticeable about some of these selected quotes (whether intended by the authors or not) is that it is as if the possible ingredients of a distinctive 'global faith' are being hinted at: A *'transcendental awareness'*; a *'distinctive spiritual journey'*. Might we say that there is a certain spiritual excitement going on here? That is, we can speak with a feeling for pluralism and we are, perhaps, beginning to enter into a 'religious sense' Such a pluralistic vision of a global spirituality might thus be presented religiously as a truth worth *caring* about. Nevertheless, before we have even begun pursuing such notions we must call a halt and ask:

Would it be wise for someone anxious to deny the exclusive claims of religions in order to facilitate the equal validity of all to talk of a pluralistic *spirituality?* It could be argued that such talk actually hinders the objective of Hick's pluralist theology of religions. Why? Because it is creating a new dogma to rival the older ones, and it would seem that the aim of an authentically pluralist view of religions is to downplay the dogmatic and adopt an approach that underlines the equal validity of all. If the pluralistic view becomes a mission to awaken some kind of global spirituality then it has pulled the carpet from beneath its feet, so to speak. That is, it cannot speak *for itself.* It does appear, therefore, that Hick could face a peculiar dilemma: he may feel a sense of inspiration in 'apprehending' a unity of world faiths (and here I mean something more than an academic enthusiasm for comparative studies) but, in order to accord with the spirit of his pluralism as a meta-theory or second-order philosophical exercise, this must stop short of passion because it is this passion that has been responsible, it would appear, for the friction between different faiths.[112] The moment we become passionate about our particular vision we inevitably begin to talk of the 'truth' of our stance. A prominent writer on interfaith dialogue, M. Braybrooke, describes the interfaith vision as that thing which '[being] awakened to a unity that transcends religious divisions has been called a "second conversion"'[113] But such language has difficulties within a pluralist philosophy of religions which is committed to creating an air of neutrality. Paradoxically, enthusiasm for pluralism can only risk the possibility of betraying it as making claims for itself, especially if there is an awakening that almost amounts to a 'conversion'.

Here, we are tending to concentrate chiefly on the pluralist perspective as a theology or *spirituality* of religions rather than a *philosophical* theory *about* religion, but it is the latter that Hick defines his hypothesis as. Whereas the former might imply the construction of satisfactory spiritual (and/or practical) responses to the reality of religious diversity, the latter seems to indicate a measure of disengagement or detachment. Such a distinction ought to be made and Hick is keen to point this out when claims that pluralism is 'just another tradition' are made. It may be that adopting pluralism as no more than a philosophical theory about religion represents the only way that pluralism can avoid becoming a 'first-order' view in its own right. Or else, we might similarly suggest that the pluralist advocating Hick's pluralism should speak only of a 'notional assent' to a pluralistic reality. (By 'notional assent' I mean the mere acknowledgement of a fact or state of affairs that has no corresponding life-changing effect). S/he would be ill-advised to attempt to *excite* us about it. Hick's (somewhat magnified) Kantian structure allows us no more than a notional assent to a Real which transcends its multifarious cultural representations. We might contrast such notionality with the real commitments offered to the fleshed-out particularities (of ultimate reality) evident in the various faiths. That Hick intends this to be the case is brought out by the fact that he does not appear to be seeking to inaugurate a 'global faith' as such; he is content to remain within his own tradition whilst appreciating the spiritual beauties contained in others.[114] He is not advocating 'a world-wide uniformity'.[115] We might crudely characterise Hick's position as: 'Stay put in whatever (salvific) faith you belong to, but keep one eye on the other faiths because they are your (equally legitimate) fellow travellers towards the Ultimate.'

Ostensibly then, it appears that Hick comes close to proposing that religious people (of whatever persuasion) should offer what is little more than a notional assent to the equal validity of other faiths, or the 'bigger picture'. However, to re-phrase the question earlier: is a purely notional assent possible as an effective response to religious diversity? Or more importantly, if a pluralist view seeks to change things, can it adequately speak to the religious mind at a purely notional level?[116] Hick does not just want us to remain unaffected by his pluralist perspective on religion. What would be the point of that? What is required is an inner spiritual change of perception in each of the conflicting faiths - a religious sense that there is something real and true to be grasped in a plural vision; (indeed, Braybrooke was right to speak of a 'second conversion'). Hick would probably acknowledge the futility of seeking only to whet the philosophical/notional appetite with his pluralistic proposals. Religious enquiry is concerned with inner-application: 'what does it mean for me?'; 'who or what am I?'; 'shall I survive death?'; 'how will my mind be transformed?'

As we saw in chapter one, when addressing the rationality of religious belief, Hick maintains that a mere notional assent (to a proof of the existence of God) is not sufficient to provoke what could be characterised as a truly 'religious' reaction. It is a religious reaction that 'turns what would be a purely abstract conclusion into an immensely significant and moving fact'.[117] This seems to imply, (in the context of making the pluralistic vision meaningful), that some sort of spiritual shift is required within each religion, that is, something that takes us beyond the purely philosophical acknowledgement of the 'bigger picture' and into an affirmation of pluralism as an 'immensely significant and moving fact'. Moreover, Hick has also said: 'In order to render a distinctive style of life both attractive and rational religious beliefs must be regarded as assertions of fact, not merely as imaginative fictions'.[118] If this is true then it is clear that the pluralist perspective cannot be content to state nothing *substantial* about the religious landscape; it cannot occupy what might be called a 'thin air position'. Hick of all people understands that if it doesn't make a difference whether the pluralist view is true then it is cognitively vacuous. But in the quote above, Hick is not just making an academic point about religious language, he is really suggesting that in terms of religious significance a non-cognitive position would be 'unattractive'. His own religious inclinations tell him that there must be a reality behind religious experiences and propositions to bestow a truly religious significance. And so this is the crux: if religious pluralism is to make religious sense - and to effect some sort of inner change - then it must somehow be *immensely significant, moving, rational and attractive*. The whole idea of pluralism occupying a kind of second-order philosophical region is religiously impotent. Those 'second-order' philosophical shoes will have to be removed if we are to step into the pluralist vision with religious feeling. Hick clearly wants the pluralist vision to have a significant impact, he does not think that the religions with their various dogmas can go unchallenged or unaltered in light of a positive acknowledgement of other faiths: he speaks of 'a positive mutual enrichment'.[119] This is, of course, something that represents a welcome and beneficial development and need not necessarily lead us in the direction of Hick's pluralistic hypothesis. But, for Hick, if the pluralist vision is embraced wholeheartedly then it is probable that each religion will 'de-emphasise that aspect of its teaching which entails its own unique superiority'.[120] Hick also envisions, to a certain extent (but not in terms of a 'convergence'), a move towards what could be labelled a 'global' liturgy. In the book, *The Rainbow of Faiths* (1995), he sets forth his 'vision' for 2056 thus:

> In those sections of the universal church in which the pluralistic vision has become established, worship is explicitly directed to God, rather than to Jesus, or to the Virgin Mary or the saints. This has been the result of a continual process of liturgical revision.[121]

Intentionally or not, is it possible that Hick's speculative picture represents a state of affairs which will eventually progress, towards the emergence of a global faith? Perhaps, beyond the year 2056, Jalaludin Rumi's famous adage: 'The lamps are different, but the Light is the same'[122] will assume a *positive* significance - maybe even a 'creedal' tone? Alternatively, it could be maintained that a global trend towards spiritual unity does not actually constitute a distinctive global faith, but merely represents the intention to draw religions together in a meaningful interactive dialogue. Nevertheless (as I have somewhat already argued), I would contend that a 'vision' of religious significance has to be provided to motivate this. Moreover, such a vision, if it is to be effective, cannot operate *incognito*: Rumi' s 'Light' has to be held aloft in order for the various 'lamps' to recognise it as their own origin and source.

Here one is not taking issue with Hick's endeavours to persuade us towards a perspective where all religions are somehow taken up into a global spirituality and vision. Moreover, we should have no complaint about someone who feels this *deeply*, or finds such a possibility 'immensely significant and moving' and seeks to develop a full-blown pluralist theology of religions. Furthermore, it is this that makes the most religious sense: If the pluralistic vision is said to be free of dogma or a passionate commitment to 'truth', that is, if its tenets don't matter - then I don't know if we ought to become excited about it. But then, in a sense, religious beliefs should be very exciting, or else there is little use for them. However, if Hick is to excite us or give us a passion for his vision then he must relinquish the notion that it somehow occupies an abstract philosophical place.

Thus, paradoxically, it seems possible to argue that if Hick's pluralist vision is to become religiously feasible then it may have to re-position itself into being a first-order discourse. Is such a move possible? Perhaps Hick could urge us to see things in a global perspective without striving for neutrality and argue that his is a fairer, or more likely, vision. But then, if this were the case it would have to take its place alongside other competing faiths - and this might contradict its purpose.

Summary

Hick's commitment to rigorous religious and philosophical reflection (in light of all the available evidence) made it inevitable that he would eventually turn his attention to the *global* experience of religion. For Hick, the philosophy of religion should be just that - the philosophy of *religion* rather than just the Judeo-Christian tradition. So, with his pluralistic hypothesis, Hick has expanded beyond his initial philosophical work that was rooted within a largely Christian discourse. This does not mean that Hick has sought to overrule his previous work in religious language, the problem of evil or life after death, but instead he has qualified it. Such qualifications reflect his Kantian-inspired epistemology with its distinction between the noumenal and phenomenal world. Hick is committed to *critical realism*. That is, he thinks that we can talk of objects that exist independently of our minds (our language refers to something that actually exists); nevertheless, such things are filtered through our conceptual apparatus and experience. Thus (echoing Kant), in the religious sphere, there is a distinction to be made between the Real in itself and the Real in its various phenomenal manifestations. Our human discourse about the

Real is not literally true of the Real in itself, instead it is mythologically true. Hick's previous work is affected by this qualification, such that his Irenaean theodicy is perceived as a 'true myth' which engenders an appropriate attitude towards the Real in itself without involving a literal ascription (like the 'divine parent') to the Real in itself. Critics have sought to interrogate this, for example claiming that the Real has to be defined more concretely as 'personal' or 'impersonal'. Hick has also developed his understanding of religious truth and cognitivity. Religious statements are not true because they literally correspond to reality, rather they are 'true' because they engender an appropriate ethical disposition. Such a soteriological criterion is gleaned from the moral teachings of all the major world faiths. Nevertheless, much criticism of Hick's pluralism has centred on the alleged incompatibilities of his commitment to the cognitive (or realist) character of religious belief and the 'realocentric' ontology of his later writings. The division between the phenomenal reality and its noumenal ground, between mythology and literality, seems to have stretched Hick's critical realism to breaking point. Or else, one might say that Hick's terminology has become broader and more inclusive. He has moved away from what might be called a detailed or 'particular' cognitivity and towards a more general or broad cognivity. For example, rather than expecting the literal Kingdom of Christ, or the Buddhist *Nirvana*, one is expecting a 'limitlessly good fulfilment' to human existence. It is the general, rather than the particular, expectations that will be 'verified' in the eschaton.

Questions might also be raised about the success of Hick's hypothesis in a postmodern intellectual climate. Hick's religious pluralism goes against the grain by seeking to be comprehensive rather than tradition-specific. It is a liberal rather than conservative vision. However, to some extent, criticism of Hick's hypothesis from this angle will only reflect current theological fads and allegiances. Nevertheless, a basic concern might be that Hick's theory seeks to adopt a neutral stance. From a postmodern perspective (with its emphasis on many different 'truths' rather than one overall truth), this is impossible, we cannot help being bound within our own modes of discourse. Even without the postmodern critique, the claim to neutrality seems an imperialistic imposition made all the worse because it is a position denied to the religions themselves. In response, Hick does not claim to stand in superior judgement over the religious landscape, his criteria (like salvation/liberation) are drawn from the religions themselves. However, his hypothesis does seem to contain a certain claim to neutrality because he has characterised it as a second-order philosophical exercise, a meta-theory which reflects on religious diversity and offers an explanation of the data. Such a characterisation might lead to further questions about the religious effectiveness of his hypothesis. Moreover, what is the end-game of Hick's hypothesis? Does it seek to change people in their attitudes towards other religions (and their own)? If so, can it remain as a meta-theory, or is it time for pluralists like Hick to speak in more first-order terms?

This is a truly ambitious project that Hick has mapped out, and his work represents probably the most systematic and thorough attempt at constructing a harmonious pluralistic model in western thought. In light of this, perhaps the challenge for Hick's future critics is not to find more ingenious ways of demolishing his proposals, rather it is to construct hypotheses of equal calibre.

Notes

1. Hick, *An Interpretation of Religion*, p.1.
2. M. Eliade, *Patterns in Comparative Religion*, p.xi, cited in *An Interpretation of Religion*, p.15.
3. See Hick, 'The Possibility of the Religious Pluralism: A Reply to Gavin D'Costa'.
4. Hick, *God Has Many Names,* p.3.
5. Hick, *The Rainbow of Faiths*, p.13.
6. For Karl Barth ('Barthian'), knowledge of God depended on the divine initiative rather than human action. Thus, he paints a picture using the sun's light on the earth as an analogy of the divine freedom towards human beings: 'That the sun lights up this part of the earth and not that means for the earth no less than this, that day rules in one part and night in the other[...]Now it is in exactly the same way that the light of the righteousness and judgement of God falls upon the world of man's religion, upon one part of that world, upon the Christian religion, so that that religion is not in the night but in the day, it is perverted but straight, it is not false religion but true.' K. Barth, 'The Revelation of God as the Abolition of Religion' in *Church Dogmatics*, Vol.I, part 2, sec.17. Cited in B. Hebblethwaite and J. Hick, (eds.), *Christianity and Other Religions*, pp.50-51.
7. Matt. 7:16.
8. For the classic expression of this typology see Alan Race, *Christians and Religious Pluralism*.
9. Voices who have spoken against the paradigm include I. Markham, 'Creating Options: Shattering the "Exclusivist, Inclusivist, and Pluralist" Paradigm'; Gavin D'Costa, *The Meeting of Religions and the Trinity*. Hick defends the paradigm in his article 'The Possibility of Religious Pluralism: A Reply to Gavin D'Costa' op.cit., pp.161-163.
10. See Karl Rahner, 'Christianity and the Non-Christian Religions' in *Theological Investigations*, Vol.5.
11. A good example of this kind of approach is R. Panikkar, *The Unknown Christ of Hinduism*.
12. See Hick, 'The Copernican Revolution in Theology' in Hick, *God and the Universe of Faiths*, pp.121-132.
13. Ibid. p.131.
14. See *An Interpretation of Religion*, pp.9-11.
15. G. D'Costa, 'John Hick and Religious Pluralism: Yet Another Revolution' in H.

Hewitt, (ed.), *Problems in the Philosophy of Religion: Critical Studies of the Work of John Hick*, pp.4-5.

16. *An Interpretation*, p.373.
17. Ibid.
18. Ibid., p.246.
19. Hick uses this analogy in *The Rainbow of Faiths*, p.25.
20. Ibid.
21. See *An Interpretation*, pp.353-361 for a discussion of religion and mythology.
22. Ibid., p.353.
23. See Hick, 'Reply' in H. Hewitt, (ed.), op.cit., p.26.
24. See Part V of *An Interpretation* for an extended discussion of 'criteria'. Also, for a study of ethical criteria from an anthropological angle, see H. Meacock, *An Anthropological Approach to Theology: A Study of John Hick's Theology of Religious Pluralism towards Ethical Criteria for a Global Theology of Religions.*
25. Hick, *The Second Christianity*, pp.86-87.
26. Hick in H. Hewitt, op.cit., pp.24-25.
27. Ibid., p.24.
28. Hick, *Problems of Religious Pluralism*, p.100.
29. Ibid.,
30. Hick, *An Interpretation*, p.355.
31. Ibid., p.356.
32. Ibid., p.361.
33. Hick in H. Hewitt, op.cit., p.25.
34. Ibid., p.6.
35. Hick, *An Interpretation*, p.361.
36. D'Costa in H. Hewitt, op.cit., p.7. For further discussion, see also K. Rose, *Knowing the Real: John Hick on the Cognitivity of Religions and Religious Pluralism.*
37. Ibid.
38. Ibid., pp.7,8.
39. St. Thomas, *In librum De Causis* 6. Quoted by F.C. Coplestone, *Aquinas*, pp.131-2. Cited in Hick, *Rainbow of Faiths*, p.58.
40. *Yogava'sistha*, I, 28. V.L.Parrisikar (ed.), *Srimad-Valmiki-Maharsi-Pannitah Yogava'sistha*, I, p.144. Cited in Ibid, p.57.
41. *Tao Te Ching*, I, trans. Ch'u Ta-Kao, p.17. Cited in Hick, *An Interpretation*, p. 237.
42. G. D'Costa raises these issues in H. Hewitt, op.cit., p.10.
43. S. Mark Heim, 'The Pluralistic Hypothesis, Realism, and Post-Eschatology', p.212.
44. See Ibid., p.213.
45. Ibid. (Emphasis mine.)
46. Ibid.
47. There is a discussion of this in Hick, *An Interpretation*, pp.177-180.
48. This example is mentioned specifically in Hick, *The Rainbow of Faiths*, p.73.
49. Hick, *The Rainbow of Faiths*, p.75.
50. See J. Kellenberger, 'Critical Response' [to G. D'Costa] in H.Hewitt, op.cit., p.22.
51. Ibid.
52. See J. Lipner, 'At the Bend in the Road: A Story About Religious Pluralism' in H. Hewitt, op.cit., p.224ff.
53. Hick, *Problems of Religious Pluralism*, pp.97-98, Cited in Ibid., p.224. (Emphasis mine.)
54. Lipner, op.cit., p.224.
55. Ibid.
56. Ibid., pp.225-226.
57. See Hick, 'Reply' [to Lipner] in H. Hewitt, op.cit., p.243.

58. See Hick, *Evil and the God of Love*, pp.271-275.
59. See Ibid.
60. For example, Hick wrote: 'I think it is clear that a parent who loves his children, and wants them to become the best human beings they are capable of becoming, does not treat pleasure as the sole and supreme value.' Ibid., p.258. See also chapter three of this book.
61. Hick, *An Interpretation*, p.359. C. Robert Mesle takes issue with this, and thinks that such a statement severely undermines his theodicy: 'On this ground, he now views his entire theodicy as "mythically true" but not "literally true". Yet he still claims that there is that "assurance" that "all shall be well". How can there be such an assurance? How can immortality be mythically true if not literally true?' 'Humanism and Hick's Interpretation of Religion' in H. Hewitt, op.cit., pp.66-67. (I endorse Mesle's complaint further on in this section).
62. Hick, *An Interpretation*, p.359-60.
63. Hick, *The Rainbow of Faiths*, p.63.
64. David Griffin, 'Response' [to Hick's theodicy] in S. Davis, (ed.), *Encountering Evil*, p.54.
65. For example, Hick writes: 'But such evidence as there is has led historians of the period to conclude, with an impressive degree of unanimity, that Jesus did not claim to be God incarnate.' *The Metaphor of God Incarnate*, p.27.
66. Hick, *Disputed Questions in Theology and the Philosophy of Religion*, p.38.
67. Ibid.
68. See, for example, 'The Logic of God Incarnate' in Ibid., pp.58-76; or chapters 5-7 of *The Metaphor of God Incarnate*.
69. 'For to say, without explanation, that the historical Jesus of Nazareth was also God is as paradoxical as to say that this circle drawn with a pencil on paper is also a square.' Hick, 'Jesus and the World's Religions' in Hick, (ed.), *The Myth of God Incarnate*, p.178.
70. Maurice Wiles, 'A Survey of Issues in the *Myth* Debate', in M. Goulder, (ed.), *Incarnation and Myth: The Debate Continued*, p.6.
71. See, for example, Frank Weston, *The One Christ: An Enquiry into the Manner of the Incarnation*.
72. See Hick, *The Metaphor of God Incarnate*, esp. chapters 6 and 7.
73. Ibid., p.78.
74. See Hick, *Disputed Questions*, p.38.
75. Hick, *The Rainbow of Faiths*, p.87.
76. Hick, *The Metaphor of God Incarnate*, pp.162-163.
77. Ibid., p.98
78. See Brian Hebblethwaite, 'The Impossibility of Multiple Incarnations', p.324.
79. Hick, *The Metaphor of God Incarnate*, pp.91-92. Hick is responding to Hebblethwaite's views expressed in B. Hebblethwaite, *The Incarnation*, p.187.
80. Ibid., p.2.
81. B. Hebblethwaite, 'The Logical Coherence of the Doctrine of the Incarnation' in M. Goulder (ed.), op.cit., p.61.
82. Ibid.
83. Stephen Davis makes a similar point in a useful article entitled 'John Hick on Incarnation and Trinity' in S.T. Davis, D. Kendall, G. O'Collins (eds.), *The Trinity: An Interdisciplinary Symposium on the Trinity*. He observes that Hick happily brings together concepts such as 'God' and 'impersonal voidness' (Buddhism) in his theory of religion. That is, there is paradox and mystery in Hick's theory also. (See pp.260-261.)
84. See A. Flew 'Theology and Falsification' in A. Flew and A. MacIntyre, *New Essays in Philosophical Theology*. See also Chapter One of this book.

85. David Hume, *Dialogues Concerning Natural Religion*, pp.108-109.

86. See D. Griffin 'Creation out of Chaos and the Problem of Evil' in ed. S. Davis, op.cit., pp.101-119.

87. J. Hick, 'Hick's Response to Critiques' in S. Davis, op.cit., p.63.

88. See J. Hick, *Evil and the God of Love*.

89. See J. Hick, 'Reply' [to G. D'Costa] in H. Hewitt, op.cit., pp.24-25.

90. P. Griffiths in a discussion about epistemic confidence and religious diversity also observes that 'religious people do, sometimes, seem to be troubled, cognitively, by coming to know of religious diversity'. *Problems of Religious Diversity*, p.70.

91. D. Hay, *Religious Experience Today*, p.35. (Emphasis mine).

92. W. Cantwell Smith, 'The Christian in a Religiously Plural World' in J. Hick and B. Hebblethwaite (eds.), op.cit. p.94.

93. E.J. Sharpe describes such a 'total life stance' as 'a totally explicit set of values which affect everything, in this world and (in its own terms) beyond it'. *Understanding Religion*, p.27.

94. C. Gillis, 'An Interpretation of *An Interpretation of Religion*' in H. Hewitt, op.cit., p.40.

95. P. Tillich, *The Shaking of the Foundations*, p.67.

96. J.V.Taylor, 'The Theological Basis for Interfaith Dialogue' in Hick and Hebblethwaite (eds.) op.cit., p.225.

97. Tillich, op.cit., p.60.

98. See Hick, *Death and Eternal Life*, Part V - A Possible Human Destiny.

99. Note that an *experiential* point is being made. The experiential consequences seem to be roughly the *same* regardless of whether one is advocating Hick's pluralism or one-tradition absolutism.

100. See, for example, John V. Apczynski, 'John Hick's Theocentrism: Revolutionary or Implicitly Excusivist?'.

101. See K. Surin, 'A Certain "Politics of Speech": "Religious Pluralism" in an Age of McDonald's Hamburger'.

102. Hick, *An Interpretation of Religion*, p.1.

103. H. Netland, *Dissonant Voices: Religious Pluralism and the Question of Truth*, pp.221-222.

104. S. Twiss, 'The Philosophy of Religious Pluralism: A Critical Appraisal of Hick and His Critics', esp. pp.540-549. This article is an excellent defence of Hick against an assortment of his critics.

105. Hick, *The Rainbow of Faiths*, p.43.

106. See, G. D'Costa, *The Meeting of Religions and the Trinity*.

107. Hick, 'The Possibility of Religious Pluralism: A Reply to Gavin D'Costa', p.164.

108. B. Williams, *Morality*, p.48.

109. E. Cousins, in F. Whaling (ed.), *Religion in Today's World*, p.330.

110. W. Nicholls, in W. Nicholls (ed.), *Religion and Modernity*, p.177.

111. E. Cousins, op.cit., p.334.

112. That is, it is when incompatible truth-claims are held with passion - or as 'matters of life and death' - that disagreements become *real* rather than purely notional.

113. M. Braybrooke, 'Religious Studies and Interfaith Developments' in U. King (ed.), *Turning Points in Religious Studies*, p.140.

114. See in particular the closing remarks of Hick, 'A Personal Note' *Disputed Questions*, pp.144-145.

115. Hick, *The Second Christianity*, p.89.

116. For example, Braybrooke expresses the need for the pluralistic vision to have a significant influence: 'The hardest task of the interfaith movement is not to establish co-operation between some members of each religion, but to effect inner change within each religion.' Braybrooke, op.cit., p.141.

117. Hick, 'Rational Theistic Beliefs Without Proofs' in P. Badham (ed.), *A John Hick Reader*, p.54.
118. Hick, *Philosophy of Religion*, p.96.
119. Hick, *The Second Christianity*, p.90.
120. Hick, *The Rainbow of Faiths*, p.30.
121. Ibid., p.136.
122. R.A. Nicholson, *Rumi: Poet and Mystic*, p.166. Cited in Hick, *An Interpretation*, p.233.

Postscript

Hick's work has a provocative quality. It is very difficult to present an account of his thinking without offering some kind of engagement with it. This is something which, I hope, this book has illustrated. Moreover, it is this quality that will ensure that Hick's work continues to have an important role in the philosophy of religion. Hick's clarity of style is such that his work is accessible to a wide audience and this will extend his importance beyond a purely academic arena. Nevertheless, the future success of Hick's work will largely depend on the future of religious liberalism. Whilst powerful intellectual forces are persuading many towards postmodern or postliberal interpretations (e.g. Radical Orthodoxy), Hick is committed to a liberal vision which extends itself beyond 'tradition-specific' boundaries. Being a liberal, he borrows from many different disciplines: scientific, psychological, sociological, historical, philosophical and so on, and from all the major world faiths as well. His is a universal vision not content to stay within a carefully staked-out Christian discourse, but open to the whole world of religious experience. Additionally, his work seems to treat religious experience, including *revelatory* experience, as raw data in a journey towards truth. Thus, for Hick, truth results from a cumulative amassing of data and experience, it does not arrive like a bolt of lightning.

Some might argue that this desire by Hick to be comprehensive and universal in scope is indicative of a truly sincere religious quest. That is, in the best religious style, Hick has sought to find an answer to *all that there is*. Indeed, we have seen that this is his preferred perspective: one that sees religious faith as a free interpretation and experience of the world rather than the committed adherence to a definitive revelatory intervention. Others will see these same characteristics as the actual weaknesses in Hick's approach. He has 'cast off' from his Christian moorings and is adrift in a sea of different faiths and philosophies.

In 1991, Hick wrote that he was in sympathy with a theological movement 'which is theologically liberal, and yet conservative in its basic affirmation of the reality of God and of human immortality…'.[1] That is, his vision is one which is open to a vast range of religious possibilities, however he is also committed to a critically realist conception of religious language. But is it possible to be both of these things? Indeed, can it be maintained that his later views about ultimate reality are so empty of content that it is possible that he has undermined and weakened the case for critical realism? This same question was posed by the conservative thinker, Brian Hebblethwaite, who when reflecting on a conference which discussed 'realism vs. non-realism' wrote the following of Hick's contribution:

> Hick's pluralism, seeking to accommodate all forms of human experience of the transcendent, theistic and monistic, personal and impersonal, into a single global interpretation of religion, tended to erode the cognitive significance of religious experience. So much has to be conceded to the constructivists. So great was the consequent agnosticism about the ultimate or the "Real".[2]

In repositioning religious propositions to a mythological status can one begin to suspect that Hick has been travelling down a road that eventually leads to non-realism? Don Cupitt, a non-realist, uses language to describe religious discourse which is strikingly similar to Hick's own. For example, he writes: '...in our modern large scale and highly communicative societies there is no single grand overarching dogmatic truth any longer. All truths, beliefs, theories, faiths, perspectives become just individual stocks in the market. They rise and fall relative to each other as conditions change.'[3] Furthermore: 'Since we have given up ideas of absolute truth and error, we can look down other perspectives without prejudice. The anti-realist viewpoint has already made it possible for us to view other people's faiths more sympathetically and to enter into them more deeply, than in the past'.[4] Finally, '...the goal of the religious life is a spiritual state that is beyond all symbols'.[5] And yet, Cupitt is an 'atheist priest'. He has dispensed with belief in a reality that is independent of human imagining or language. The *later* Hick uses the same language when speaking of religious discourse and so it becomes hard to resist the temptation to re-classify Hick into the non-realist camp. It is perhaps this kind of continual philosophical journeying that has made it difficult for commentators to form a judgement concerning his influence and future legacy. That is, where is his theological constituency? Does he speak for those who embrace some sort of pluralist 'interfaith' religious persuasion? The answer would appear to be yes and no. For, although he would advocate a pluralistic perspective on a second-order philosophical level, he would eschew the idea of embracing a first-order confessional pluralism.

Setting aside his pluralism, the more theologically conservative will find much in Hick's early epistemological work on faith and knowledge, his contribution to Christian theodicy, his ideas on human immortality that can be supported. And yet, it is possible that conservatives in all religions will feel that the later religious pluralism in his work inevitably entails an unacceptable reinterpretation, or discarding, of important doctrines (for example, the Incarnation for Christians, or the finality of the Qur'an for Muslims). This is because Hick does not speak for those whose positions are already fixed, rather he will appeal to those who prefer to continue travelling.

As an intellectual traveller, Hick has changed in his attitudes to his own work. For example, from the point of view of *The Fifth Dimension* (1999), there is a sense that all that has gone before is not really very important. That is, the debates about such matters as a viable theodicy, or the nature of the resurrection body, or the characteristics of a disembodied world are largely irrelevant. Hick has come a long way. From now on, he thinks that we should operate on a 'need-to-know' basis only. And, for Hick, what we need to know are only those things that help us in our journey away from 'self' and towards a limitlessly good fulfilment for our lives.

> Going beyond questions about the origin and structure of the physical universe, we do not know what happens to us after death. *All that we know, if our big picture is basically correct, is that nothing good that has been created in human life will ever be lost* [...] We have our theories, but they are only theories.[6]

Notes

1. Hick, 'Reply' [to P. Badham and L Stafford Betty], in H. Hewitt, (ed.), *Problems in the Philosophy of Religion*, p.104.
2. B. Hebblethwaite, 'Reflections on Realism vs. Non-Realism', in J. Runzo, (ed.), *Is God Real?*, p.210.
3. D. Cupitt, 'Anti-Realist Faith', in J. Runzo, Ibid., p.48.
4. Ibid., p.53.
5. Ibid., p.54.
6. Hick, *The Fifth Dimension*, p.224. (Emphasis mine.)

Bibliography

John Hick

Faith and Knowledge (London: Macmillan, 1966), [1957].
'The Christology of D.M. Baillie' *Scottish Journal of Theology* 11/1, 1958.
'Theology and Verification' *Theology Today* 27/2, 1960.
'God as Necessary Being' *The Journal of Philosophy* 57/22-23, 1960.
'Necessary Being' *Scottish Journal of Theology* 14/4, 1961.
Philosophy of Religion (Englewood Cliffs: Prentice Hall, 1990) [1963].
(ed.), *Classical and Contemporary Readings in the Philosophy of Religion* (Englewood Cliffs: Prentice Hall, 1964).
(ed.), *Faith and the Philosophers* (London: Macmillan, 1964).
(ed.), *The Existence of God* (London: Macmillan, 1964).
Evil and the God of Love (New York: Harper & Row, 1978), [1966].
Christianity at the Centre (London: Macmillan, 1968).
'God, Evil and Mystery' *Religious Studies* 3/2, 1968.
'The Problem of Evil in the First and Last Things - Reply to I. Trethowan' *Journal of Theological Studies*, NS, 19/Pt. II, 1968.
'Freedom and the Irenaean Theodicy Again' *Journal of Theological Studies* 21/Pt. II, 1970.
Arguments for the Existence of God (London: Macmillan, 1971).
Biology and the Soul (Eddington Memorial Lecture: Cambridge University Press, 1972).
'Mr Clarke's Resurrection Also' *Sophia* 11/3, 1972.
God and the Universe of Faiths (London: Macmillan, 1988) [1973].
'Resurrection Worlds and Bodies' *Mind*, LXXXII/327, 1973.
'Coherence and the God of Love Again' *Journal of Theological Studies* 24/Pt. II, 1973.
(ed.), *Truth and Dialogue in World Religions: Conflicting Truth Claims* (Philadelphia: The Westminster Press, 1974).
Death and Eternal Life (London: Macmillan, 1985) [1976].
The Centre of Christianity (London: SCM Press, 1977).
(ed.), *The Myth of God Incarnate* (London: SCM Press, 1977).
'Eschatological Verification Reconsidered' *Religious Studies* 8/2, 1977.
'Christian Theology and Inter-religious Dialogue' *World Faiths* 103, 1977.
'Present and Future Life' (The Ingersoll Lecture) *Harvard Theological Review* 71/1 - 2, 1978.
and Hebblethwaite, B. (eds.), *Christianity and Other Religions* (Glasgow: Fount, 1980).
God has Many Names: Britain's New Religious Pluralism (Philadelphia: Westminster Press, 1982).

'An Irenaean Theodicy' (also: 'responses to' and 'critiques of' J.K. Roth, S.T. Davis, D.R. Griffin, F. Sontag, J.B. Cobb) in S. Davis (ed.), *Encountering Evil.*
The Second Christianity (London: SCM Press, 1983).
and Goulder, M., *Why Believe in God?* (London: SCM Press, 1983).
'The Philosophy of World Religions' *Scottish Journal of Theology* 37, 1984.
Problems of Religious Pluralism (London: Macmillan, 1985).
and Knitter, P., *The Myth of Christian Uniqueness* (New York: Orbis, and London: SCM Press, 1987).
An Interpretation of Religion (London: Macmillan, 1989).
'Response to Nielsen' in S. Davis (ed.), *Death and Afterlife.*
'The Logic of God Incarnate' *Religious Studies* 25/4, 1989.
'Rational Theistic Beliefs Without Proofs' in P. Badham (ed.), *A John Hick Reader.*
'Religious Faith as Experiencing-as' in P. Badham (ed.), *A John Hick Reader.*
'Religion as Fact-Asserting', in P. Badham (ed.), *A John Hick Reader.*
'A Response to Gerard Loughlin' *Modern Theology* 7/1, 1990.
'Response', in C.R. Mesle, *John Hick's Theodicy: A Process Humanist Critique.*
Replies to G. D'Costa, J. Kellenberger, C. Gillis, C.W. Ernst, C.R. Mesle, J. O'Connor, P. Badham, L.S. Betty, W. Rowe, L. Zagzebski, F.B. Dilley, S.T. Davis, D.R. Stiver, H. Hewitt, G. Loughlin, J. Lipner and J. Prabhu, in Hewitt, H. (ed.), *Problems in the Philosophy of Religion: Critical Studies of the Work of John Hick.*
Disputed Questions in Theology and the Philosophy of Religion (London: Macmillan, 1993).
The Metaphor of God Incarnate (London: SCM Press, 1993).
The Rainbow of Faiths (London: SCM Press, 1995).
'The Possibility of Religious Pluralism: A Reply to Gavin D'Costa' *Religious Studies* 33/2, 1997.
The Fifth Dimension (Oxford: Oneworld, 1999).
Dialogues in the Philosophy of Religion (New York: Palgrave, 2001).

Secondary Texts

Abraham, W.J., *An Introduction to the Philosophy of Religion* (Englewood Cliffs: Prentice Hall, 1985).
Alston, W., 'John Hick, *Faith and Knowledge*' in A. Sharma, *God, Truth and Reality.*
Anderson, R.S., *Theology, Death and Dying* (Oxford: Blackwell, 1986).
Anselm, *Proslogion*, trans. M.J. Charlesworth (Oxford: Clarendon Press, 1965).
Apczynski, J.P., 'John Hick's Theocentrism: Revolutionary or Implicitly Inclusivist?', *Modern Theology*, 8/1, 1991.
Aquinas, *In Librum De Causis*, in F.C. Coplestone, *Aquinas.*
-----,*Quaestiones Disputatae: De Malo*, 6 in D.J. O'Connor, *Freewill* (London: Macmillan, 1971).

-----,*Summa Contra Gentiles Book Four* trans. English Dominicans (London: Burns Oates & Washbourne Ltd, 1929).

Armstrong, D.M., *Materialist Theory of Mind* (R.K.P., 1968).

Augustine, *City of God*, trans. H. Bettenson (London: Penguin, 1972).

-----,*Confessions*, trans. R.S. Pine-Coffin (London: Penguin, 1961).

-----,*De Correptione et gratia* (33,34), H. Bettenson, *The Later Christian Fathers* (Oxford: Oxford University Press, 1970).

-----,*De Genesi ad litteram* (6.36) cited in H. Bettenson *The Later Christian Fathers* (Oxford: Oxford University Press, 1970).

-----,*On Free Will*, trans. A.S. Benjamin and L.H. Hackstaff (Indianapolis: Bobbs Merrill, 1964).

Ayer, A. J., *Language, Truth and Logic* (New York: Dover, 1952).

Badham, P., *Christian Beliefs About Life After Death* (London: Macmillan, 1976).

-----,and Badham, L., *Immortality or Extinction?* (London: SPCK, 1984).

-----,(ed.), *A John Hick Reader* (London: Macmillan, 1990).

-----,'Introductory Essay' in P. Badham (ed.), *A John Hick Reader* (London: Macmillan, 1990).

Barnes, P.L., 'Continuity and Development in John Hick's Theology' *Studies in Religion* 21/4, 1992.

Barth, Karl, *Dogmatics in Outline* (London: SCM Press, 1949).

-----,*Church Dogmatics*, *Vol. II*, trans. G.W. Bromiley (Edinburgh: T & T Clark, 1957).

Berger, A., Badham, P., Kutscher, A.H., Berger, J., Perry, M., Beloff, J. (eds.), *Perspectives on Death and Dying* (Philadelphia: Charles Press, 1989).

Bettenson, H., *The Early Christian Fathers* (Oxford: Oxford University Press, 1956).

-----,*The Later Christian Fathers* (Oxford: Oxford University Press, 1970).

Bohm, D., *Wholeness and the Implicate Order* (London: Routledge & Kegan Paul, 1980).

Bowker, J., *Meanings of Death* (Cambridge: Cambridge University Press, 1991).

Braithwaite, R.B., 'An Empiricist's View of the Nature of Religious Belief' in B. Mitchell (ed.), *Philosophy of Religion* (Oxford: Oxford University Press, 1971).

Braybrooke, M., 'Religious Studies and Interfaith Developments' in U. King (ed.), *Turning Points in Religious Studies* (Edinburgh: T & T Clark, 1990).

Brummer, V., *Speaking of a Personal God* (Cambridge: Cambridge University Press, 1992).

Bullock, A., and Stallybrass, O. (eds.), *The Fontana Dictionary of Modern Thought* (London: Collins, 1977).

Campbell, K., *Body and Mind* (London: Macmillan, 1970).

Cantwell-Smith, W., 'The Christian in a Religiously Plural World' in J. Hick and B. Hebblethwaite (eds.), *Christianity and Other Religions*.

Cheetham, D., 'John Hick, Authentic Relationships and Hell' *Sophia* 33/1, 1994.

-----,'Pulp Fiction, a God of Love and an Authentic World' *Modern Believing* 27/3, 1996.

-----,'Evil and Religious Pluralism: The Eschatological Resolution' *New Blackfriars*, May, 1997.

-----,'Hell as Potentially Temporal' *Expository Times* 108/9, 1997.

-----,'Religious Passion and the Pluralist Theology of Religions' *New Blackfriars*, May 1998.

Chrzan, K., 'When is gratuitous evil really gratuitous?' *International Journal of Philosophy of Religion* 24/1-2, 1988.

Clarke, J.J., 'John Hick's Resurrection' *Sophia* 10/3, 1971.

Cockburn, D., *Other Human Beings* (London: Macmillan, 1990).

Coplestone, F.C., *Aquinas* (Harmondsworth: Penguin, 1955).

Cullmann, O., *Immortality of the Soul or Resurrection of the Dead?* (London: Epworth Press, 1958).

Cummins, G., *The Road to Immortality* (London: Ivor Nicholson & Watson, 1932).

Cupitt, D., 'Anti-Realist Faith' in Runzo, J. (ed.), *Is God Real?*

-----,*The Time Being* (London: SCM Press, 1992).

D'Costa, G. (ed.), *Christian Uniqueness Reconsidered* (New York, Orbis Books, 1990).

-----,'John Hick and Religious Pluralism: Yet Another Revolution' in H. Hewitt (ed.), *Problems in the Philosophy of Religion* (London: Macmillan, 1991).

-----,'Whose Objectivity? Which Neutrality? The Doomed Quest For A Neutral Vantage Point From Which To Judge Religions' *Religious Studies* 29/1, 1993.

-----,'The Impossibility of the Pluralist View of Religions' *Religious Studies* 32, 1996.

-----,*The Meeting of Religions and the Trinity* (Edinburgh: T & T Clark, 2000).

Davies, P., *God and the New Physics* (London: Penguin, 1983).

-----,*Superforce* (London: Penguin, 1986).

-----,*The Mind of God* (London: Penguin, 1992).

Davis, S. (ed.), *Encountering Evil* (Edinburgh.: T & T Clark., 1981).

-----,(ed.), *Death and Afterlife* (London: Macmillan, 1989).

-----,'The Resurrection of the Dead' in S. Davies (ed.), *Death and Afterlife* (London: Macmillan, 1989).

-----,*Risen Indeed* (London: SPCK, 1993).

-----,(ed.) with D. Kendall, G. O'Collins, *The Trinity: An Interdisciplinary Symposium on the Trinity* (Oxford: Oxford University Press, 1999).

-----,'John Hick on Incarnation and Trinity', in S. Davis, D. Kendall, G. O'Collins, *The Trinity: An Interdisciplinary Symposium on the Trinity.*

Dilley, F.B., 'Resurrection and the "Replica Objection"' *Religious Studies* 19, 1983.

Doctrine Commission of the General Synod of the Church of England, *Doctrine of the Church of England* (London: SPCK, 1962).

-----,*The Mystery of Salvation* (Church House Publishing, 1995).

Donovan, P., *Religious Language* (London: Sheldon Press, 1976).

-----,'The Intolerance of Religious Pluralism' *Religious Studies* 29/2, 1993.

Dostoevski, *The Brothers Karamazov* trans. C. Garnett (Encyclopaedia Britannica Inc., 1971).

Easwaran, E. (trans.), *The Upanishads* (London: Arkana - Penguin, 1988).

Eliade, M., *Patterns in Comparative Religion* trans. Rosemary Sheed (New York: New American Library, 1958).

Emmett, D.E., *The Nature of Metaphysical Thinking* (London, 1945).

Farmer, H.H., *Towards Belief in God* (London: Student Christian Movement Press, 1942).

Farrer, A., *A Science of God?* (London: Geoffrey Bles, 1966).

Flew, A., 'Theology and Falsification' in A. Flew and A. MacIntyre, *New Essays in Philosophical Theology* (London: SCM Press, 1955).

-----, and MacIntyre, A., *New Essays in Philosophical Theology.*

-----, 'Divine Omnipotence and Human Freedom' in Flew and MacIntyre, *New Essays in Philosophical Theology.*

-----, *The Presumption of Atheism* (London: Elek/Pemberton, 1976).

Forrester, D., 'Professor Hick and the Universe of Faiths' *Scottish Journal of Theology* 29, 1976.

Fremantle, F., and Trungpa, C., *The Tibetan Book of the Dead* (London: Shambhala Publications, 1975).

Friedman, R. Z., 'Evil and Moral Agency' *International Journal of Philosophy of Religion* 24, 1988.

Geach, P., *God and the Soul* (London: Routledge & Kegan Paul, 1969).

Geivett, R.D., *Evil and the Evidence for God: The Challenge of John Hick's Theodicy* (Philadelphia: Temple University, 1993).

Gillis, C., 'An Interpretation of *An Interpretation of Religion*' in H. Hewitt (ed.), *Problems in the Philosophy of Religion.*

Gorman, U., *A Good God?: A Logical and Semantical Analysis of the Problem of Evil* (Stockholm: Verbum, Lund: H. Ohlssons, 1977).

Goulder, M., (ed.), *Incarnation and Myth: The Debate Continued* (London: SCM Press, 1979).

Griffiths, B., *A New Vision of Reality* (London: Fount, 1989).

Griffiths, P.J., *Problems of Religious Diversity* (Oxford: Blackwell, 2001).

Haldane, J.B.S., *Possible Worlds* (London: Chatto & Windus, 1927).

Halkes, C.J.M., *New Creation* (London: SPCK, 1989).

Hamnett, I. (ed.), *Religious Pluralism and Unbelief* (London: Routledge, 1990).

Hanfling, O., *Logical Positivism* (Oxford: Blackwell, 1981).

Hay, D., *Religious Experience Today* (London: Mowbray, 1990).

Hebblethwaite, B. and J. Hick (eds.), *Christianity and Other Religions.*

----- *The Christian Hope* (Marshall, Morgan & Scott, 1984).

-----, *The Incarnation* (Cambridge: Cambridge University Press, 1987).

-----, 'Reflections on Realism v. Non-Realism' in Runzo, J. (ed.), *Is God Real?* (London: Macmillan, 1993).

-----, 'The Impossibility of Multiple Incarnations' *Theology*, Sept/Oct., 2001.

Heim, S.M., 'The Pluralistic Hypothesis, Realism, and Post-Eschatology' *Religious Studies* 28/2, 1992.

Hendry, G.S., *Theology of Nature* (Philadelphia: Westminster Press, 1980).

Herbert, R.T., *Paradox and Identity in Theology* (Ithaca: Cornell University Press, 1979).

Hewitt, H. (ed.), *Problems in the Philosophy of Religion* (London, Macmillan, 1991).

Hollis, M., *Invitation to Philosophy* (Oxford: Blackwell, 1985).

Hume, D., *Dialogues Concerning Natural Religion*, M. Bell (ed.) (London: Penguin, 1961).

Irenaeus, *Against Heresies* , trans. D.J. Ungar (New York: Paulist Press, 1992).

Julian of Norwich, *The Revelations of Divine Love* trans. James Walsh (London: Burns and Oates, 1961).

Kellenberger, 'Critical Response' [to G. D'Costa] in H. Hewitt (ed.), *Problems in the Philosophy of Religion.*

King, U. (ed.), *Turning Points in Religious Studies* (Edinburgh: T. & T. Clark, 1990).

Lash, N., and Tracy, D. (eds.), *Cosmology and Theology* (Edinburgh: T. & T. Clark Ltd., 1983).

Lipner, J.J., 'Hick's Resurrection' *Sophia* 18/3, 1979.

-----,'A Bend in the Road: A Story About Religious Pluralism' in H. Hewitt (ed.), *Problems in the Philosophy of Religion.*

Livingston, J.C., *Modern Christian Thought* (London: Macmillan, 1971).

Loughlin, G., *Mirroring God's World - A Critique of John Hick's Speculative Theology* (Unpublished Ph.D. thesis, Cantab., 1986).

-----,'Prefacing Pluralism: John Hick and the Mastery of Religion' *Modern Theology* 7, 1990.

-----,'Squares and Circles: John Hick and the Doctrine of the Incarnation' in H. Hewitt (ed.), *Problems in the Philosophy of Religion.*

Lucas, J.R., *Freedom of the Will* (Oxford: Oxford University Press, 1970).

MacGregor, G., *Reincarnation as a Christian Hope* (London: Macmillan, 1982).

MacIntyre, A., 'Faith and the Verification Principle' in A. MacIntyre and R.G. Smith (eds.), *Metaphysical Beliefs.*

-----,and Smith, R.G. (eds.), *Metaphysical Beliefs* (London: SCM Press, 1957).

Macquarrie, J., *The Christian Hope* (London: Mowbray, 1978).

Markham, I., 'Shattering the "Exclusivist, Inclusivist and Pluralist" Paradigm' *New Blackfriars*, January, 1993.

Mathis, T.R., *Against John Hick* (Boston: University Press of America, 1985).

Meacock, H., *An Anthropological Approach to Theology: A Study of John Hick's Theology of Religious Pluralism. Towards Ethical Criteria for a Global Theology of Religions* (Boston: University Press of America, 2000).

Mesle, C.R., *John Hick's Theodicy: A Process-Humanist Critique* (London: Macmillan, 1991).

Mitchell, B. (ed.), *Philosophy of Religion* (Oxford: Oxford University Press, 1971).

Moltmann, J., *Theology of Hope* (London: SCM Press, 1964).

-----,*The Future of Creation* (London: SCM Press, 1979).

-----,*Experiences of God* (London: SCM Press, 1980).

-----,*The Trinity and the Kingdom of God* (London: SCM Press, 1981).

-----,*The Coming of God: Christian Eschatology* (London: SCM Press, 1996).

Montefiore, H., *The Probability of God* (London: SCM Press, 1985).

Netland, H., *Dissonant Voices: Pluralism and the Question of Truth* (Leicester: Apollos, 1991).

Newbigin, L., 'Religion for the Marketplace', in G. D'Costa (ed.), *Christian Uniqueness Reconsidered*.

Nicholls, W. (ed.), *Religion and Modernity* (Waterloo/Ontario, 1987).

Nicholson, R.A., *Rumi: Poet and Mystic* (London: Allen & Unwin, 1978).

Nielsen, Kai, 'God, the Soul, and Coherence: A Response to Davis and Hick' in S. Davis (ed.), *Death and Afterlife* (London: Macmillan, 1989).

Nietzsche, F., *The Gay Science with a Prelude to Rhymes and an Appendix to Songs* (New York: Random House, 1974).

O'Connor, D. J., *Freewill* (London: Macmillan, 1971).

Olding, A., 'Resurrection and Resurrection Worlds' *Mind*, Oct. 1970.

Panikkar, R., *The Unknown Christ of Hinduism* (London: Darton, Longman and Todd, 1964).

Parfit, D., *Reasons and Persons* (Oxford: Oxford University Press, 1986).

Parrisikar, V.L. (ed.), *Srimad-Valmiki-Maharsi-Pannitah Yogava'sistha, I*, (Bombay: Tukaram Javaji, 1978).

Penelhum, T. (ed.), *Immortality* (California: Wadsworth Publishing Company, 1973).

-----,'Review and Critique of *Death and Eternal Life*' *Canadian Journal of Philosophy* 9, 1979.

-----,'Reflections on the Ambiguity of the Universe' in A. Sharma, *God, Truth and Reality*.

Phillips, D.Z., *The Concept of Prayer* (London: Routledge & Kegan Paul, 1965).

Plantinga, A., *God and Other Minds* (Ithaca, NY: Cornell University Press 1967).

-----,*God, Freedom and Evil* (London: Allen & Unwin, 1975).

Polkinghorne, J., *Reason and Reality* (London: SPCK, 1991).

Price, H.H., *Essays in the Philosophy of Religion*, (Oxford: Oxford University Press, 1972).

-----,'Survival and the Idea of "Another World"' in T. Penelhum (ed.), *Immortality* (California: Wadsworth Publishing Company, 1973).

Puccetti, R., 'The Loving God, Some Observations on John Hick's *Evil and the God of Love*' *Religious Studies* 2/2, 1967.

Quinton, A., 'Logical Positivism' in A. Bullock and O. Stallybrass (eds.), *The Fontana Dictionary of Modern Thought*.

Race, A., *Christians and Religious Pluralism* (London: SCM Press, 1994).

Rahner, K., *Theological Investigations, Vol. 5* (London: Darton, Longman & Todd, 1966).

Reichenbach, B.R., 'Price, Hick and Disembodied Existence' *Religious Studies* 15, 1979.

Richards, H.J., *Death and After* (London: Fount Paperbacks, 1980).

Rose, K., *Knowing the Real: John Hick on the Cognitivity of Religions and Religious Pluralism* (Frankfurt am Main; Oxford: Peter Lang, 1996).

Rosher, G. *Beyond the Horizon* (London: James Clark, 1961).

Rowe, William, 'Paradox and Promise: Hick's Solution to the Problem of Evil' in H. Hewitt (ed.), *Problems in the Philosophy of Religion*.

Runzo, J. (ed.), *Is God Real?* (London: Macmillan, 1993).

Russell, B., *A History of Western Philosophy* (London: Allen & Unwin, 1984).

Sartre, Jean-Paul, *Being and Nothingness* (London: Methuen, 1957).

Schlick, M., 'Meaning and Verification' *Philosophical Review*, 1936.

Schmidt, K.R., *Death and Afterlife in the Theologies of Karl Barth and John Hick: A Comparative Study* (Amsterdam: Rodopi, 1985).

Selby, P., *Look for the Living* (London: SCM Press, 1976).

Sharma, A. (ed.), *God, Truth and Reality* (London: Macmillan, 1993).

-----,*Philosophy of Religion and Advaita Vedanta* (Philadelphia: Pennsylvania State University Press, 1995).

Sharpe, E., *Understanding Religion* (London: Duckworth, 1992).

Sinkinson, C., *The Universe of Faiths: A Critical Study of John Hick's Religious Pluralism* (Carlisle: Paternoster Press, 2001).

Smith P., and Jones, O.R., *An Introduction to the Philosophy of Mind* (Cambridge: Cambridge University Press, 1986).

Soelle, D., *Suffering* (London: Darton, Longman & Todd, 1975).

Stanley-Kane, G., 'Soul-Making Theodicy and Eschatology' *Sophia*, IX-XIV 1970-1975.

Stiver, D., *The Philosophy of Religious Language: Sign, Symbol and Story* (Cambridge, MA: Blackwell, 1996).

Stocker, M., 'Desiring the Bad: An Essay in Moral Psychology' *Journal of Philosophy*, Vol. LXXVI, 1979.

Surin, K., *Theology and the Problem of Evil* (Oxford: Blackwell, 1986).

-----,'Towards a Materialist Critique of Religious Pluralism' in I. Hamnett (ed.), *Religious Pluralism and Unbelief*.

-----,'A Certain "Politics of Speech": "Religious Pluralism" in an Age of McDonald's Hamburger' *Modern Theology* 7/1, 1990.

Swinburne, R., *The Coherence of Theism* (Oxford: Clarendon Press, 1977).

-----,*The Existence of God* (Oxford: Oxford University Press, 1979).

-----,'A Theodicy of Heaven and Hell' in A.J. Freddoso (ed.), *The Existence and Nature of God* (Notre Dame: University of Notre Dame Press, 1983).

Ta-Kao, C. (trans.), *Tao Te Ching, I* (London: Mandala Books, 1982).

Talbott, T., 'The Doctrine of Everlasting Punishment' *Faith and Philosophy* 37/7, 1990.

Taylor, J.V., 'The Theological Basis for Interfaith Dialogue' in Hick, J. and Hebblethwaite, B. (eds.), *Christianity and Other Religions*.

Tertullian, *De Resurrectione Carnis*, 12 in H. Bettenson, *The Early Christian Fathers* (Oxford: Oxford University Press, 1956).

Tilbury, A., *Soul* (B.B.C. Education, 1992).

Tillich, P., *Shaking of the Foundations* (London: SCM Press, 1949).

-----,*Systematic Theology III* (Chicago: University of Chicago Press, 1951).

-----,*The Courage To Be* (London: Fontana, 1962).

Travis, S., *Christian Hope and the Future of Man* (Leicester: IVP, 1980).

Trethowan, D.I., 'Dr. Hick and the Problem of Evil' *Journal of Theological Studies*, Oct. 1967.

Twiss, S., 'The Philosophy of Religious Pluralism: A Critical Appraisal of Hick and His Critics' *The Journal of Religion*, 70/4, 1990.

Urban, L., *A Short History of Christian Thought* (Oxford: Oxford University Press, 1986).

Ward, K., 'Freedom and the Irenaean Theodicy' *Journal of Theological Studies*, Vol.20, 1969.

-----,'Truth and the Diversity of Religions' *Religious Studies*, 26, 1990.

-----,*Religion and Human Nature* (Oxford: Clarendon Press, 1998).

Welman, M., 'Introduction' in E.D. Mitchell, *Psychic Exploration* (Putnam's, 1974).

Weston, F., *The One Christ: An Enquiry into the Manner of the Incarnation* (London: Longmans, Green, 1914).

Whaling, F., *Religion in Today's World* (Edinburgh: T & T Clark, 1987).

Wiener, N., *The Human Use of Human Beings* (London: Sphere Books, 1968).

Wiles, M., 'A Survey of Issues in the *Myth* Debate', in M. Goulder, *Incarnation and Myth: The Debate Continued*.

Williams, B., *Morality* (London: Penguin, 1972).

Williams, H.A., *True Resurrection* (London: Mitchell Beazley, 1972).

Wilson, C., *Afterlife* (London: Grafton Press, 1987).

Wilson, I., *The After-Death Experience* (London: Sidgwick & Jackson, 1987).

Wisdom, J., 'Gods' *Proceedings of the Aristotelian Society* (London, 1944-5).

Wittgenstein, L., *Philosophical Investigations* trans. G.E.M. Anscombe (Oxford: Blackwell, 1953).

-----,*Culture and Value* trans. P. Winch (Chicago: University of Chicago Press, 1980).

Yandell, K., 'Hell and Moral Philosophy' *Religious Studies* 28/1, 1992.

Zagzebski, Linda, 'Critical Response' [in response to William Rowe], in H. Hewitt (ed.), *Problems in the Philosophy of Religion*.

Zeis, J., 'To Hell with Freedom', *Sophia* 25/1, 1986.

Index